Teleological Realism

Teleological Realism

Mind, Agency, and Explanation

Scott R. Sehon

A Bradford Book
The MIT Press
Cambridge, Massachusetts
London, England

MIT Press books may be purchased at special quantity discounts for business or sales
promotional use. For information, please email special_sales@mitpress.mit.edu or
write to Special Sales Department, The MIT Press, 5 Cambridge Center, Cambridge,
MA 02142.

Set in Stone sans and Stone serif by The MIT Press. Printed and bound in the United
States of America.

Library of Congress Cataloging-in-Publication Data

Sehon, Scott Robert, 1963–
Teleological realism : mind, agency, and explanation / Scott R. Sehon.
p. cm.
"A Bradford book."
Includes bibliographical references (p.) and index.
ISBN 0-262-19535-6 (alk. paper)
1. Causation. 2. Teleology. 3. Philosophy of mind. 4. Intentionalism. 5. Agent
(Philosophy). 6. Psychology, Applied. I. Title.

BD591.S44   2005
128'.2—dc22   2005043350

10 9 8 7 6 5 4 3 2 1

for Jackie, Hayden, and Josephine

Contents

Acknowledgments

According to Hofstadter's Law, "it always takes longer than you expect, even when you take in to account Hofstadter's Law" (Hofstadter 1979, p. 152). That law has certainly applied to the writing of this book. Through the years I have accumulated debts, philosophical and otherwise, to many people, more than I will be able to remember or properly acknowledge here.

Some of the central ideas in this book, and some isolated bits of text, go back to my doctoral dissertation, written over a decade ago. Accordingly, I am once again indebted to my dissertation advisor, Mark Johnston, and I am also grateful to Paul Benacerraf, Sarah Buss, Harry Frankfurt, Richard Moran, Christian Perring, Abraham Roth, Michael Smith, and the late David Lewis.

Some material derives from previously published articles: "Teleology and the Nature of Mental States," *American Philosophical Quarterly* 31 (1994): 63–72; "Deviant Causal Chains and the Irreducibility of Teleological Explanation," *Pacific Philosophical Quarterly* 78 (1997): 195–213; "Natural-Kind Terms and the Status of Folk Psychology," *American Philosophical Quarterly* 34 (1997): 333–344; "An Argument against the Causal Theory of Action Explanation," *Philosophy and Phenomenological Research* 60 (2000): 67–85.

I thoroughly reworked the extant draft during a sabbatic leave generously granted by my institution, Bowdoin College. I have inflicted some of this material on my students at Bowdoin, and the results were useful for my education if not for theirs. I am also grateful to colleagues at Bowdoin for years of philosophical discussions and a great work environment: Denis Corish, Jordi Fernandez, Lawrence Simon, and Matthew Stuart; and to Gerlinde Rickel for running the show.

I am indebted to a number of friends and colleagues who read and commented on part or all of the manuscript: Lynne Rudder Baker, Paul Bethge,

Nico Cornell, Thomas Gardner, Kevin Johnson, Laurel Jones, Alfred Mele, Stephen Naculich, Jacqueline Sartoris, G. F. Schueler, Sergio Tenenbaum, and Donald Stanley.

I am especially grateful to George Wilson. His book *The Intentionality of Human Action* first convinced me of the importance of action explanation to philosophy of mind and of the irreducibility of teleological explanation. My philosophical debt to his work goes beyond the scattered references that appear in the pages below. Moreover, he read and commented incisively the penultimate version of the manuscript. His comments, along with those of G. F. Schueler, caused me weeks of additional work when I thought I was all but done; this both kept me out of trouble and, I hope, resulted in an improved book.

I

1 | Introduction

1.1 The Mystery

When we speak of ourselves as agents with minds, we use the language of *common-sense psychology* (CSP). Within the common-sense psychological project, we attempt to understand people (including ourselves) as agents who act for reasons, who have moral responsibility for our actions, who act freely at least some of the time, who have purposes and goals and projects, who are loci of value, and for whom things have value. We attribute mental states in an effort to understand the point or purpose of behavior; we justify our own actions by referring to the way we believe or desire the world to be, we attribute mental states in the course of allocating moral praise or blame, and so on. CSP will deliver claims like the following: Jackie went to the kitchen in order to get wine. People who prefer beer to wine will typically choose beer if offered both. Tom Seaver threw a curveball because he thought the batter was expecting a fastball.

When we think of human beings as physical objects, we use the language of physical science, and we give causal accounts. The specific terminology we employ depends on the nature of the event we are attempting to explain or predict. If we want to know how fast a person falls if dropped from a plane, we will be concerned with the body's mass and aerodynamic properties. If we want to know why a certain medicine reduces inflammation, our explanation will be couched in terms of chemical properties of the medicine and the human organism. If we want to know how a given subject will react to a particular stimulus, we would have to look deep into the neurological properties of the brain. Although the latter sort of predictions are, in general, quite beyond our current abilities, there seems to be no barrier in principle to neurologically based predictions of human behavior.

Both CSP and physical science have the aim of understanding, explaining, and predicting human behavior. However, talk of mind and agency does not seem to mesh well with the language of physical science. Notions like *action* and *purpose*, the cornerstones of our descriptions of agents, appear to have no role in purely physical descriptions of the world. Normative notions like *moral responsibility* and *criticizable irrationality*, also central to the common-sense perspective, likewise do not belong to the conceptual arsenal of physics. We would never say that an asteroid was morally responsible for its motion, even if it crashed into Earth, nor would we say that an elementary particle was being irrational. Moreover, beliefs, desires, and other mental states have the odd feature of being *about* objects and states of affairs. This feature of beliefs and desires—given the label of "intentionality"—is not a property attributed by physics to physical objects. On the other hand, since human beings are physical objects, they must ultimately be appropriate subject matter for physical science, and they must behave in accord with physical laws. Physical science must be able, in principle, to provide detailed causal accounts of all bodily motions. But physical science will presumably not use the language of CSP in describing human beings as physical objects, and hence it will apparently not make the sorts of claims about persons that we are accustomed to making in CSP.

Thus, there is an apparent philosophical mystery. Putting aside substance dualist views according to which we have nonphysical souls, it seems that a human being is, in some sense, nothing more than a very complicated collection of physical particles. (I will discuss the reasons for rejecting substance dualism in the next chapter.) Thus, it seems that human behavior should be within the explanatory domain of physical science. Moreover, there is reason for thinking that, within its explanatory domain, physical science will ultimately provide *complete* explanations of human behavior. This makes it appear that, if common-sense talk of mind and agency is to have any validity, it must somehow be subsumed within physical science. However, the language of CSP is also quite different from the language of physical science, so it appears unlikely that the claims of CSP can simply be subsumed within the claims of physical science. At the broadest level the problem is this: It seems that mind does not fit with the rest of the physical universe, and yet it seems that mind *must* fit with the rest of the physical universe. The problem is hardly new; it is the mind-body problem, and it is the problem of discovering the place of rational agency. It is the problem of ascertaining the place of human beings in the natural world and of seeing whether the common-sense facts about mind and agency can be squared with a naturalistic, scientific perspective on the world.

1.2   Reformulation of the Mystery

This philosophical mystery has been couched in rather vague terms so far. I have talked metaphorically about whether CSP will *mesh well* with physical science, and have claimed that *in some sense* human beings are nothing over and above collections of physical particles. We feel the mystery strongly, but much of the task of philosophy of mind consists in formulating the problem in a tractable, clear, and precise way. We can, I think, make progress toward this goal by asking the following question: What is the logical relationship between the claims put forward by CSP and the claims that will ultimately be put forward by physical science?

If we consider two propositions p and q, we can classify their possible logical relationships as follows:

(1) p and q contradict each other.

(2) One of p and q entails the other.

(3) p and q are logically independent.

We would have the first of these options if the two propositions were "Only adults are at the beach" and "Hayden is at the beach, and Hayden is not an adult." The second relationship holds between "Water is wet, and water is H_2O" and "H_2O is wet." The third relationship, that of logical independence holds between "Tom Seaver was the best pitcher the Mets ever had" and "Grass is green."

Applying this to the relationship between CSP and physical science, there are three options.

option 1: CSP and physical science contradict one another.

option 2: Physical science entails CSP, CSP entails physical science, or CSP and physical science are equivalent.

option 3: CSP and physical science are logically independent.

However, we must tread somewhat carefully in characterizing these options, since CSP and physical science are *sets* of propositions, and we need to be explicit about what we mean when we say that one set of propositions bears a certain logical relationship to another. One way to go would be to say that CSP and physical science contradict each other if any proposition or conjunction of propositions within CSP contradicts any proposition or set of propositions within physical science. Similarly, we could say that physical science entails CSP if the conjunction of the propositions of physical science logically implies each of the propositions of CSP. However, it will be preferable to take a somewhat more relaxed approach. If, for example, only one or two of the claims of CSP conflict with those of science, we would be hesitant to say that, in general, CSP and physical science contradict one another. We would reach this conclusion only if science contradicts some substantial subset of CSP. Similarly, we would say that physical science entails CSP if the propositions of physical science entail the bulk of CSP, without requiring that every single proposition of CSP be entailed by science in this way. Finally, we would say that CSP and physical science are independent if the bulk of CSP is logically independent of science. Of course, since "substantial subset" and "bulk of" are vague, there could be a corresponding degree of vagueness concerning which option holds.

An example involving something other than CSP might help at this point. Instead of common-sense psychology, consider astrology. In the words of one of its proponents, astrology is "the science which treats of the influence upon human character of cosmic forces emanating from celestial bodies" (N. de Vore, past president of the Astrological Research Society, quoted in Culver and Ianna 1988, p. 2). Within this purported science, numerous claims can be made, such as the following:

There is "an observable parallelism between the timing of events in the universe and in the individual consciousness." (Rudhyar, quoted in Culver and Ianna 1988, p. 1)

If Mars is in the first house at the time of your birth, then you are likely to be an aggressive individual with a muscular body.

If the Sun is in the fifth house at the time of your birth, then you are likely to have great creative talents.

Most of us see no great philosophical mystery regarding astrology. However, for the 25 percent of Americans who believe in astrology, there is a mystery, for astrology and science do not seem to mix well. Physical science does not claim that astronomical bodies have any astrological influence on human events and human character. The planet Jupiter, for example, does exert a force on me; however, according to physical science, the force is that due to gravity, and the gravitational attraction between Jupiter and a human body on Earth is minuscule. One might then wonder why physical science—our best attempt to make sense of the nuts and bolts of the universe—does not include astrological claims or principles. One might then also wonder about the nature of astrological forces.

As with CSP and physical science, I suggest that a "philosopher of astrology" could sharpen these worries by asking what the logical relationship is between astrology and physical science. And again we have the same three options. Option 1 is that astrology and science contradict one another and that at most one is right. Option 2 is that physical science ultimately entails the truths of astrology, or that, in an even more unlikely scenario, all facts of physical science are entailed by the astrological facts about the world. Option 3 is that astrology and physical science are logically independent, meaning that neither contradicts the another neither is entailed by the other. If we can determine which of these relationships holds, and why, we are well on our way to resolving any sense of philosophical mystery about astrology. If, as seems all but certain, astrology and our best physical science contradict one another, then at most one can be right. If we reject astrology on these grounds, we have resolved the mystery by demoting astrology to the realm of falsehood and illusion. On the other hand, if option 2 turns out to be correct, then the principles and methods of astrology follow from the facts of physical science. This would resolve the mystery by *vindicating* astrology; astrology would be true if science is true. Astrology would in this sense be subsumed within physical science. Finally, if we could produce reasons for maintaining that astrology and science are logically independent of each other, then we would thereby have resolved any tension between astrology and science, and we would have shown that astrology and science can both be true.

Similarly, in the case of CSP and physical science, if we can determine which of the three logical relationships holds, then we will resolve the philosophical mystery. Option 1 gives us the following resolution to the mystery: we are right to feel a tension between claims about the mind and claims about the physical universe, for typical CSP claims about the mind actually contradict what we know or will discover through physical science. Thus, we would be forced to reject either CSP or physical science. Since bets placed against science have a sorry history, we would conclude that the claims of CSP are generally false.

Option 2 is a disjunction of three possibilities; however, only one of them has any plausibility. No one would maintain that all the facts of physical science, including the value of the gravitational constant, are implied by the facts of CSP. Thus, option 2, as we will consider it, is this claim: The facts of CSP are ultimately implied by the facts of physical science. As was noted above, this might be a matter of degree, for it might be that a few of the alleged facts of CSP ultimately contradict physical science and have to be rejected. But so long as the facts of physical science imply the bulk of CSP, we have a resolution to our philosophical mystery. On this view, CSP, despite its apparent differences with the language of physical science, is implied by physical science. If CSP simply follows from the propositions ultimately put forward by science, then CSP is vindicated. CSP would thus be neatly subsumed within physical science.

Rather than affirm either of the first two options, we might take a more cautious approach. We could say that CSP will either be implied by science or it will contradict science, but that before we can determine which we will have to wait for more scientific results. We might, for example, have to learn more about the brain before we can say with confidence either that CSP fits nicely within physical science or that it contradicts physical science. That is, we might say that either option 1 or option 2 is correct, but only further empirical research in science will be able to determine which. I will refer to this approach as *strong naturalism*.

Finally, there is option 3, according to which CSP and physical science are logically independent and psychological facts about the mind and physical facts about bodies can coexist peacefully. This would resolve the initial mystery by showing that there is no conflict between the two after all—i.e., that the conflict had been merely apparent rather than real. One way to support the third option would be to adopt substance dualism, the claim that minds are immaterial substances; this would make it natural to assume that propositions about mind and propositions about material bodies simply have different subject matters. CSP and physical science would then each be about different things, and would independent for the same reason that "Grass is green" and "Snow is white" are independent.

1.3 Addressing the Reformulated Question

Determining the logical relationship between two individual statements is typically a straightforward affair, although there is no mechanical procedure that is guaranteed to determine, in a finite number of steps, the logical relationship between two arbitrary propositions. It is similarly straightforward, though more complicated, to determine the logical relationship between two well-defined, finite sets of statements. But our problem is more complicated than that. CSP is an ill-defined mass of propositions including individual attributions of mental states to particular agents, explanations of the behavior of individual agents, and generalizations concerning behavior and mental states. Even if we could produce all the generalizations that are held true in CSP, attributions and explanations can arise in an indefinitely large number of circumstances, and thus there is no effective way of specifying all of the propositions of CSP.

The propositions of physical science will likewise include an indefinitely large number of ascriptions, explanations, and generalizations concerning physical objects. Moreover, we are not merely concerned with the propositions that are *currently* put forward by physical science. As I will explain below, if we were to limit ourselves to present-day science it would be quite clear that CSP and physical science are logically independent of one another. If we want to know how mind and agency fit in the physical universe, we will have to ask about the logical relationship between the propositions of CSP and the actual physical *facts* about the world—i.e., the propositions ultimately put forward by a completed physical science.

Our task of evaluating the logical relationship between CSP and physical science would thus appear to involve some speculation about the progress of science. However, the task is mostly conceptual, for we will be concerned primarily with the differing *vocabularies* of CSP and physical science rather than the specific claims each makes. As has already been noted, on the face of it the crucial bits of CSP vocabulary do not seem to have any role in physical science. As will be argued in chapter 5, if physical science entails the facts of CSP then the psychological terms in CSP must have necessary and sufficient conditions that can be spelled out purely in the terms of physical science. Similarly, to show that CSP contradicts physical science one must claim that psychological terms in CSP at least have physically specifiable necessary conditions. If in fact there are physically specifiable necessary and sufficient conditions for psychological properties, this shows that either option 1 or option 2 is correct, and which one is correct is determined by the empirical question of whether there is anything that fulfills the necessary and sufficient conditions. But the logically prior question is whether psychological properties *have* physically specifiable necessary and sufficient conditions, and this is a largely conceptual question that can be addressed in a relatively a priori fashion.

To say that the problem is largely conceptual is not to say that it is easy. In recent decades most philosophers of mind have been, in effect, proponents of option 2. As has already been noted, this view requires that CSP vocabulary be brought into line with that of physical science. However, as will be discussed in part II, there are major obstacles to specifying necessary and sufficient conditions for mental terms.

On the other hand, according to option 3, facts about the mind are independent of physical science, and CSP in some sense has a different subject matter than does physical science. This might seem palatable if one is a substance dualist and thinks of the mind as a kind of nonphysical stuff. However, most philosophers have given up substance dualism and will acknowledge that human beings are composed of the same elementary particles as are the rest of the objects in the universe. This would *seem* to mean that there are no limits on the scope of the subject matter of physical science; in particular, it is hard to see how CSP could carve out a distinct subject matter if the human beings that are its central concern are composed of physical particles. Moreover, given that human beings are composed of physical particles, it seems that, in principle, physical science must be able to explain and predict human behavior; but that is, in large part, also what CSP does. If CSP and physical science both give explanations for the same events, then it seems that either their answers must be ultimately the same (i.e., option 2) or their answers contradict one another (option 1); it is hard to see how their respective explanations could be logically independent of one another.

1.4 Why Care?

Why does it matter which option turns out to be correct? The question, as I have stated it, will not have antecedently concerned the average person. Is it merely a philosopher's puzzle, of no more intrinsic and general interest than the Sunday *Times* crossword? No. I think that there is a great deal at stake, even for the ordinary person who would not normally pay much attention to philosophical inquiry. In the previous two paragraphs, I quickly sketched reasons for thinking that each of option 2 and option 3 is untenable. If this turns out to be correct, then we are stuck with option 1—the claim that CSP and the ultimate claims put forward by physical science contradict one another. This would be a truly momentous conclusion. The ultimate claims put forward by physical science represent our best and most considered efforts at gaining knowledge. Giving up physical science would undermine any confidence we have in our ability to gain any knowledge about the world. On the other hand, if we are stuck with option 1 and we hold on to science as a reliable means of gaining knowledge, then our only alternative would be to deny the claims of CSP.

The denial of CSP would be an equally radical conclusion. We constantly engage in CSP in our interaction with one another; indeed, seeing one another as agents with minds seems obligatory in more than one sense. First, insofar as we wish to predict and explain the behavior of human beings, we are in practice forced to use the language of CSP. In principle, an omniscient physicist might be able to predict our bodily motions with nearly perfect accuracy based on knowledge of the state of every elementary particle in and around our bodies; in practice, of course, such a task is impossible. If you want to know what I will be doing tomorrow, it will work far better simply to ask me what my intentions are. Second, insofar as we abandon the CSP approach to another human being, we give up treating that human being as a *person*. To see someone as a person is to see someone as an agent with a mind, and the language of mind and agency is precisely what CSP provides. To give up CSP would be to give up seeing ourselves and our compatriots as persons. It would mean acknowledging that nearly everything we care about (indeed, even the notion of caring itself) has been an illusion. If such a view is coherent at all, it must surely be seen as a desperate last resort, a view to be adopted only if it is conclusively demonstrated that the other two options are untenable.

In fact, one might be convinced that option 1 is so unattractive that *nothing* could ever rationally convince us of its truth; that is, one might argue that we have no theoretical commitments deeper than CSP and the general reliability of science, and hence there is no commitment from which we could launch an argument that would dislodge us from our belief in both CSP and physical science. If this is right, then either option 2 or option 3 *must* be right; i.e., it must be the case that CSP and physical science are not in conflict with one another. I have considerable sympathy for this line, and I firmly agree that it would take powerful considerations to convince us that CSP is wrong; however, it might be a bit hasty to rest on the claim that such considerations will never be put forward.

In any event, even if we could remove option 1 from consideration, there would still be a considerable philosophical mystery; the choice between option 2 and option 3 is not a technical matter of little significance. First, as I will argue much later in the book, other significant philosophical questions can turn on the question of option 2 versus option 3: I will argue that a certain brand of skepticism about moral value becomes much more plausible given option 2. (See chapter 11.) I also think that the problem of free will and determinism likewise looks rather different depending on which option is correct, but a treatment of that issue will have to await another time. Second, there is a genuine intellectual curiosity to be satisfied here, one concerning the nature of the universe and the place of mind and value within it. If option 2 is correct, then mental facts are, in the end, a species of physical fact; if physics can arrive at a grand unified theory of elementary particles and forces, then any facts about the mind will simply be entailed and subsumed by this theory. On the other hand, if option 3 is correct, then there are facts about the world that are logically independent of physical science, even if everything in the world is composed of physical particles. We would have to accept that CSP, in some sense, has a different realm—the realm of mind (or the space of reasons)—than does physical science. Facts about mind and value would not rest on the foundation of the physical sciences. In particular, the normative notions that are central to CSP (e.g., *rational, irrational,* and *responsible*) would not rest on, or be reducible to, physical facts and laws.

In a related vein, Martin Luther King Jr. once claimed that we needed to rediscover the following principle:

. . . that all reality hinges on moral foundations. In other words, that this is a moral universe and that there are moral laws in the universe just as abiding as the physical laws. (King 1954)

Depending on the details, the proponent of option 3 might accept King's formulation. Regardless of whether one accepts King's claim, option 3 would require a more limited principle, resembling this: This is a rational universe, in the sense that there are normative principles of psychological explanation that are just as abiding as, and are independent of, the physical laws of the universe. This might sound supernatural and mystical to the strong naturalist, and indeed King's own comments came in an overtly religious context. I will argue that the proponent of option 3 need not be wedded to anything recognizably supernatural, but that option 3 still amounts to a very interesting claim about the nature of mind and the nature of the universe. Ultimately, there will also be a lesson here about the foundationlessness and yet firmness of facts about mind and value.

1.5 Preview of the Teleological Realist Answer

I will defend option 3; that is, I will claim that the facts of CSP and physical science are logically independent. Thus, although I agree that human beings are composed of physical particles, I will claim that the facts about the mind are not ultimately a species of physical fact, and that they are not going to be subsumed within physical science.

The nature of psychological explanation will be paramount. Explanations of human behavior do not exhaust the content of CSP, but they do constitute an essential part of CSP. In physical science, explanations are typically causal explanations: We explain an event by giving its antecedent cause. For example, we explain an eclipse of the sun by citing the position of the moon (i.e., the moon's position and size is cited as the cause for the sunlight's not reaching particular portions of Earth), the general warming of the Northern Hemisphere during summer is explained by citing the tilt of Earth's axis as cause, and an increase in global temperatures generally is explained by citing the increase in the amount of certain greenhouse gases in the atmosphere. Most philosophers of mind assume that CSP explanations are causal too; thus, when CSP says, "Vera went to the kitchen because she wanted tea," this is construed as making the claim that Vera's desire for tea caused her going to the kitchen. However, we also know that physical science will presumably produce a perfectly good causal explanation of Vera's movement to the kitchen, an explanation that will cite some brain state. If both common-sense and physical science are offering causal explanations of human behavior, it is hard to avoid seeing them as competitors. Either the common-sense explanation will somehow reduce to the scientific explanation (if, e.g., Vera's desire for tea just *is* the brain state cited in the physical explanation), or the two causal explanations will conflict with each other and at most one can be right. In other words, if common-sense psychological explanation is causal, then it is hard to avoid the conclusion that either the option 1 or option 2 must be correct. (See chapter 12.)

As the crucial part of my defense of the third option, I claim that CSP explanations are not causal; instead, I claim that they are *teleological*. A teleological explanation explains by citing the *purpose* or *goal* of the behavior in question; thus teleological explanations cite a future state of affairs toward which the behavior was directed, rather than an antecedent state that caused the behavior. Many common-sense explanations already have this form—e.g., "Vera went to the kitchen in order to get tea." "Vera went to the kitchen because she wanted tea" can be given an explicitly teleological construal as follows: "Vera went to the kitchen in order to bring it about that her desire for tea was satisfied." According to this account, common-sense explanations of behavior are simply answering a different question than are physical science explanations: in physical science we ask for the antecedent cause of the behavior, whereas when we give psychological explanations we ask for the end at which the behavior was directed. If, as I claim, teleological and causal explanations are independent of one another, then we can begin to see how the common-sense facts about mind and agency can be independent of the physical facts about human beings. I call the view *teleological realism*, and it is the subject of part III.

In the opening chapter, in merely setting up the problem with which this book is concerned, I explicitly ruled out a view of the mind that is probably more common than any other. I described a mystery: How can we be agents with minds while also being completely constituted by inanimate physical particles? However, it is widely thought that we are *not* completely constituted by physical particles. Rather, our mind is said to be an immaterial substance over and above our physical bodies; accordingly, the view is referred to as *substance dualism*. In suggesting that this view is more common than any other, I mean that it is maintained, implicitly or otherwise, by most nonphilosophers. For example, in a statement that affirmed Darwinian evolutionary theory, Pope John Paul II said:

. . . if the origin of the human body comes through living matter which existed previously, the spiritual soul is created directly by God. . . . As a result, the theories of evolution which, because of the philosophies which inspire them, regard the spirit either as emerging from the forces of living matter, or as a simple epiphenomenon of that matter, are incompatible with the truth about man. They are therefore unable to serve as the basis for the dignity of the human person. . . . With man, we find ourselves facing a different ontological order—an ontological leap, we could say. (1996)

Although I have no hard data, I suspect that most nonphilosophers, religious and otherwise, would sympathize with the pope's claim that the mind is quite different in kind from mere matter.

On the other hand, among philosophers, and particularly among philosophers of mind, substance dualism is nearly universally rejected. (This disparity between philosophical and lay opinion is perhaps a symptom of analytic philosophy's lack of concern with presenting some of its work in a form accessible to the layperson; here philosophy stands in stark contrast to the sciences, which have had an array of writers like Isaac Asimov, Richard Dawkins, Stephen Jay Gould, and Carl Sagan.) Nonetheless, a discussion of substance dualism will be worthwhile, for it can help us answer some very general questions about theory selection. Moreover, an objection similar to that which is fatal to substance dualism will appear to threaten teleological realism too. (See chapter 13.)

2.1 Why People Believe Substance Dualism

People are drawn to dualism for a number of reasons. First, according to many religious views, people can survive their bodily deaths, and, on most accounts of personal identity, this would seem to require the independence of mind and body. Of course, for this to count as an argument for dualism, there would have to be reasons for thinking that the religious views are correct. Although there is presumably good reason to *want* life after death, there is no obvious evidence that there is life after death (unless one accepts certain religious texts as authoritative, but one would then presumably need some independent rationale for that acceptance). Dualism may well be a prerequisite for immortality, but to affirm dualism on these grounds alone would simply be wishful thinking.

On the other hand, thoughts about an afterlife may arise from a deeper reason for believing substance dualism: even if I only hope, rather than believe, that I will survive my bodily death, such survival at least seems *conceivable*. We can at least imagine what it would be like to go on thinking and perceiving while our physical bodies rot in the grave. Such survival could come in two forms: a disembodied existence or a reincarnation into some new body. We can also, apparently, imagine two people suddenly coming to occupy one another's body (at least one short-lived television show and one movie were based on this premise); and one can imagine having out-of-body experiences in which one perceives events quite distant from one's physical body. The apparent conceivability of such scenarios seems to be symptomatic of a fundamental sense or feeling that the mind is something quite different from the body and that my thoughts, beliefs, and feelings are fundamentally independent of my physical embodiment. Indeed, it is hard to shake the sense that it is at least possible to exist apart from one's body. Moreover, if such scenarios are even possible, then this can seem to show that one's mind is constituted by some sort of substance that is independent of one's body. So the argument for dualism would be this:

Certain scenarios (e.g., life after death) are possible.
Such scenarios are possible only if substance dualism is true.
∴ Substance dualism is true.

However, one might ultimately question both premises in this argument. First, while allowing that life after death *seems* to be possible, one might deny that it is *really* possible. Alternatively, one might claim that the second premise is false as it stands, for all that we can really say is that such scenarios are possible only if substance dualism is *possible*. That is, one might grant that it is possible that I will survive my bodily death precisely because it is *possible* that I have an immaterial soul that will go on after my body ceases to function. No materialist needs to deny the logical possibility that substance dualism is true, just as no expert on cows need deny the logical possibility that a cow might jump over the moon. But of course it does not follow that we should believe substance dualism, just as it does not follow that cows have a latent flying ability.

2.2 Against Substance Dualism

Whatever one thinks of the case for substance dualism, there is a strong argument against it. The argument is based on very fundamental features of what makes one theory better than another, and I will illustrate this feature by considering a patently absurd theory far removed from philosophy of mind.

2.2.1 The Simplicity Principle and the Five-Minute Theory

According to current cosmology, the universe is about 15 billion years old, and Earth is approximately one-third that age. On the other hand, according to some creationists, God brought the whole universe into existence less than 10,000 years ago. (According to some, we can be more specific yet and say that the year was 4004 BCE.) Such creationist views have to explain many features of the world that seem to be much older than this: fossils, distant galaxies, and so on. The creationist might respond by disputing the scientific methods and theories that lead us to infer that these objects are older than 10,000 years. But there is another, more devious, tack that the creationist might take. The creationist might claim that God brought the world into existence 6,000 years ago, but that he created it with dinosaur fossils already in place, and with light from distant galaxies already in transit (or apparently already in transit—the photons never actually left the galaxy but were instead created in space). In other words, God created the world 6,000 years ago, and he created it such that it looks exactly like our scientific theories say that it looked at that time—with buried fossils, photons spread throughout the universe in particular ways, etc. This version of creationism need not fear being contradicted by any empirical evidence about the apparent age of the universe.

This type of creationism is an absurd theory, but not quite absurd enough for my purposes. So I will propose a different theory of the universe, one which changes the creationist theory in two crucial respects. First, the universe, on this theory, is only five minutes old rather than 6,000 years; second, there was no God who brought the universe into existence—instead, it just popped into existence without any cause. Bertrand Russell employs this example for a slightly different purpose in *The Analysis of Mind* (1921, p. 159) and in *Human Knowledge* (1948, p. 212). As with creationism, the five-minute theory need not fear being directly contradicted by any empirical evidence. For example, although I appear to have many memories of times before five minutes ago, the five-minute theory simply claims that I came into existence with those memories already in place. Similarly, I am looking at a compact disc that bears a copyright date of 1992, but the compact disc simply came into existence five minutes ago with that marking already on it.

W. V. Quine has emphasized that individual claims about the world are not susceptible of verification or falsification by sensory data; any particular claim about the world can withstand any empirical test, so long as we are willing to make the requisite compensatory moves in the rest of our theory (Quine 1951). The five-minute theory is, in essence, the extreme illustration of this Quinean holism. As long as I am willing to make the compensating moves recommended by the five-minute theory, there is no empirical test that can show that the world is more than five minutes old.

Of course, the five-minute theory is patently absurd, and anyone who genuinely believed it would be irrational. But why? Since it is not susceptible of empirical disconfirmation, there must be some other reason. I take it that the reason is simply this: In contrast with the normal view (in which the world is much older than five minutes), the five-minute theory posits an enormous number of brute, inexplicable coincidences or mysteries. First, there is the mystery of why the world popped into existence at all; however, an atheistic scientific account of the world has that same mystery, and a theistic account of the world has the analogous mystery of why God exists. So no theory appears to be free of inexplicable mysteries. But the five-minute theory adds hugely to the list. For example, my apparent recollection of the whereabouts of various things around my house is reasonably accurate. I would have no trouble finding the bathroom or the kids' bedrooms, despite the fact that I have not seen any of these rooms in the last five minutes. The accuracy of my apparent recollection is easily explained on the normal view of the world, for I have seen those rooms many times, and I now remember their locations. In contrast, the five-minute theory must simply leave my ability to find these rooms as a brute and inexplicable mystery. Another example: It seems that sunlight is streaming in the window. On the ordinary view, this is the result of the photons' having been emitted from the sun about eight minutes ago. The five-minute theory cannot adopt this explanation; at best it can say that the photons came into existence five minutes ago traveling on a path that happened to look as if they had come from the sun, but there would be no further explanation for why they were on that path. Indefinitely many such examples could be offered.

Thus the fundamental reason for rejecting the five-minute theory is that it fails to provide explanations for many events and states of affairs that are explicable on the alternative view of the universe. So far as I can tell, there is no other reason for rejecting the theory. That we do reject the theory, then, strongly suggests that we assume something like the following general principle:

(S) Given two theories, it is unreasonable to believe one that leaves significantly more unexplained mysteries.

I will call this the *simplicity principle*. I take it to be a version of Occam's Razor (the principle that entities ought not to be multiplied beyond necessity). In this version the entities in question are unexplained mysteries. Our reaction to the five-minute theory shows the depth of our commitment to this principle. Were it not for our commitment to the simplicity principle, we would have no reason at all for rejecting the five-minute theory and all manner of other nonsense.

The simplicity principle does not provide an easy, mechanical means of testing theories, for the principle is unavoidably vague. It is not always clear how to count mysteries, and thus it is not always clear when one theory leaves more mysteries than another. It is also not obvious which events or states of affairs are to be categorized as mysteries. For example, suppose I flip a coin ten times and the sequence of heads (H) and tails (T) is T H H H T H T T T H. Then suppose I flip another coin and the sequence is H H H H H H H H H H. Intuitively, the second series calls out for an explanation; one is inclined to point out that the odds against 10 heads in a row are 1,024 to 1. One would then proceed to closely examine the coin or the circumstances to find the reason that this particular sequence was achieved. The first sequence, on the other hand, seems to call for no such explanation. However, the odds against that particular sequence's occurring are likewise 1,024 to 1. On the other hand, if I had predicted in advance that I would flip exactly that sequence, then we probably would seek some sort of explanation. The point is simply that there is no clear and obvious criterion for when an event constitutes a mystery that requires explanation.

Nonetheless, even if there are no obvious mechanical rules by means of which the simplicity principle can be applied, there are still many cases in which its application is clear. Consider an example from science: The Ptolemaic model of the solar system placed the sun and all the planets in orbit around Earth. To make this consistent with the observed positions of these objects, Ptolemaic astronomers had to assume not only that the planets and sun moved in circles but also that they moved around a circle within the main circle. To accord with the data, however, epicycles had to be added to the epicycles. Moreover, each of the main circles was centered on a different point—each a point somewhere near Earth, but not Earth itself. And some of these points themselves moved in circles—i.e., planets did not move around a fixed point. With all these assumptions in place, the model provided reasonably accurate predictions of the locations of the planets against the background stars—Copernicus's model was not appreciably more accurate. But a great many questions are simply left unanswered by the Ptolemaic model. For one thing, why does each of the planets move in such a strange orbits? Each epicycle (and there were more than 40) raises the question of why the epicycle is there and why it has the particular diameter that it has. Compare this with the post-Copernicus, post-Kepler, post-Newton model according to which the planets orbit the sun in ellipses and their motion is determined by the law of gravity. Granted, Newton had no explanation for why gravity works the way that it does, but the answer to this one question could in essence answer the question of why each of the planets moves as it does. Under the Ptolemaic system, the orbit of each planet is unique, and there is no one law that could possibly cover them all; thus, Ptolemy had no answer to "Why does Mercury moves the way it does?" and "Why does Venus moves the way it does?" and so on, and these look to be independent questions. Moreover, because of the epicycles, each of these questions subdivides into a number of other apparently independent questions. In addition, Newton's gravitational law also explains the tides and why apples fall to the ground; whatever mechanism Ptolemy might have dreamed up to explain the odd motion of the planets, it presumably would not have had anything to do with tides or with ordinary objects' falling to the ground—those would have been separate mysteries. The Copernican model, particularly after Kepler and Newton, explains far more for less; i.e., it leaves fewer inexplicable mysteries.

2.2.2 Applying the Simplicity Principle to Substance Dualism

When the simplicity principle is applied to substance dualism, substance dualism fares very poorly, for it leaves many inexplicable mysteries. Here are a few:

• Humans evolved from single-cell organisms. Such organisms presumably do not have immaterial minds. So, according to dualism, somewhere along the evolutionary chain an organism that had no mind produced offspring that did have minds. Why and how would that happen? Was a certain kind of physical genetic mutation necessary for the addition of an immaterial mind? What kind of mutation? Why was it necessary? Why sufficient?

• Why don't we see obvious evidence that people survive bodily death? If they do, why do we no longer see any effects from their presence? If they don't, why not?

• Why do minds stay attached to particular bodies? Why doesn't it happen that my mind and yours change places now and then?

• Why do drugs and alcohol affect the mind?

• Why does mental ability deteriorate with age?

• Why does damage to the brain (e.g., from strokes or accidents) affect the mind?

• Why do certain mental states explain certain behaviors?

The materialist who claims that the mind is constituted by material particles does not have any difficulty with the first three questions above; if our minds are constituted by our brains, then it is no mystery at all why my mind stays attached to my body, and it is no mystery at all why, for example, I fail to see any evidence of my deceased father's continued existence. To be fair to the dualist, on the last four questions, the materialist does not yet have full answers either; we don't know that much, for example, about exactly why and how strokes have the effects that they do. But nonetheless, at a certain level it is not utterly mysterious: If the mind is constituted by the brain, and if there is damage to the brain because of a restricted blood flow, then it is not surprising that there will be some mental effects, even if we are not now in a position to explain and predict them exactly. The situation is similar with the other remaining questions.

Materialism brings with it the promise of a rather full understanding of mental functioning, such that, e.g., we would be able to predict how damage of a certain sort (damage we have not yet seen) would affect mental capacity—for we would be able to understand and model how actual mental functioning works in the brain, and then see what would happen in the model if certain features were changed or damaged. The dualist could never do this, for the dualist must claim that we can never observe the actual mental functioning. At best we can come up with a list of correlations of physical states and corresponding mental states. Without an understanding of the mechanism, we would never really understand *why* certain brain states are correlated with certain mental states. Thus we would never be able to move on to prediction in unseen cases, and we wouldn't really have explained why the brain states were correlated with the mental states in the first place. For the dualist, *each* physical-mental correlation is a unique and apparently forever inexplicable phenomenon.

2.3 Prospects for Dualism

Perhaps the substance dualist can begin to answer some of these objections by providing a more fully worked-out theory, one that provides an explanatory framework such that at least some of the above questions appear to have answers. The dualist might try to formulate some principles concerning the relation between the immaterial mind and the physical body; the hope would be that a relatively small number of such principles would suffice to explain most or all of the mysteries laid out above. For example, the dualist might propose that it is a fundamental law of nature that an immaterial mind is sustained and kept vital by being attached to an organism with a certain type of physical structure and complexity. This would go some way toward answering the first three questions. Of course, this raises the further question of *why* such a principle holds true, and the dualist presumably has no further answer to that question. But even so, if the principle could be formulated appropriately it would at least trade a number of apparently distinct mysteries for the one mystery of why that principle holds. And perhaps a similar strategy could be tried for the remaining mysteries: attempting to formulate general principles of mind-body correlation that lump a number of apparently distinct mysteries under a smaller number of distinct headings. And this is, of course, a perfectly respectable enterprise if fruitful. It is essentially the same as what physicists do when they isolate the fundamental forces of nature. We, as yet, have no account of why the gravitational force or the strong force works the way it does, or why those forces have the strength they have. But by positing this small number of unexplained mysteries, physicists can explain a range of phenomena that would otherwise constitute an enormous list of unexplained mysteries. And at the theoretical edges of physics there are efforts to unify the known fundamental forces, thus simplifying further.

The dualist, however, will have some special difficulties trying to ascertain principles correlating mental and physical states. When formulating the law of gravitation, physicists are able to observe the motions of massive bodies (planets, etc.) directly, so they have a fairly direct way of ascertaining whether their formulation is correct (e.g., through various observations, they can determine whether the force due to gravity varies inversely with the square of the distance). But when the dualist attempts to formulate analogous principles, observation is a little trickier. Evidently, the immaterial soul posited by the dualist can be directly observed, if at all, only by introspection. For example, we have no way of directly observing which sort of organisms have minds at all, and even in the case of humans there is no way for more than one person to directly observe the same token mental state. And introspection itself hardly seems infallible.

Even if the dualist manages to formulate a small number of principles that seem to be in accord with observable data and to offer some explanation for the mysteries cited above, the truth of these principles themselves would presumably be left unexplained. By itself this is not a problem, for all theories leave something unexplained—the materialist cannot explain why the basic physical laws of nature are true. Nonetheless, materialism would still appear to leave fewer inexplicable mysteries than even a fully articulate dualistic theory. The dualist does not, of course, abandon physical theory, so new dualistic mind-body principles will simply add further mysteries. Thus, it seems that materialism would be preferable even to a fully formulated dualist theory.

There is still a way in which substance dualism might come to seem preferable to materialism. Materialism would be undermined if there were observations and data which the new dualistic theory could explain but which materialism could not. For example, suppose that neuroscientists regularly saw brain events occur without any observable physical cause; the dualist could explain this by saying that the immaterial mind produced those events, whereas the materialist would be at a loss. Or suppose that some people could regularly produce information about past events, information that they could not have known otherwise. Depending on the nature of the dualist theory, the dualist might be able to explain such things by saying that the person's immaterial mind lived through those past events and was then reincarnated into its present body. (However, the dualist would have to be careful here. If the theory is formulated such that it is possible for immaterial minds to detach from dead bodies and move to different bodies, the dualist will have to face the mystery of why such mind-body switches don't happen regularly, even with bodies that are alive. Perhaps there is some formulation of the dualist theory that could have it both ways.) The materialist would be at a loss. I am not suggesting that we have any such evidence against materialism, and I think it extremely unlikely that we will ever run into any such evidence, but there is no point in denying the *possibility* of such occurrences. If such things happened regularly, dualism might leave fewer mysteries overall.

To sum up: Substance dualism need not be thought of as unscientific mystical gobbledygook. It could be formulated as a real theory with a chance of being true. However, so far no one has presented a full formulation of the theory such that it can answer the mysteries above or have other compensating explanatory advantages over materialism. And finding such a formulation will not be easy. Thus, because dualism so far appears to fail so badly when the simplicity principle is applied, we must say that the evidence points overwhelmingly against it.

2.4   Preview of the Simplicity Objection against Option 3

As I mentioned, few philosophers have any inclination toward substance dualism. I have belabored the case against it two reasons: to make explicit to nonphilosophers *why* philosophers reject the theory and to bring out and illustrate the simplicity principle. One reason for discussing the simplicity principle, apart from its intrinsic interest and importance, is that this principle can appear to raise serious prima facie objections to any option-3 account of the mind.

According to option 3, the common-sense claims about mind and agency are logically independent of the claims of physical science. If we accept both CSP and physical science as making true claims, option 3 would appear to automatically increase the number of inexplicable mysteries. Why? As discussed above, no theory explains everything; even a completed physical science will presumably leave certain fundamental laws of nature or other features of the world unexplained. Similarly with CSP—although many of the truths of CSP will presumably be subsumed under more general claims about minds and agents, there will, according to option 3, be some basic claims of CSP that are not explained further. If option 2 were correct, these basic claims would be entailed by the truths of physical science and would thus be explained by physical theory. Thus, with option 2 we are only stuck with the unexplained mysteries at the base of physical science, whereas option 3 adds new mysteries to those we already inherit from physical science. Thus it seems that we should prefer option 2 to option 3.

On the other hand, the situation is a little different here than it was with dualism. The apparent mysteries that dualism introduces are eliminated by materialism. Materialism claims that dualism is false, and with the falsity of dualism most of the mysteries evaporate. Option 2 accepts the truth of the core of CSP, but it avoids any new mysteries by saying that such truths are actually entailed by physical science. But saying that they are entailed does not make it so. If one accepts the truth of CSP, and if it turns out that CSP's claims simply are not implied by the truths of physical science, one is stuck with the additional mysteries, like it or not. That is to say: If reductionism fails, the additional mysteries introduced by CSP are left unexplained by physical science. And this is basically the line that teleological realism will take in answer to the objection. However, at this point it is a bit premature to fully judge how teleological realism fares when the simplicity principle is applied. We will take a much fuller look in chapter 13.

Entailment and the Three Options

I began the first chapter by presenting the mind-body problem as a vaguely felt mystery: How does our common-sense view of mind and agency fit with what physical science tells us about human beings? I suggested that we can sharpen the mystery by considering the logical relationship between the facts of physical science and the claims of common-sense psychology. There were three possible options: contradiction, entailment, and independence. If the first of these options is correct, we should ultimately reject the claims of CSP; hence this would be tantamount to eliminativism. On the second option, the facts of physical science imply the claims of CSP, and thus CSP would be vindicated. This option can be called *reductionism*, for it holds that the claims of CSP will be reduced to the claims of physical science. According to the third option, the claims of CSP and the facts of physical science are simply independent of one another. In this chapter I will characterize these options more carefully and explicitly. In essence, we are at our third layer in setting up the problem: First we had the intuitive setup of the mystery, then we had a somewhat more precise way of putting the mystery in terms of the three options, and now we aim to find an even more precise way of characterizing exactly what these options mean. I will focus on option 2 and the notion of *reduction*.

My account of reduction will follow, at least in outline, the account of theoretical reduction elaborated by Ernest Nagel (1961), although there will be some significant deviations. In the last section of this chapter I will discuss an altogether different model of reduction, sometimes known as *Hooker-Churchland reduction*; I will argue that this model of reduction is not at all useful in discussing the mind-body problem.

Most philosophers of mind do not explicitly count themselves as reductionists; in particular, many philosophers think that the prevailing functionalist theory of mind is not reductionist. In chapter 4, I will argue that functionalism does fall squarely within option 2 reductionism, at least as I have characterized it. The dispute may be in part a simple quibble over how to use the word 'reduction'. Since the notion of theoretical reduction is not a staple of pre-philosophical discourse, there can be no real question of one or another philosopher's getting the notion right. The real questions can only concern the philosophical fruitfulness of the concept. However, I will argue that those who claim that functionalism is not a reductionist view have a notion of reduction that is hard to motivate in the context of the mind-body problem as I have presented it.

3.1 Reduction and the Need for Bridge Laws

In describing the three options, the critical concept is that of *implication* or *entailment*. This is most explicit in option 2, which I characterized as the view that the claims of physical science will entail those of CSP. I described option 1 as the view that CSP and physical science contradict one another, but this can likewise be put simply in terms of entailment: According to option 1, the ultimate facts of physical science will entail the negation of the claims of CSP. Option 3—the view that CSP and physical science are independent—can be defined as the claim that neither option 1 nor option 2 holds. The notion of entailment is given a precise meaning in the context of symbolic or formal logic. This concept is familiar from dozens of formal logic textbooks.

As a first pass, we can say that option 2 is the view that the claims of CSP are formally implied by the facts of physical science. Or, if 'P' denotes the claims of physical science and 'M' denotes the claims of CSP, option 2 claims that P entails M. We need not be strict about this; it will suffice if physical science entails the bulk of CSP but not quite all of it, particularly if physical science entails an acceptable *revision* of CSP.

However, there is an immediate obstacle for option 2, insofar as the vocabularies of CSP and physical science differ. CSP makes claims like "Joan wants a glass of wine." The problem is that the concept of *wanting*, which figures crucially in this attribution, is presumably not a predicate that will appear in the statements of physical science. This means that there is no way that the statements of physical science could formally entail "Joan wants a glass of wine." In general, when two schemata or logical formulas do not share any predicate letters or sentence letters, there will be no entailment relationship between them[1]; accordingly, when two statements do not share any predicates, there is no reason to think that one entails the other. Thus, since there are predicates of CSP that do not appear in the statements of physical science, the facts of physical science alone cannot entail the claims of CSP. Of course, even if two statements lack common predicates, the first might entail the second if we can also assume the truth of an additional sentence that links the predicates in the right way. Thus, the statements of physical science might entail the statements of CSP, if we can also assume the truth of some general statements linking the disparate vocabularies. Such general statements can be referred to as *bridge laws*.

However, we will have to restrict what can count as a bridge law. We could trivially produce *a* general statement that allows physical science to entail CSP: "If P then M" (where, again, P is the entire set of statements of physical science and M the entire set of CSP claims). The combination of P and "if P then M" does entail M. Moreover, insofar as we believe M, we also believe "if P then M" (since a conditional is true if either the consequent is true or the antecedent is false). Nonetheless, if we simply assume "if P then M" on the grounds that we already accept M, we beg an important question. At minimum, for the purpose of showing that P entails M, we should not assume a bridge law that presupposes the truth of M; any bridge law should be a claim to which we are committed to regardless of our commitment to CSP.

An illustration might help. Consider the following two statements:

(1) Tom Seaver was the best pitcher the Mets ever had.

(2) Tom Seaver was the best hurler the Mets ever had.

Statement (1) does not entail statement (2). Nonetheless, there does seem to be an implication relationship here, especially for anyone who knows that to be a pitcher just is to be a hurler and who, in particular, knows the following:

(3) One person is a better pitcher than a second if and only if the first is a better hurler than the second.

Statements (1) and (3) taken together do suffice to imply statement (2). Of course, this is still not to say that (1) formally implies (2). But, given the nature of (3), one might be forgiven for claiming that (1) does imply (2); not only is (3) a true statement, but it is also a statement we would affirm regardless of our opinion of Tom Seaver.

A bridge law linking the vocabulary of CSP to physical science would have to work in an analogous fashion. At minimum, the bridge law would have to be something that we practitioners of CSP would accept (implicitly or explicitly) quite apart from our affirmation of the substantive claims of CSP. In particular, the bridge laws would be claims that we accept about the mental irrespective of our commitment to the actual existence of mental states. In essence, the bridge laws would constitute our own best reflections on the meaning or implications of the language of CSP; they would amount to something like methodological observations. In this respect, my account of bridge laws differs significantly from Nagel's. Nagel himself says that a bridge law might be merely the factual discovery that "the occurrence of the state of affairs signified by a certain theoretical expression 'B' in the primary science is a sufficient (or necessary and sufficient) condition for the state of affairs designated by 'A'" (Nagel 1961, p. 354). Nagel's words are susceptible of more than one interpretation, but he seems to suggest that bridge laws are empirically discovered correlations between physical properties and mental properties. For example, we might discover that anybody who has mental state K has a particular brain state, Q. In that case, a Nagelian bridge law would have the form

(NBL) $(\forall x)(x$ has mental state $K \equiv x$ has brain state $Q)$.

However, there is an oddity about bridge laws of this form. To discover that such a bridge law is true, we would have to be able to know when a person has mental state K. Presumably we would do that simply by using the normal means employed by CSP, since before finding some appropriate bridge law we would have no other way. So, in the very process of finding the bridge laws, we would be effectively assuming the correctness of CSP. This is odd, for our project had been to see whether physical science showed that CSP was correct. If we presuppose the correctness of CSP in the very process of finding the needed bridge laws, one might question how much vindication of CSP can result.

More specifically, I contend that with Nagelian bridge laws it would never be possible to show that CSP is actually inconsistent with physical science. First consider an analogous situation: There are people who believe that ghosts exists, and they have what we might refer to as a folk theory of ghosts. Suppose we want to consider whether this theory is vindicated or contradicted by physical science. Of course, physical science does not employ the concept *ghost*; thus, if the facts of physical science are to show either that there are or are not ghosts, we will need some sort of bridging statement between the folk theory and the scientific theory. If we follow Nagel's lead, we would say the relevant bridge law would be an empirically discovered correlation of the form

(GBL) $(\forall x)(x$ is a ghost $\equiv x$ has physical property Q).

But if there are in fact no ghosts, how could we ever discover a correlation of this form? Of course, we could make the following empirical discovery:

$(\forall x)(x$ is a phenomenon that the folk *call* a ghost $\equiv x$ has physical property Q).

But this will not yield a bridge law of the Nagelian form unless we further assume

$(\forall x)(x$ is a phenomenon that the folk *call* a ghost $\supset x$ is a ghost).

But if we assumed this, then, since there are phenomena that the folk *call* ghosts, it would already follow that ghosts exist. The net result is this: If the required bridge laws are empirically discovered correlations, it will be impossible to discover that the facts of science are inconsistent with the existence of ghosts.

An analogous argument can be run concerning mental states. If it is to be possible for physical science to imply that no one in fact has mental state K, we will need a bridge statement. Nagel tells us that the bridge laws will be empirically discovered correlations of the form of (NBL). But if CSP is mistaken and no one is really in mental state K, then the most we could hope to discover empirically is

$(\forall x)(x$ is a person whom the folk *say* has mental state $K \equiv x$ has brain state Q).

But just as with the ghost case, this will not get us any closer to the needed bridge statement unless we further assume something like

$(\forall x)(x$ is a person whom the folk say has mental state $K \supset x$ has mental state K).

But since there are people who are *said* to have mental state K, it would follow that those people really do have mental state K. So if bridge laws are supposed to be empirically discovered correlations between mental states and physical states, then it will be impossible to discover that the facts of physical science entail the falsity of CSP. This strongly suggests that something has gone awry with Nagel's approach to bridge laws. If you are in the game of trying to either vindicate or contradict CSP through empirical study, the rules of the game should not eliminate the possibility of contradiction. None of this provides any reason to reject the bridge-law approach entirely, but it does suggest that we should accept the modified proposal rather than Nagel's original suggestion.

3.2   The Options Revisited

We started with an intuitively felt mystery about mind and body, and my aim has been to give a more precise characterization of the philosophical worry. It now makes sense to stand back and assess whether the three options, as characterized, genuinely speak to the philosophical worry with which we began. As I presented the problem in the opening chapter, there is an apparent tension between our common-sense conception of ourselves as agents with minds and our recognition of the fact that we are physical objects. Our status as agents with minds can appear mysterious next to the conception of human beings derived from physical science, for physical science does not speak in terms of agency or responsibility, nor does it attribute intentional states to the objects it studies.

How would option 2, as characterized in this chapter, constitute a solution to this problem? Option 2 yields a picture in which the common-sense facts about mind and agency are neatly subsumed within physical science; the apparent tension is resolved, for the claims of CSP are simply logical implications of the ultimate claims of physical science. That is not quite right: the claims of CSP are logical implications of physical science *and* the bridge laws, where the bridge laws themselves are not scientific claims. However, given the required special status of the bridge laws, the overall picture does not change substantially. The bridge laws were required to be claims about CSP to which we would be committed even apart from our commitment to the existence of mental states; i.e., these would be claims that we practitioners of CSP think are true about mental states *if there are any*. Option 2 claims that the substantive assertions of CSP logically follow from the truths of physical science plus these bridge laws. Thus, given the truths of physical science, the claims of CSP essentially come along for free. According to option 2, the facts of CSP ultimately are facts of physical science, albeit packaged somewhat differently. This would indeed look like a vindication of CSP—a showing that not only are the truths of CSP not mysterious from the scientific perspective, but, given a proper understanding of the nature of CSP claims (an understanding provided by the bridge laws), the truths of CSP are in fact simply logical implications of the facts of physical science. Surely this would resolve our original mystery.

What about option 1? I originally suggested the three options as an exclusive listing of the possible logical relationships between physical science and the claims of CSP. However, option 2 is now defined as the claim that CSP is entailed by physical science plus bridge laws. Thus, instead of talking about the logical relationship between physical science *simpliciter* and CSP, we are now considering the relationship between physical science plus certain commitments about the nature of CSP, on the one hand, and the substantive claims of CSP, on the other. Accordingly, option 1 would be the claim that the substantive claims of CSP are inconsistent with physical science plus the bridge laws; to put it in equivalent terms, the claims of physical science plus the bridge laws suffice to entail the *negation* of the claims of CSP. This would naturally provide a starkly different way of resolving the original mystery: The apparent tension between science and CSP is resolved by seeing that we should in fact reject the claims of CSP.

It should be noted again that reduction need not be an all-or-nothing matter. Perhaps most but not all of CSP will follow from physical science plus the appropriate bridge laws. Or perhaps certain parts of CSP will follow from physical science only if we revise the bridge laws we are inclined to accept about CSP. This would amount to a partial *reconstrual* of our claims about mind and agency. There is nothing particularly mysterious about either of these possibilities, and there is nothing to be gained by insisting on a sharp line between vindicating and rejecting CSP.

Option 3 arises quite naturally here, at least as a coherent alternative that must be on the table, for it is clear that between any two given sets of propositions there is logical space for the two sets not to be inconsistent and for one not to imply the other. Hence the third option: that the claims of CSP and physical science are logically independent of one another. On the face of things, such a view would resolve the tension by showing that the claims of physical science at least pose no threat to the truth of CSP.

3.3 Hooker-Churchland Reduction

There is another model of reduction, developed by C. A. Hooker and by Patricia and Paul Churchland and explained and refined by John Bickle.[2] Bickle dubs the approach *H-C reduction*, and he claims that it is quite different from standard bridge-law reduction. If H-C reduction is indeed quite different from the Nagelian account, and if it would help in solving the philosophical mystery with which we began, then it too should be brought into consideration. However, I will argue that H-C reduction is altogether unsatisfactory; to the extent that it differs from broadly Nagelian bridge-law approaches, H-C reduction makes reduction trivial and, in any event, misses the point of having a reductive theory of the mind.

Like the Nagelian account, the H-C model sees reduction as a certain kind of relation between two theories. On the one hand we have the new theory,

T_N, which is the scientific account of the behavior of human beings; on the other hand we have the old theory, T_O, which in this case is the common-sense psychological theory of mind. According to Nagelian reduction, the new theory, T_N, plus appropriate bridge laws, entails T_O, i.e., CSP. On the H-C account, there is no deduction of T_O; instead, "what gets deduced is rather *an analogue structure* I_N, already specified within (a restricted portion of) the vocabulary of T_N. This I_N is the approximately equipotent isomorphic image of the T_O: approximate, since most reductions imply corrections to the reduced theory." (Bickle 1992, p. 222)

I_N is, in essence, a subset of the claims made by T_N; in particular, it has the same vocabulary, and hence the deduction of I_N from T_N does not require bridge laws. However, I_N is still said to be the approximately equipotent iso-morphic image of the T_O. If the H-C reductionist can justify the claim that I_N is indeed the equipotent isomorphic image of CSP, then H-C reduction would seem to accomplish what option 2 sets out to do: It would provide a picture in which the common-sense facts about mind and agency are neatly subsumed within physical science. And yet it would apparently do so with-out the need for traditional bridge laws.

Bickle provides the following hypothetical and abstract illustration of H-C reduction:

T_N & limiting assump. & boundary cond.
logically entails
I_N (a set of theorems of (restricted) T_N)
e.g.,
$(x)(Ax \supset Bx)$,
$(x)((Bx \& Cx \supset Dx)$,
which is relevantly isomorphic with T_O (the older theory)—e.g.,
$(x)(Jx \supset Kx)$
$(x)((Kx \& Lx) \supset Mx)$. (1992, p. 222)

The crucial question is what it means for I_N to be *equipotent* or *relevantly iso-morphic* with T_O (i.e., CSP). Bickle tells us the following:

. . . cross-theoretic identity statements play no role in . . . in the comparison between the syntactic structures of I_N and T_O. The I_N is already specified with (a portion of) the language of T_N, so there is no need for cross-theoretic statements to effect its non-trivial derivation. Elements analogous in one functional respect to the bridge laws of the logical empiricists do appear in the comparison of the I_N and T_O. But these ele-ments are merely ordered pairs of terms, drawn from the descriptive vocabularies of the two theories, which indicate the term substitutions in I_N that yield the actual laws of T_O (or approximations of the actual laws, if that is all a given case allows). Bridge laws in the logical empiricist's sense are hence no part of an H-C intertheoretic reduction. (ibid., p. 223)

Thus, all that is required for I_N to be isomorphic to T_O is that there be a set of ordered pairs of terms such that T_O results if the second in each pair is substituted for the first within I_N. In Bickle's schematic example, the following set of ordered pairs will do the trick:

$\{\langle Ax,Jx\rangle,\langle Bx,Kx\rangle,\langle Cx,Lx\rangle,\langle Dx,Mx\rangle\}$.

That is, if we substitute "Jx" for each occurrence of "Ax" in I_N, "Kx for each occurrence of "Bx" in I_N, etc., the result of the substitution will be equivalent to T_O. On the bridge-law approach, a successful reduction requires laws linking the new theory to the terminology of the old theory, where the laws must be true and must reflect our commitments *about* the old theory apart from any commitment to the theory itself. The requirement of H-C reduction is much more minimal. We do not need to produce any propositions, true or otherwise, that link the vocabulary of T_N and I_N to T_O. Instead, the test of whether T_O has been successfully reduced is merely syntactic: Reduction is accomplished so long as there is a set of substitutions into I_N such that the result is equivalent to T_O. If there exists such a set of substitutions, I_N is deemed to be the "equipotent isomorphic image" of T_O.

Bickle tells us that "on the H-C account, an intertheoretic reduction is a proof of displaceability, demonstrating that a more comprehensive theory T_N contains explanatory and predictive resources parallel to those of the reduced theory T_O" (1992, p. 222). In other words, if the reduction is successful, then T_O is, at best, superfluous, for all of its explanatory and predictive resources have been shown to be matched by the new theory T_N. However, it is hard to see why Bickle thinks that this result would have been shown by the mere fact that a set of substitutions into T_N yields an expression of T_O. In general, the fact that one can get from one true proposition to another proposition by substitution is hardly a justification for the claim that the second proposition has been displaced or shown to be superfluous.

Suppose that T_N is Newtonian physics, and that I_N is a particular claim of T_N:

(1) Between any two masses, there is a force that is inversely proportional to the square of the distance between them.

We could represent this schematically as

(2) $(\forall x)(\forall y)(Mx \mathbin{\&} My \supset (\exists z)(Fz \mathbin{\&} Izxy))$,

where "Mx" means "x is a mass," "Fz" means "z is a force," and "$Izxy$" means "z is inversely proportional to the square of the distance between x and y." Now consider the common-sense (and rather dubious) claim about human relations, that opposites attract. In other words, the T_O claim is as follows:

(3) Between any two people, there will be an attraction that is inversely proportional to the similarity of their personalities.

And this could be put schematically as

(4) $(\forall x)(\forall y)(Px \ \& \ Py \supset (\exists z)(Az \ \& \ Szxy),$

where "Px" means "x is a person," "Az" means "z is an attraction," and "$Szxy$" means "z is inversely proportional to the similarity of the personalities of x and y." There is an obvious set of substitutions into (2) such that (4) results:

$\{\langle Mx,Px \rangle, \ \langle Fz,Az \rangle, \langle Izxy,Szxy \rangle\}.$

This case has been set up so that it appears to meet the formal requirements of an H-C reduction. We could thus conclude that the old theory that opposites attract has been displaced and shown superfluous by the claim that gravitational force varies inversely with the square of the distance between two bodies. But, of course, this is absurd. The mere fact that a set of substitutions will transform (2) into (4) is simply irrelevant to the logical relationship between (2) and (4).

Perhaps the H-C reductionist would reply that one could only get such absurdities when the two theories involved are extremely short. If instead of (3) we considered our entire common-sense theory about human relations, the schematic presentation would obviously be much more complex; in particular, the predicates that appear in (4) would also appear in many other claims about human beings. Given this, it would then be highly unlikely that any subset of Newtonian mechanics would be able to map onto the common-sense theory in the way required by H-C reduction.

However, adding complexity to T_O does not change the situation, and the proposed criterion for reduction is still clearly inadequate. To see this, let us first look back at Bickle's schematic example of a successful reduction. In his example, I_N was

(5) $(\forall x)(Ax \supset Bx) \ \& \ (\forall x)((Bx \ \& \ Cx) \supset Dx).$

And Bickle said that this was relevantly isomorphic with the old theory, T_O,

(6) $(\forall x)(Jx \supset Kx) \ \& \ (\forall x)((Kx \ \& \ Lx) \supset Mx),$

for there is an obvious set of substitutions into (5) that will yield (6). However, it is first worth noting that there is a set of less obvious substitutions that will also transform (5) into an equivalent of (6):

(7) {⟨Ax, Jx & –Kx v Kx & Lx & –Mx⟩, ⟨Bx, –Jx & –Kx v –Jx & –Lx v –Jx & Mx v Kx & –Lx v Kx & Mx⟩, ⟨Cx, Jx & –Kx v Kx & Lx & –Mx⟩,⟨Dx, –Jx & –Kx v –Jx & –Lx v –Jx & Mx v Kx & –Lx v Kx & Mx⟩}.

That is, for every occurrence of the one-place predicate "Ax" we substitute the one-place predicate "Jx & –Kx v Kx & Lx & –Mx," and for every occurrence of the one-place predicate "Bx" we substitute the one-place predicate "–Jx & –Kx v –Jx & –Lx v –Jx & Mx v Kx & –Lx v Kx & Mx," etc. This set of substitutions will yield a monstrously long schema in place of (5), but that schema is logically equivalent to (6). What I have done is substitute for each predicate of (5) a predicate gerrymandered in a way that guarantees that the end result will be equivalent to (6). So far, this is of no particular moment, for we already knew that (5) could be transformed into (6) by a given set of substitutions; there was no need for the madness of the substitution pattern given in (7). However, there was a method to the madness in (7). In fact, given two schemata X and Y, one can in general provide a recipe for substituting into X such that the result is a schema equivalent to Y. Suppose, for example, that instead of (6) we have

(6a) (∀x)(Jx ⊃ Kx) & (∀x)((–Kx & Lx) ⊃ Mx)

—that is, suppose a negation is thrown into the second conjunct. If this is the schematic representation of T_O, then it may at first *appear* that there is no way that the theory I_N is equipotent or isomorphic in the sense defined by Bickle. If we do the straightforward substitution that yielded (6) from (5), then of course we do not get (6a) or anything equivalent to (6a). But there is a different set of substitutions which, when made in (5), will yield an equivalent of (6a):

(8) {⟨Ax, Jx & –Kx v –Kx & Lx & –Mx⟩,⟨Bx, –Jx & –Kx v –Jx & –Lx v –Jx & Mx v Kx & –Lx v Kx & Mx⟩, ⟨Cx, Jx & –Kx v –Kx & Lx & –Mx⟩, ⟨Dx, –Jx & –Kx v –Jx & –Lx v –Jx & Mx v Kx & –Lx v Kx & Mx⟩}.

So even if our old theory T_O were (6a) instead of (6), when judged by Bickle's criteria, I_N would still be its "equipotent, isomorphic image." Clearly, something has gone badly awry if (5) is said to be the isomorphic image of both (6) and (6a); and the situation is even worse since (5) can be transformed by substitution into any number of schemata—we need merely gerrymander the substitution in the right way and the result is automatic.[3]

The result is that H-C reduction is empty. Given any T_N and any T_O, one can gerrymander correlations such that Bickle's purely syntactic requirements are met. One might try to rule out the gerrymandered substitution patterns by some further syntactic restrictions, but I'm dubious about the chances for success here. The syntactic restrictions on the substitution patterns would have to be sufficiently restrictive to rule out the possibility that an intuitively unrelated T_O is reducible to some theory T_N. On the other hand, the restrictions would also have to allow for cases of theoretical reduction that intuitively seem clear and genuine. It is not at all clear that there is a way of avoiding both of these obstacles. The fundamental difficulty is one I noted earlier in this section when discussing the law of gravitation and opposites attracting: that one can transform one sentence into another by substitution says little or nothing about the logical relationship between the sentences.

Proponents claim that H-C reduction is superior to Nagelian reduction precisely because H-C reductionist do not try to deduce the old common-sense theory from the new scientific theory. This would seem to indicate immediately that the new-wave reductionists are on the wrong track. Recall that reductionism is put forward as an answer to a strongly felt mystery: It seems that our ordinary ways of thinking about minds and agents do not fit well with our scientific approach to the human organism. The Nagelian reductionist has a way of resolving that mystery; according to reductionism, our ordinary claims about the mind are, contrary to their initial appearance, entailed by the scientific approach to human beings. Whatever problems such a view has (and we will be exploring a number of these), at least the Nagelian reductionist provides an answer to the original mystery. With H-C reduction, things are much less clear. As its proponents admit, the cross-theoretic correlations posited by the H-C reductionist do not do any substantive work, and H-C reductionism does not even aim at showing that the old theory follows from the new theory. In essence, the H-C reductionist simply wants to walk away from T_O rather than show that it has any substantive relationship to T_N. But, at least in the mind-body case, that simply amounts to walking away from the original mystery and then proclaiming it solved.

4 | Functionalism and Option 2

It is fair to say that, among philosophers, some form of functionalism is the most widely accepted view of the nature of mental states. As was mentioned in the last chapter, it is sometimes thought that functionalism is not a reductive view, at least not when "reduction" is construed in a broadly Nagelian sense. However, I contend that functionalism clearly does fall within the option-2 project of subsuming common-sense psychology within physical science, and thus I see functionalism as a reductive account. In this chapter I defend that appraisal. In the first two sections of this chapter I lay out the functionalist view, loosely following David Lewis (1972), and I argue that, given functionalism, the truths of CSP are entailed by the propositions of physical science plus appropriate bridge laws. In the next two sections I respond in more detail to some of the reasons standardly given for thinking that functionalism is not reductionist.

4.1 Basic Exposition of Functionalism

The most direct and obvious way to reduce the language of CSP to that of physical science would seem to be through straightforward identity theories. According to a simple version of the identity theory, we will discover through empirical research that each type of mental state is identical to some particular type of brain event. Thus, for example, we could discover that desires for coffee just are instances of brain state P200, and we might also discover that a particular person has an instance of P200. This combination of discoveries would allow us to infer the CSP claim that the person desires coffee:

Desire for coffee = brain state P200.
Bill has brain state P200.
∴ Bill has a desire for coffee.

However, this would not show that the facts of physical science entail the CSP claim, for the identity in the first premise is not a truth of physical science, since it uses the CSP term "desire for coffee." The identity could play the role of a bridge law if it were a truth *about* CSP to which we were committed irrespective of our commitment to the existence of mental states. However, the particular identity as stated is clearly not something to which we CSP practitioners are antecedently committed. Thus, such correlations between brain states and mental states could not have the status of genuine bridge laws, and thus could not support a reduction of CSP to physical science.

There was also a further objection to standard identity theories: we can imagine an alien who does not have anything like our brain states but who does have mental states. Since the identity theory thus denies mental states to beings that have mental states, the theory is unduly restrictive—or, as Ned Block (1978, p. 270) puts it, "chauvinist."

Functionalism entered the philosophical scene, in part, as a response to these problems with the identity theory. (See, for example, Putnam 1967.) I say "in part" because functionalism was also seen as a direct improvement on behaviorism.) The functionalist starts with the thought that the alien who desires coffee must have *something* in common with us by virtue of which it has this desire. The common feature, according to the functionalist, is a state that plays the same causal role. We can spell this out in more detail as follows. Alongside our ordinary explanations of individual actions, CSP also includes a vast body of common-sense platitudes or generalizations relating mental states and behavior. For example, we presumably believe the following:

(1) Agents who desire coffee and believe that coffee can be obtained in the kitchen will, ceteris paribus, go to the kitchen.

(2) If an agent smells coffee in the kitchen, then she will, ceteris paribus, come to believe that coffee can be obtained in the kitchen.

The functionalist reads such claims as *causal* generalizations. In other words, the functionalist will construe (1) and (2) as follows:

(1) If an agent has a desire for coffee and a belief that coffee can be obtained in the kitchen, then, ceteris paribus, the desire and belief will cause her to go to the kitchen.

(2) If an agent smells coffee in the kitchen, then this will, ceteris paribus, cause her to believe that coffee can be obtained in the kitchen.

According to functionalism, if we gather together all such folk generalizations, we will have the central theoretical core of CSP. This theory implicitly defines mental-state types. A belief that coffee can be obtained in the kitchen just *is* the sort of thing that plays the causal role specified by the generalizations of CSP. Thus CSP serves to specify the *causal role* that is definitive of that kind of mental state.

The CSP generalizations will link the propositions of physical science on the one hand and the individual mental-state attributions of CSP on the other. For example, physical science might discover that there is a state of Bill's brain that has certain characteristic causes and effects. If these characteristic causes and effects match the causal role of desires for coffee, as defined by the generalizations of CSP, then we will get the following inference:

Bill is in P200. [discovery by physical science]
P200 is typically caused by such and such and typically causes so and so. [discovery by physical science]
Anything that is typically caused by such and such and typically causes so and so is a desire for coffee. [CSP characterization of the desire-for-coffee causal role]
∴ Bill desires coffee.

Thus, functionalism would allow for the ordinary facts of CSP to be entailed by the facts of physical science. The entailment also requires the CSP characterization of the desire-for-coffee role; however, according to functionalism, this characterization is a truth about CSP to which we are committed irrespective of our commitment to the existence of mental states. Thus, the CSP characterization can serve as a bridge law. So functionalism would appear to be an option-2 or reductionist view. However, since there are those who deny that functionalism is a reductive view, it will perhaps be worthwhile to lay this out in more explicit detail; that is what I will do in the next section, largely following Lewis (1972).

First, however, I should note that functionalism is not necessarily committed to option 2 or reductionism per se, for the functionalist need not assume that physical science will make the required empirical discoveries. The peculiarly philosophical commitment of functionalism is just this: CSP defines a causal role for each kind of mental state, and CSP asserts that anything that plays the right causal role is the associated kind of mental state. This philosophical position is agnostic about whether physical science will discover, for example, that there is some brain state in my head right now playing the causal role specified by CSP for the belief that it is a warm, humid day. If there is no such state, then, according to functionalism, I do not have the belief that it is a warm and humid day, regardless of how obvious it seems from the CSP perspective. If, in general, no physical states play the roles specified by CSP, then this would mean that people do not have mental states after all, and CSP is wrong. The specifically philosophical commitment of functionalism leaves open the eliminativism/reductionism question. That is, functionalism claims that either option 1 or option 2 is correct, depending on the results of empirical science.

4.2 More Detailed Exposition of Functionalism

As explained by Lewis (1972), according to functionalism, the central theoretical core of CSP consists of a vast store of generalizations relating mental states to sensory inputs and behavioral outputs. These common-sense generalizations will typically take the following form:

If A is in mental state t_i and receives sensory stimuli I_j, she will tend with so-and-so probability to be caused thereby to go into mental state t_k and produce behavioral response B_l.

Here "I_j" and "B_l" are terms denoting types of sensory input and behavioral output, and "t_i" and "t_k" are terms denoting kinds of mental states. For example, "t_{25}" might be "desire for coffee." For the purpose of showing that functionalism is a reductive theory, it will be useful to distinguish between mental-state types and tokens. So the common-sense generalization will look as follows:

If A has an instance of mental state t_i and receives sensory stimuli I_j, she will tend to be caused thereby to have an instance of mental state t_k and produce behavioral response B_l.

In quasi-formal language, this can be put as follows:

$(\forall y)(A$ receives input I_j & A has y & $y \approx t_i \supset (\exists w)(w \approx t_k$ & y and I_i cause A to have w and cause A to produce behavior response $B_l))$,

where $\approx$ symbolizes the copula and thus "$y \approx t_i$" is read as "y is a t_i."

According to Lewisian functionalism, the conjunction of such conditionals constitutes our common-sense account of mental states; we will refer to the entire conjunction as T. The conjunction serves to implicitly define the mental terms (the t terms) in terms of the B terms and the I

terms, which are given in physicalistic language; thus the remaining free variables in T are the mental terms (the t terms) and the variable for the agent, "A." Our common-sense theory of the mental is intended to hold generally of all agents, so we can universally generalize, and then abbreviate the whole theory as

$(\forall z)T[z,t_1,t_2, \ldots, t_n]$.

We can follow Lewis in allowing a bold $\mathbf{t}$ to represent an n-tuple of t terms, and we can thus represent the common-sense theory as

$(\forall z)T[z,\mathbf{t}]$.

According to Lewisian functionalism, our common-sense theory asserts the existence of states that play the roles specified by T; i.e., the theory asserts that for each agent there is a set of states that play the specified causal roles. We can formalize this as follows (continuing with convention that boldface variables represent n-tuples):

$(\forall z)(\exists \mathbf{x})T[z,\mathbf{x}]$.

The functionalist next claims that if the theory T is realized, then the states that realize it *are* instances of the corresponding mental states. In other words, if T is realized in a particular person, z, then if z has an instance of any one of those realizer states, the instance is also an instance of the corresponding mental state. Put more formally,

$(\forall z)[(\exists \mathbf{x})T[z,\mathbf{x}] \supset (\forall \mathbf{x})(T[z,\mathbf{x}] \supset (\forall v)(v \approx x_i \ \& \ z \text{ has } v \supset v \approx t_i))]$.

This is logically equivalent to

$(\mathrm{BL_A}) \quad (\forall z)(\forall \mathbf{x})(T[z,\mathbf{x}] \supset (\forall v)(v \approx x_i \ \& \ z \text{ has } v \supset v \approx t_i))$.

On the other hand, if there is no set of states that realizes T in a particular thing, then that thing has no mental states:

$(\mathrm{BL_B}) \quad (\forall z)[-(\exists \mathbf{x})T[z,\mathbf{x}] \supset -(\exists v)(z \text{ has } v \ \& \ v \approx t_i)]$.

The last two claims are designated "BL" because they will serve as bridge laws. What remains to be shown is that, on the functionalist account, these bridge laws, along with the appropriate empirical discoveries by physical science, will allow us to infer the truths of CSP. For the purpose of showing this, we will divide the claims of CSP into three categories: attributions of mental states, explanations of behavior, and generalizations about mental states and behavior.

Consider first the individual attributions of mental states. Physical science could discover about a particular person, z, that a certain set of states realizes the T theory for z. In other words, scientists could make the following general empirical discovery:

(GED) $T[z,\mathbf{r}]$.

Next, physical science could discover that z currently has one of those states; i.e., we might make the following specific empirical discovery:

(SED) $(\exists y)(y \approx r_i \,\&\, z$ has $y)$.

From (GED) and (BL$_\mathrm{A}$), it follows that

$(\forall v)(v \approx r_i \,\&\, z$ has $v \supset v \approx t_i)$.

And from this and (SED) it follows that

$(\exists y)(y \approx t_i \,\&\, z$ has $y)$.

And this is the assertion that z has an instance of mental state t_i, and thus is the individual mental-state attribution.

Explanations of behavior will also follow from (BL) and the appropriate discoveries. If, after ascertaining the truth of (GED), physical science discovers that

$(\exists y)(y \approx r_i \,\&\, z$ has $y \,\&\, y$ caused behavior $B)$,

it will follow from these and (BL$_\mathrm{A}$) that

$(\exists y)(y \approx t_i \,\&\, z$ has $y \,\&\, y$ caused behavior $B)$.

And this is the assertion that z's instance of mental state t_i caused behavior B—i.e., that z did B because he was in mental state t_i. (Of course, I am assuming for the sake of argument that CSP explanations of behavior are causal explanations; but this construal of action explanation is clearly a part of the functionalist doctrine.)

Of course, things might not turn out nicely for CSP. Physical science might discover that there is no set of states that plays the role specified by T in a particular person (or for people in general). Thus we would discover that

$-(\exists \mathbf{x})T[z,\mathbf{x}]$.

For any such z, it would follow from this and (BL$_\mathrm{B}$) that z has no mental states.

Finally, the basic CSP generalizations about mental states and behavior will follow trivially, for they are already part of the common-sense theory

T. According to functionalism, our common-sense theory *T* defines what it is to have mental states. We also typically assume that people actually have mental states and thus that our common-sense generalizations about the mental are instantiated. This assumption can be vindicated only through empirical discoveries. However, according to the Lewisian functionalist, even prior to empirical research, we can know that anyone who does have a certain combination of mental states will tend to behave in a certain kind of way.

The outcome of the discussion is this: According to functionalism, there are bridging statements that, in combination with empirical discoveries of physical science, will suffice to imply either the truth or the falsity of the claims of CSP. Of course, this might be a matter of degree; it might turn out that some of CSP is implied and some of it is not. Moreover, it is explicitly a part of the Lewisian picture that the candidate bridge laws, (BL$_A$) and (BL$_B$), are statements that practitioners of CSP accept *about* CSP irrespective of our commitment to the existence of mental states. Lewis claims that such statements embody "platitudes" that we accept about mental states; they amount to our reflections on the meanings of our mental-state terms; they have an "odor of analyticity" (1972, p. 213). Thus, (BL$_A$) and (BL$_B$) indeed meet the criteria suggested above for status as bridge laws, and functionalism is an option-2, reductive view.

4.3   Biconditionals and Bridge Laws

Jerry Fodor says that the conventional wisdom in philosophy of mind is that "psychological states are multiply realized and that this fact refutes psychophysical reductionism once and for all" (1997, p. 149), and Fodor himself endorses this consensus. However, I have argued that functionalism, according to which mental states are multiply realized, still counts as a reductionist view. My dissent from the consensus might lead one to suspect that I am operating with a nonstandard notion of *reduction*. More sharply yet, one might think that my setup of the mind-body problem fails to divide the possible views in a useful way and is, in any event, behind the times. Of course, this dispute is in danger of being a mere verbal quibble over how to use the word 'reduction'. Nonetheless, it is worth sorting out the issue, for I think that Fodor and others place ill-motivated constraints on the notion of *reduction*.

On one line of thought, functionalism is not reductionist because its bridge laws are of the wrong form. In his classic paper "Special Sciences,"

Fodor assumes that bridge laws will be biconditionals (1974, p. 128). Similarly, when Jaegwon Kim attacks the idea of bridge-law reduction, he specifies that the bridge laws will be biconditionals correlating mental and physical properties:

Standardly, these bridge laws are taken to be biconditionals in form ('if and only if' statements), providing each property in the domain of the theory to be reduced with a nomologically coextensive property in the reduction base. For a mind-body reduction, then, the Nagel model requires that each mental property be provided with a nomologically coextensive physical property; that is, a law of the following form must hold for every mental property M:

(BL) $M \leftrightarrow P$

where P is some physical property. (1998a, p. 13)

The propositions that I called bridge laws in the previous section, (BL_A) and (BL_B), do not have the form specified by Kim or Fodor; (BL_A) and (BL_B) are conditionals rather than biconditionals, and they do not explicitly link mental properties with natural physical properties. Thus, on Fodor's characterization, the account I propose is not really a bridge-law account of reduction at all.

But why think that bridge laws must be biconditionals? We should keep in mind that we seek theoretical reduction as a response to a mystery. In this case the mystery is how to square our common-sense psychological conception with the conception of human beings we receive from physical science. The problem is that these two ways of talking about human beings seem to be in tension. We could resolve the mystery if we could show that physical science entails CSP—and that is, in essence, what the reductionist tries to do. Because of the divergent vocabularies of CSP and physical science, bridge laws of some sort are required for this task. But why should the bridge laws specifically have to be in the form of biconditionals? The aim of reduction is to show that the claims of CSP are subsumed by and hence compatible with physical science, despite initial appearances to the contrary. As we saw in the previous section, bridge laws of the form of (BL_A) and (BL_B) would be adequate to this task, for, given appropriate empirical discoveries by science, these bridge laws would imply the claims of CSP.

In any event, even if Fodor and Kim were justified in demanding biconditionals, the functionalist approach could easily accommodate them. The bridge law, (BL_A), had the form of a quantified conditional that basically said this: Anything that plays the role of a mental state is a mental state. We could make this slightly stronger and say that someone has a mental state if and only if she has something that plays the role of that kind of mental state. For example, someone is in pain if and only if she has a state that plays a particular causal role. Formally, this would look like

$$(\exists v)(z \text{ has } v \ \& \ v \approx t_i) \equiv (\exists \mathbf{x})(T[z,\mathbf{x}] \ \& \ z \text{ has } x_i).$$

This is a biconditional with a mental predicate on the left and a predicate from physical science on the right. There would be analogous characterizations for each kind of mental state. The right side of the biconditional characterizes mental states in terms of their causes and effects and is, by hypothesis, spelled out in non-intentional terms. So my claim is this: By any reasonable standard, the functionalist account of mental states, even with its multiple realizability, *is* an instance of a bridge-law reduction of the mental to the physical.

However, Fodor would presumably be unimpressed, for Fodor imposes further requirements on bridge laws. According to Fodor, reduction requires that "there are natural kind predicates in an ideally completed physics which correspond to each natural kind predicate in any ideally completed social science" (1974, p. 131). Of course, with functionalism and multiple realizability, we will not get this kind of correspondence, for the right side of the biconditional above is not a natural-kind predicate. But why should this be the goal of reduction? Some comments by both Fodor and Kim suggest that the goal of reduction should be that of ontological simplification; if we could identify mental kinds with natural physical kinds, then we would indeed have fewer kinds in our overall ontology. In particular, Fodor (1974, p. 129) and Kim (1998b, p. 97) both argue that certain forms of substance dualism would still be consistent with a Nagelian reduction unless the mental properties are *identified* with physical properties of the right sort. Technically, they might be correct. That is, Nagelian reduction might be logically consistent with the existence of a separate immaterial mind—an immaterial mind that in some way mirrors all of the physical properties. Thus Nagelian reduction, by itself, does not guarantee the simplified physicalist ontology that we might want. But this would be an awfully odd variety of dualism. By hypothesis, if the full Nagelian reduction succeeds, then all of the facts of CSP are entailed by physical science plus the bridge laws. Any form of substance dualism compatible with this result would posit the existence of a purely epiphenomenal immaterial mind. There would be no reason to believe in such a thing, any more than there is a reason to think that each electron in the universe has an immaterial soul whose properties mirror its physical properties. So, yes, bridge-law reduction as I have presented it does not guarantee the sort of ontological simplification one might want; but option-2 reduction would completely undermine the motivation for such a dualist view.

In the end, Fodor and I might simply be seen as drawing lines between possible views at different places. Moreover, it is not as if there is a common-sense notion of *reduction* and we are disagreeing about its analysis. By requiring biconditionals between natural-kind predicates, Fodor puts more stringent requirements on reduction. So within the class of views that I would count as option 2, Fodor makes a further distinction between those that offer a nice neat ontological reduction and those that do not. But Fodor's further distinction does not seem to me to be important to the mind-body problem as I have set it up; whether or not functionalism gives us a nice ontological simplification, functionalism would, if true, show that the claims of CSP can be neatly subsumed within physical science. If functionalism is correct, and if the appropriate physical discoveries are forthcoming, then physical science essentially entails CSP, and the apparent tension between CSP and physical science is resolved. The reduction might not be as neat as one would like, but the mystery about the relation between mind and body would be solved.

In any event, even if one does view this as a semantic quibble, it should be noted that my notion of reduction is weaker than Fodor's, for I place less stringent requirements on reductionist views. Since teleological realism is ultimately an option-3 nonreductionist view, I am only making things harder for myself by having such a weak notion of reduction.

4.4 Missed Generalizations and Autonomy?

Fodor and others also offer a different reason for thinking that psychological facts are not reducible to physical facts: They claim that psychology can make discoveries that cannot be made with the resources of physical science alone. If this is right, and there are facts of CSP that are not entailed by the facts of physical science plus bridge laws, then that would be enough to show that CSP does not reduce to physical science. I have already argued that if functionalism is true, the individual mental-state attributions do follow from the physical facts plus bridge laws; I have also argued that the explanations of individual actions will likewise follow from the physical facts plus bridge laws.

Fodor argues that it is the *generalizations* or *laws* that will not reduce: He claims that the laws of the special sciences, particularly psychology, will not be reducible to the claims of the physical sciences. Insofar as the laws he has in mind are part of our common-sense conception of the mental, then, as argued above, the laws will follow trivially; perhaps Fodor is thinking of laws that are not part of common-sense psychology. In any event, Fodor's explicit argument for this claim again presupposes that the bridge laws will have the form of biconditionals. He begins as follows:

Let formula (1) be a law of the special science S.

(1) $S_1x \rightarrow S_2x$

Formula (1) is intended to be read as something like 'all events which consist of x's being S_1 bring about events which consist of y's being S_2.' (Fodor 1974, p. 128)

Fodor then argues as follows:

A necessary and sufficient condition for the reduction of formula (1) to a law of physics is that formulae (2) and (3) should be laws, and a necessary and sufficient condition for the reduction

(2a) $S_1x \leftrightarrow P_1x$

(2b) $S_2y \leftrightarrow P_2y$

(3) $P_1x \rightarrow P_2x$

of S to physics is that all its laws should be so reduced.

A good part of the rest of Fodor's paper then argues that we will not be able to get the likes of (2a) and (2b), and his argument assumes that the predicates in question will have to be natural-kind predicates. Of course, I have already argued that reduction does not require biconditionals correlating natural-kind predicates, so I disagree that the conditions Fodor gives are necessary for reduction. So, at least as I am using the word 'reduction', Fodor's argument does nothing to establish that the special sciences are irreducible.

Like Fodor, Antony and Levine (1997) claim that CSP is autonomous from the physical sciences, and they affirm a basic functionalist understanding of the mind. However, they acknowledge the point (made above) that the generalizations that are part of our original common-sense theory—those that, in Lewis's words, have an "odor of analyticity"—are not irreducible. But they claim that there will be other generalizations, or "contingent regularities" in psychology, and that the availability of these regularities is sufficient to guarantee the autonomy of the mind. They first illustrate the point through a different example of a functionally defined property: *dormitivity*. Generalizations like "dormitive substances cause sleep" are merely analytic and don't illustrate autonomy. But Antony and Levine suggest that things are different with a generalization such as

"Dormitive substances, if ingested before driving, cause traffic accidents."
Concerning this generalization, they write:

Note in this connection that while this is a *ceteris paribus* law, there is no reason to
expect that the exceptions will be systematic with respect to the realizations; the conditions that must be equal may all have to do with extrinsic contingencies (like the
density of traffic at the time the driver falls asleep) that are themselves realization-
independent. We contend that the availability of this sort of generalization certifies
"dormitivity" as a genuine property, associated with a distinctive set of causal powers.
(1997, p. 93)

Antony and Levine next argue that there are analogous contingent generalizations involving mental properties.

However, before turning to their claims about mental properties, we
should more closely examine the dormitivity example. I need not quibble
with Antony and Levine's claim that dormitivity is in some sense a distinctive property—that it is associated with a set of causal powers that is distinct
from any natural kind in the physical sciences. However, unless we assume
that reduction requires a neat one-to-one correlation between natural properties of the special science and natural kinds of the physical sciences, no
claim about irreducibility will follow. More specifically, I think that the contingent generalization about dormitivity *is* deducible from the physical
facts plus bridge laws. I assume that the relevant bridge law would look
something like this:

(B) Dormitive substances tend to cause sleep.

The following is an empirical discovery we have made:

(E) Drivers falling asleep are very likely to cause traffic accidents.

And from these it will follow pretty quickly that drivers' ingesting dormitive substances will tend to cause traffic accidents.

Antony and Levine are right about at least this much: If we focused
solely on the physical facts without the functional concept *dormitive*, we
would be unlikely to discover that ingesting dormitive substances causes
traffic accidents; this generalization is not a natural one from the perspective of the physical sciences, for dormitive substances do not form a
natural kind (and, for that matter, neither do traffic accidents). But this is
far from establishing that contingent generalizations about dormitive
substances are somehow beyond the realm of physical science. The contingent generalization is deducible from empirical discovery and an
appropriate bridge law.

Similarly, we can grant Antony and Levine that there will be contingent generalizations involving mental terms; i.e., there will be generalizations that are *not* part of our original common-sense theory. Nonetheless, it scarcely follows that these generalizations lie beyond the realm of the physical sciences, nor does it follow that these generalizations cannot be deduced from the physical facts plus bridge laws. Let us start with a fairly simple generalization that seems to hold, albeit roughly, of people in the United States: People who believe that capital punishment should be abolished tend to believe that abortion should be legal. This is presumably not part of our folk theory of the mental, especially since there is no obvious logical connection between the two beliefs. However, if functionalism is true, then this generalization would follow from the physical facts plus the bridge laws. As was explained above, the individual mental-state attributions will follow from empirical discoveries plus bridge laws. Once we have used these means to determine the relevant mental states of a sample population, it is a simple matter to correlate empirically the beliefs in question.

The situation is similar for other contingent generalizations invoking mental terms. Antony and Levine use the example "Repetition facilitates learning." Scientists could use the bridge laws and empirical discoveries to determine the degree to which a sample population has learned some specified information or skill, and then empirically correlate this with the degree to which the material or skill was repeated by the subject. So, although Antony and Levine are surely right that there are generalizations invoking mental states that are not part of the old common-sense theory, it is hard to see why this poses any problem for full reduction, assuming the truth of functionalism. Thus, despite persistent claims to the contrary, I see no reason to think that multiple realizability generally, or functionalism specifically, will yield autonomy or irreducibility for CSP. Functionalism is a fully option-2, reductionist view.

II

5   Strong Naturalism and Common-Sense Psychology

Recall from the opening chapter that there were three options for the relationship between common-sense psychology and physical science. According to the first, CSP and physical science contradict one another; according to the second, the facts of physical science ultimately imply the truths of CSP; according to the third, CSP and physical science are logically independent. I define *strong naturalism* as the following claim: either option 1 or option 2 is correct, and further developments in physical science will tell us which. In the three chapters of part II, I will argue against strong naturalism.

As a description of a philosophical position, 'naturalism' presumably derives from 'nature'; naturalism is, first and foremost, the doctrine that nature, or the natural world, is all there is. Naturalism denies the existence of supernatural forces or beings, such as God, angels, or ghosts. A naturalistic account of the mind appeals to nothing beyond the natural world and thus, for example, does not invoke immaterial souls. (However, I assume that one could have a naturalistic account of the mind without denying the existence of God.) Strong naturalism about mind goes further: By claiming that talk of mind either is entailed by scientific truths or is inconsistent with them, the position rules out the possibility that there are claims about mind that are independent of the natural sciences. Thus, strong naturalism holds that the claims of the natural sciences exhaust all truths (whether in general or about a particular area). By distinguishing strong naturalism from naturalism, I am implicitly suggesting that there is room for what might be called weak naturalism. A weak naturalist would not appeal to anything recognizably supernatural, and would not assert the existence of anything beyond the natural world, but a weak naturalist might nonetheless claim that there are *facts* about the world that go beyond the facts of the natural sciences. I will put forward teleological realism as a version of weak naturalism—as occupying a middle ground between supernaturalism and strong naturalism.

Before getting into the details of my attack on strong naturalism, I should mention two topics that will *not* figure in my arguments: consciousness and intentional content. Some philosophers would claim that consciousness is the most pressing problem for strong naturalism. David Chalmers (1997), for example, claims that it is possible to give a reductionist account of intentionality, but he argues at length that no such account can be given of consciousness. My own view is roughly the opposite of Chalmers's. I am convinced that there will be no reductionist account of intentionality, agency, or normativity, but I am not convinced of the impossibility of a reductionist account of consciousness. There is nothing inconsistent about this, of course; the teleological realist can maintain that some mental properties are subsumable within a scientific account while still maintaining that much of CSP will resist such reduction. In any event, any adequate discussion of consciousness would take us much too far afield, so the topic will have to be put off until another time.

The other traditional challenge for strong naturalism is intentionality. The reductionist will have to show how the physical, non-intentional facts about a human being could suffice to imply that a person has a state with a particular intentional content. Providing this sort of reductionist account of intentionality has been a central project within philosophy of mind for a number of decades. Some philosophers propose accounts falling under the broad framework of functionalism as described in chapter 4 above. Others, including Fodor (1990) and Dretske (1981), propose information-theoretic or indicator theories. I don't think that any of these accounts are successful, but I will not get involved in the details of these debates. The questions I am addressing are in a certain way prior to naturalistic theories of content. Such theories typically take it for granted that action explanation is causal; in other words, they take it for granted that the notion of *agency* can be reduced to causal terms. Indeed, much of the debate about theories of content concerns how to preserve the causal relevance of the mental. Since the cornerstone of teleological realism is that action explanation is not reducible to causal terms, I deny the assumption that initiates and motivates naturalistic theories of content.

5.1 The Proto-Science View of CSP

What I have been calling common-sense psychology comprises a great variety of practices: attributing mental states in an effort to explain and predict behavior, justifying actions by reference to the way we believe or desire the world to be, attributing mental states in the course of allocating moral praise or blame, and so on. Alongside these ordinary activities, we have a body of mostly tacit general beliefs about the relationship between mental states and behavior. According to strong naturalism, the claims made by CSP either contradict or are implied by the truths of physical science. This already commits the strong naturalist to a fairly substantive view of the nature of CSP, for it implies that the propositions of CSP have the same subject matter as those of physical science and that CSP and physical science are, so to speak, playing the same game. In part, this means that the strong naturalist sees CSP as itself a scientific or proto-scientific theory, a theory that will either be vindicated or eliminated by the ultimate claims of physical science proper. This requirement is perhaps clearest in the case of option 2, or reductionism. If, as option 2 maintains, CSP is to be subsumed within physical science, then CSP must be doing the same sort of thing as science, even if in a somewhat unsystematic and immature way. But even with option 1, if CSP contradicts science, then some central portion of CSP must make claims that conflict with those of physical science; thus, even if CSP is wildly unscientific in its methods, option 1 requires that some of its claims at least purport to be scientific assertions. The strong naturalist maintains that the choice between the two options will be made later on empirical grounds, but either way CSP will have to be a proto-science.

For many within the strong naturalist camp, the view of CSP as a proto-scientific theory is not seen as particularly contentious. This "theory theory" of CSP is taken not only to be true but to be virtually self-evident. Paul Churchland, for example, asserts that "not only is folk psychology a theory, it is so *obviously* a theory that it must be held a major mystery why it has taken until the last half of the twentieth century for philosophers to realize it" (1981, p. 71). Michael Devitt and Kim Sterelny are equally explicit in their view of CSP: ". . . folk psychology, like all folk theories, is a *proto-science*. It differs from a science proper in being immature: it is imprecise, inexplicit and unsystematic; it is held uncritically; it is not associated with a methodology for its development. Nonetheless, it has the same general characteristics as a science." (1978, p. 242)

Of course, a pivotal question in this context is exactly what one means by "theory" or "proto-science." If a proto-scientific theory is simply any set of practices involving some explanation and prediction, then Churchland, Devitt, and Sterelny are right, and CSP obviously is a proto-scientific theory. For the purposes of strong naturalism, however, this is not enough. The strong naturalist needs to align CSP with paradigmatic sciences (e.g. physics, chemistry, and biology); CSP must have the same goals and must move in the same conceptual space as physical science.

However, I will argue in this chapter that CSP does not look like a proto-scientific theory of the mind and thus that CSP is not a candidate for subsumption within, or rejection by, physical science. I will claim in section 5.2 that CSP has a normative dimension unlike anything seen in physical science. I will argue in section 5.3 that CSP assertions exhibit a sensitivity to context that is likewise uncharacteristic of the physical sciences. In section 5.4 I will argue that mental-state terms do not function semantically as natural-kind terms. (Though I shall often use the "mental state," my concern throughout is specifically with the propositional attitudes—belief, desire, and the like.) If mental-state terms do not function as natural-kind terms, then CSP is not a theory in the sense maintained by strong naturalism.

5.2 Normativity

5.2.1 Reasons and Action

The normative element of CSP appears in a number of distinct ways. First, mental states such as desires and intentions give us a *reason* or *justification* for acting. For example, if I want to have some tea, this desire provides me with a justification for taking the steps necessary to make a cup of tea. Of course, other considerations might override, but nonetheless my desire gives me *a* reason to act. Suppose I do act; I put water on to boil. Now, according to strong naturalism, mental states are causes of behavior and explanations of action are causal explanations. Thus, when we say that I put water on to boil because I wanted tea, the strong naturalist construes this as asserting that my desire for tea caused my behavior of putting water on to boil. But this creates a problem for the strong naturalist, for it seems that the justifying or normative force of the reason has been lost. As Christine Korsgaard notes, "causal connections cannot be wrong" (1996, p. 139). If causes cannot be wrong, then they cannot be *right* either. "*A* caused *B*" does not carry any normative force; it is simply the statement of a non-normative fact about the world. When the cue ball goes crashing into the eight ball, it does not give the eight ball a *reason* to move; we would not hold the eight ball to be criticizably unreasonable if it failed to move upon being struck by the cue ball. So why should we say that my desire for tea, qua cause of my behavior, gave me a normative reason to put water on to boil?

We say of someone who fails to act on her intentions that she is weak-willed, and we intend this as a criticism: she is failing to live up to the standards of rationality or agency. But why should we make these normative judgments if the explanations of our action are simply causal claims? We might well say that someone who does not act on her intentions is "causally abnormal," but that would simply mean that, in her, intentions to φ do not typically cause φing. Statistical abnormality in a mechanism is not grounds for normative criticism.

So the problem for the proto-science view is this: CSP explanations of human behavior typically imply that the agent had a normative reason to behave in the way she did. Causal explanations in the natural sciences do not carry any such implication. Thus it would appear that CSP explanations are not part of a proto-scientific theory of human behavior.

5.2.2 Inference

We see an even more explicit normative element to CSP when we look at inference and reasoning, for we criticize certain inference patterns as fallacious or wrong. For example, we make claims such as the following:

It is unreasonable for a well-informed person to believe that the earth is flat.

It is a mistake to infer that God does not exist merely because no one can *prove* that God does exist.

It is a mistake to infer that homosexual behavior is wrong merely because you find the thought of it unpleasant.

These claims are explicitly normative, for they imply that certain beliefs ought not to be held and certain inferences ought not to be made. These are not the sorts of claims we would expect to see a scientific theory make about its subject matter. Physicists do not assert that elementary particles make mistakes. In the physical sciences, we are first and foremost concerned with making causal explanations and finding explanatory laws; but, again, causes and laws of nature are never right or wrong—they just are.

To be more specific, suppose a reductionist claims that inferential reasoning is a matter of one brain state's causing another. Thus, if I see thunderclouds on the horizon and infer that rain is likely soon, this simply means that my belief that there were thunderclouds on the horizon caused a new belief: that rain is likely soon. The first belief was presumably a brain state of some sort, and, through the normal causal laws that govern the particles which constitute the brain state, this brain state caused the brain state that is the belief that rain is likely soon.

On the other hand, suppose that someone has the belief "If astrology is reliable, then I will have a good day today" and "I am having a good day today" and proceeds to infer that astrology is reliable. The reductionist would say that this is likewise a matter of two brain states' causing a third brain state. But this creates a problem. The latter inference is, of course, fallacious; it is wrong to infer that astrology is reliable from the first two beliefs. But the inference was said to consist of two brain states' causing a third, and the particles making up the brain states were simply behaving in accord with the fundamental physical laws governing the universe. It seems that the reductionist would be committed to saying that a particular causal chain was *wrong*. But what can that mean? What can it mean to say that the first two brain states ought not to have caused the third?

A reductionist might stipulate that a *wrong* inference is one that is not in accord with the laws of logic, and then, by definition, the above inference counts as wrong. But this simply makes 'wrong' into a descriptive term, and the normative force is lost. The reductionist has simply lumped together a set of causal chains with a certain feature, and has used the label 'wrong' for any member of that set. But simply using a label does not capture the normative force—the idea that the inference was a *mistake*, that it *ought not* to have occurred, that the person ought not to have made it.

The reductionist might point out that fallacious inferences fail to preserve truth, and then say that if the person *wants* her beliefs to be true, she should not reason in that way. And while what the reductionist says is true, it is not enough, for the reductionist has so far not said anything at all about the inference's being a mistake or being wrong. The reductionist then might claim that any action or inference contrary to a person's desires is a mistake, and thus the inference is a mistake because reasoning in this way will fail to serve the person's desire to have true beliefs. Here the reductionist tries to reduce the normative force of certain claims to a set of descriptive facts about the person's beliefs. But this still does not suffice; the normative force cannot be tied simply to failure to satisfy the person's desires. The normative force does not come down to the person's desires: the inference would still count as wrong—as unreasonable and criticizable—even if the person said she had no desire to have true beliefs in this context. More generally, a person's desires are not taken as the sole determinant of what it is reasonable for the person to do or to infer, for we can coherently ask whether it is reasonable for the person to act on that desire. (See Nagel 1997.)

The reductionist can try ever more sophisticated ways of reducing normative force to some descriptive fact about the agent's mental states, but the same problems will continue to reoccur. In any event, there is a related and more fundamental reason that the reductionist will have trouble with normative claims in CSP.

5.2.3 Interpretation

As Donald Davidson has long argued, normative elements enter into CSP at a level much more general than those considered so far. Davidson argues that "we cannot intelligibly attribute any propositional attitude to an agent except within the framework of a viable theory of his beliefs, desires, intentions and decisions" (1980, p. 221). This "viable theory" of the agent's attitudes will be one that "finds him consistent, a believer of truths, and a lover of the good" (ibid., p. 222). More generally, when we ascribe mental states, we do so against the controlling assumption that we are dealing with a *rational* agent; i.e., we attribute propositional attitudes to an agent against our background conception of what she *ought* to believe and desire. When we interpret a person with the resources of CSP, we apply a principle of charity—we assume that, roughly speaking, she believes what she ought to believe and desires what she ought to desire.

To see the Davidsonian point, consider a typical example of interpretation. Josephine looks outside at the dark clouds, and then says "I'd better get my umbrella." She then picks up her umbrella and heads out the door. On that basis, we would ascribe to Josephine the belief that rain is likely today. We could also ascribe various other, more or less tacit, beliefs and desires: the desire not to get wet and the belief that an umbrella can help one avoid getting wet in the rain. But consider the same example if we did not apply the principle of charity. Then all manner of bizarre interpretations become perfectly consistent with the known facts. We could, for example, imagine that Josephine believes that one is morally obligated to carry an umbrella on cloudy days, although she sees no connection between dark clouds and rain. Nothing in what we have seen in the purely non-normative facts would disallow this conclusion. Moreover, someone could claim to interpret Josephine's behavior in a yet more bizarre way (for example, denying that Josephine has any beliefs concerning the desirability of carrying her umbrella), or the interpreter might suggest that Josephine picked up the umbrella because she believed that rain was *not* likely. Such an interpreter might allow that it would be *unusual* for that belief to cause that behavior but insist that there is no non-normative fact that can rule out such an interpretation.

So, apart from the normative principle of charity, the behavioral evidence available to the interpreter will generally allow for indefinitely many attributable sets of beliefs and desires; all else being equal, the interpreter will choose the set that maximizes the rationality of the agent. Attributing a completely irrational set of beliefs to an agent defeats the purpose of belief attribution, and the attribution itself loses sense. By attributing beliefs and desires to others, we see them as rational agents, as beings like us. If we were to attribute an utterly irrational set of attitudes, we would, by hypothesis, not be able to make sense of the person's beliefs and desires, and we would have failed in our effort to reach even a minimal understanding of the *person* with whom we are confronted.

The overtly normative aspect of attitude ascription is not what we would expect if CSP were a proto-scientific theory of human behavior. In scientific theorizing about natural kinds, choice between competing theories can involve appeal to certain criteria for good scientific theories: simplicity, conservativism, etc. However, scientific theorizing does not appeal to overtly normative standards in the way that mental-state ascription does. Our choice of theories is not guided by an ideal conception of how the world *ought* to behave. A scientist might well initially formulate a theory on the basis of a conception of how "mother nature" ought to behave if she is rationally motivated, but such appeals to a normative standard would be, at best, no more than heuristic. We don't claim that we should be able to understand, even minimally, the world's "motivation" for behaving in the way that it does. The world as a whole does not have to have rational reasons for having the causal laws or the physical constants that it has. Regardless of what our best theory of the world says, we would not accuse the world of being *criticizably* irrational or *criticizably* arbitrary.

The Davidsonian point about interpretation becomes all the more important when we consider again the more explicitly normative features of CSP noted in sections 2.1 and 2.2. The problem there for reductionism was that CSP sometimes has directly normative implications, and this made it seem quite unlike the proto-science it has to be for strong naturalism to be tenable. The obvious response was for the reductionist to attempt to reduce normative claims to something not overtly normative. For example, the reductionist might say that the valuable (i.e., that which we have reason to do) is that which we desire; or, in a more sophisticated vein, the valuable is that which we desire to desire. I have already suggested that I don't think such proposals fare well. (For more on this point, see Lewis 1989 and Johnston 1989.) However, if the Davidsonian claim about interpretation is correct, then such proposals, construed as attempts reduce the normative to the non-normative, are nonstarters. Even if we could successfully analyze all claims about normative reasons as claims about what we desire to desire, we would have made no progress, for the attribution of desires involves an irreducibly normative element.

5.3 Sensitivity to Context

Our judgments concerning mental-state ascription are sensitive to differences in context in ways we would not expect were our practices the embodiment of a proto-scientific theory. Consider how we would determine whether an agent understands an utterance of the sentence "Reich mir doch bitte das Salz." There is no straightforward list of behaviors that would manifest or fail to manifest an understanding of that sentence. A number of different abilities could be relevant, depending on the context: the ability to translate the sentence into English, the ability to rephrase or explain the meaning of the sentence (whether in German or in another language), the ability to explain the significance of the sentence in a particular context, the ability to follow the instruction correctly. Moreover, whether or not to attribute one of these abilities to an agent may also depend on particularities of the context in an unsystematic way. When does one exhibit an ability to follow the instruction given by the sentence? Not simply by passing the salt; a non-German-speaker might gather that something on the dinner table had been requested, then proceed to pass the salt because it was the nearest thing. On the other hand, a native German speaker might pass the pepper without thinking. Whether or not we would ascribe an understanding of the speaker's utterance could depend on any number of contextual factors, and it does not seem likely that these factors could be systematically characterized. (On the importance of context and circumstances in the ascription of understanding, see also Goldfarb 1989.)

Simple ascriptions of belief are also highly sensitive to context. I could correctly say of an eight-year-old child who voluntarily says prayers at night, goes to church with her parents, and thinks of God as a bearded man in a white robe that she believes in God. However, if I find out that the little girl's father also thinks that God is a bearded man in a white robe, I might well deny that he believes in God (even if the father too voluntarily says prayers at night). Circumstances can also affect ascriptions of desires. On the basis of a college student's idle fantasies of her future, we might say that she wants to be president, even though she has no thoughts about how this might come to pass and has formulated no plans involving this desire. We might be more hesitant to ascribe the same desire to the current Senate majority leader if he has not thought about how or when this might be achieved.

An eliminativist might take this context sensitivity as evidence that our folk theory is a good candidate for eventual replacement by something more rigorous. (See Stich 1983.) In a sense, I sympathize with the eliminativist's reasoning: *If* you take our practices to embody a scientific theory of psychological natural kinds, the context sensitivity and hetero- geneity of our attributions make it likely that the theory is not a good one. However, to my mind, these considerations point most directly to the falsity of the antecedent of that conditional; the sensitivity to context exhibited by our ascription practices make those practices look quite unlike a proto-scientific theory of psychological natural kinds.

5.4   Mental States and Natural Kinds

One relevant feature of the physical sciences is that their subject matter is presumed to consist of *natural kinds*, where a natural kind is, roughly speak- ing, a kind that nature itself divides into, independently of human classifi- catory interests. For example, kinds like *electron* and *charge* are presumably more natural than a kind like *game* or *road*; all electrons have intrinsic sim- ilarities, whereas roads can vary widely in their size, composition, etc. If CSP is a proto-science, then its theoretical terms will likewise purport to denote natural kinds. Devitt and Sterelny are quite willing to accept this: they admit that "if psychological kinds are not natural kinds, then folk cognitive psychology cannot be protoscience" (1978, p. 242). I will argue that mental kind terms (e.g. "desire for coffee") do not function semantically as natural- kind terms. Of course, there are substantive disputes in the literature con- cerning the nature of natural kinds. I will attempt to remain as neutral as possible regarding the competing views here; my contention will be that mental-state terms turn out not to be natural-kind terms on a wide variety of plausible accounts of natural kinds.

As was noted above, CSP includes a body of mostly tacit general beliefs about mental states, their relationship to each other, and their relationship to behavior. If mental-state terms do purport to denote natural kinds, then one of two theses will be true about this set of general beliefs. Either these beliefs will purport to *fix the reference* of mental-state terms onto natural kinds, or they will *not* serve this reference-fixing role and instead will sim- ply function as associated, empirical beliefs.

By way of illustration, consider our general, qualitative beliefs about tigers. Perhaps we can say that these general beliefs constitute our folk theory of tigers. They would include "A tiger is a large carnivorous quadrupedal feline, tawny yellow in color with blackish transverse stripes and white belly." (This description is borrowed from Kripke 1980.) Numerous less central beliefs could be included: that tigers have sharp teeth, that tigers hunt alone, that tigers make bad pets, and so on. On the first semantic option, these beliefs about tigers collectively serve to fix the reference of the word 'tiger' onto some particular natural kind of thing existing in the actual world. Roughly, a tiger is the actual *kind of thing* that matches our beliefs about tigers—that a tiger is the actual kind of thing that is a large carnivorous quadrupedal feline, tawny yellow in color, and so on. The associated-beliefs view denies that our qualitative beliefs fix the reference of the word 'tiger'. Our general, qualitative beliefs about tigers, even our most central ones, are just contingent, empirical beliefs that we have about a particular natural kind. That which is definitive of the kind, that which makes something an instance of that kind, is not necessarily accessible to ordinary observation—hence our qualitative beliefs about the kind are mere empirical generalizations. Accordingly, because the definitive features of tigers are hidden from ordinary view, our beliefs about them could undergo wholesale revision while still maintaining tigers as their subject matter.[1]

Thus, if mental-state terms function as natural-kind terms, one of the following two theses must be true:

(RF) Mental-state terms purport to refer to natural kinds, and our qualitative beliefs about mental kinds serve to fix the reference of those terms.

(AB) Mental-state terms purport to refer to natural kinds, and our qualitative beliefs are merely associated beliefs that do not play a reference-fixing role.

In this section I will argue that neither (RF) nor (AB) is true, and I will conclude that our mental-state terms do not function as natural-kind terms. I will discuss (AB) first.

5.4.1 The Associated-Beliefs View

If (AB), then that which is definitive of mental kinds is potentially hidden from ordinary view, and consequently our ordinary common-sense psychological beliefs could be dramatically false. Future science could well discover that our naive folk theory of the mental is very much in error and yet still manages to be about the "real," natural mental kinds. We can distinguish here between two different sorts of error that might, on this picture, infect our folk beliefs:

(E1) Things that *fail* to satisfy our folk requirements for mental state K could nonetheless be in mental state K.

(E2) Things that *satisfy* our folk requirements for being in mental state K could nonetheless fail to be in mental state K.

If the definitive feature of mental kinds is hidden from view, we would expect both of these sorts of errors to be possible. However, I will argue that neither of these sorts of errors is really a coherent possibility, and hence (AB) is false.

Suppose that Ann is sitting on the couch, reading the newspaper. She is aware that there is a baseball game on television, but takes no action toward turning it on. She has no strong desire to do something incompatible with watching the game, she has no strange ideas about the importance of self-sacrifice, and she doesn't think there would be anything wrong in any way with her watching the baseball game. Moreover, she reports that she has no desire to watch the game, and she has no desire to deceive us about her desires. None of this surprises those who know Ann, for no one has ever known her to express anything but contempt for baseball. In other words, all CSP requirements for attributing to Ann a desire to watch the game are absent here. In the face of this, can we make sense of the hypothesis that Ann in fact does have a strong desire to watch the baseball game right now? I say that we cannot, that it would make no sense to attribute to Ann a desire to watch the game, and that complete failure of our normal criteria would make any such attribution utterly bizarre and ultimately unintelligible.

We can imagine a context in which someone might *claim* that Ann had a strong desire to watch the game despite the failure of the normal criteria. A neuroscientist might say that, according to the latest theory of cognition, "strong desire to watch a baseball game" refers to a particular type of brain state; usually this state causes the subject to turn on the television or exhibit some other sort of appropriate behavior, but in some cases the state leads to no stereotypically appropriate behavior and leads to no awareness on the part of the agent that she has the desire in question. This neuroscientist might then look into Ann's brain and find that Ann is in the appropriate brain state; the neuroscientist would then conclude that Ann does, after all, have a desire to watch the game. The scientist can of course define her theoretical terms any way she likes, but we can question whether her term "strong desire to watch a baseball game" has the same meaning as our ordinary term of the same form. I contend that it does not. The scientist's attribution to Ann of a desire to watch the game amounts to a *change of subject*. This then returns us to the same moral as above: without equivocating on the meaning of "desire to watch the game," it is ultimately incoherent, given the circumstances as described, to attribute to Ann a desire to watch the game.

If this interpretation of the Ann story is correct, (AB) is false. The associated-beliefs view implies (E1), and (E1) asserts that certain sorts of errors should be intelligible. In fact, errors of this sort do not seem to be intelligible. Hence, desires cannot be natural kinds that are the subject matter of an entirely contingent folk theory. I think we could tell stories analogous to the Ann story about beliefs, intentions, and various other mental states. Consider, for example, ascribing to an agent the belief that it is raining when in fact it is sunny and the agent is commenting on what a gorgeous day it is. Perhaps we would have to describe the story a bit more fully, but it seems clear that at some point it would make no sense to ascribe to that agent the belief that it is raining. If this is correct, the associated-beliefs view cannot be right for mental states in general.

As was noted above, (AB) also implies (E2), the claim that things that satisfy our common-sense criteria for being in a mental state may nonetheless fail to be in that state. Just as with Twin-Earth's XYZ and Earth's water, there could be some hidden definitive feature of desire that distinguishes one who truly has a particular desire from one who meets the common-sense requirements but does not have the desire. But this is implausible too. Imagine, for example, that in the house next to Ann's there is a woman named Cheryl. Cheryl tells us that she wants to watch the baseball game. She picks up the television listings, notes that the game is on channel 9, and proceeds to turn on the television and tune it accordingly. These actions are not in the least surprising to those who know Cheryl, for Cheryl is a big fan of the Mets and rarely misses one of their televised games. Moreover, Cheryl is not attempting to deceive us, and there is no reason to think that she is self-deceived. On the associated-beliefs view, there could be, nonetheless, some hidden definitive feature of desiring to watch the game, and a mature psychology might discover that Cheryl does not exhibit this feature and consequently has no desire to watch the game. However, I have trouble making sense of the hypothesis. Hidden features of Cheryl that are unrelated to our ordinary criteria will simply be irrelevant.

So far I have argued against (AB) by relying on the intuition that (E1) and (E2) are false—that common-sense psychology is not subject to the sorts of errors to which it would be subject if (AB) were correct. I want to bolster these intuitions by giving a diagnosis of *why* the associated-beliefs view is inapplicable in this realm. The diagnosis involves a more careful consideration of the cases in which this semantic view is appropriate. The kinds about which the associated-beliefs story can be told (e.g., tigers, gold, water, etc.)

typically have *paradigmatic instances* which are clearly demarcated prior to scientific investigation. We say that tigers are *that kind of animal*, focusing on certain samples. (See Kripke 1980, p. 122; Putnam 1988, p. 33.) We can identify instances of the kind through ostension, although the properties we ultimately decide are definitive of tigers may be hidden from normal view. Of course it would be difficult to spell out a complete causal theory of reference along these lines; to see these difficulties we need merely note that what we point to as instances of *tiger* could equally be seen as instances of *cat* and *mammal*, not to mention *undetached tiger part*. Nevertheless, regardless of the details of the full referential story, where the associated-beliefs view is appropriate, we do seem able to identify ostensively paradigmatic instances. Moreover, it is precisely the identifiability of paradigmatic samples that allows our qualitative beliefs about the kind to be so flexible. Once we have fixed the subject matter of our discourse by saying that tigers are *that kind of animal*, our beliefs about tigers can change dramatically while still retaining their subject matter, and this opens the possibility that we might be very wrong about the *nature* of tigers while still being correct in affirming the reality of tigers as a natural kind.

However, this sort of story will not work for mental states such as belief and desire. Instances of mental kinds are not antecedently demarcated or identifiable in a way that would allow ostensive fixing of the subject of discourse; we cannot ostensively identify even a single instance of a belief or desire, much less can we point to a number of paradigmatic instances. We cannot point to beliefs in the same way that we can point to tigers or whales. I can, of course, point to *believers*, but this doesn't help. If I am around the pope, I can point to a paradigmatic believer of the proposition "God exists," but I cannot point to his belief that God exists. Because the subject matter of our supposed theory of the mental cannot be fixed ostensively, (AB) becomes highly dubious. Our "folk theory" concerning propositional attitudes cannot be treated as mere empirical claims, subject to significant revision by scientific discovery. In particular contexts we will associate various behaviors with a belief that *p*; if a neurophysiologist were to claim that beliefs that *p* actually had rather different sorts of behavioral connections, we would have no reason to believe that the neurophysiologist was talking about the same thing as we were—we would have no reason to think that he meant the same thing by "belief that *p*" as we do.

One might respond that (AB) does not require that we be able to point to the actual mental state. We would be sufficiently able to fix the subject matter of our discourse if we could identify paradigmatic instances of the immediate causal consequences of mental states. For example, even if we cannot point to the state of anger per se, we can (arguably) identify paradigmatic instances of behavior caused by anger. We would then say that anger is whatever typically causes that behavior, and the remainder of our beliefs about anger could be viewed as highly revisable, empirical claims. My reply is that this story might work for affective states such as anger, but that it will not do for propositional attitudes such as belief and desire, which are my present concern. As we learned from the demise of behaviorism, there are no straightforwardly identifiable behaviors that can be regarded as immediate causal consequences of beliefs, desires, hopes, wishes, etc.

5.4.2 The Reference-Fixing View

The alternative to the associated-beliefs view was (RF), according to which our common-sense qualitative beliefs serve to fix the reference of mental-state terms onto natural kinds. This view appears designed to succeed where the associated-beliefs view failed. In particular, this view takes into account the fact that mental states do not have antecedently well-demarcated instances about which we can have an utterly flexible and revisable theory. Our common-sense theory serves to specify the referent of mental-state terms; hence the theory itself serves to demarcate the mental kinds.

The investigation into (AB) did not force acceptance of any particular view concerning the nature of natural kinds; regardless of what makes a natural kind natural, it is not the case that our qualitative beliefs about the mental are as revisable as (AB) would allow. Ultimately, my rejection of (RF) will likewise remain fairly neutral concerning the nature of natural kinds. However, the specific arguments brought to bear against (RF) will depend in part on what its proponent says about what makes mental kinds natural. I can see two possible options for the proponent of (RF), meaning that there are two possible subversions of (RF):

(RFa) Our qualitative beliefs fix the reference of a given mental-state term onto tokens that share a common physiological structure.

(RFb) Our qualitative beliefs fix the reference of mental-state terms onto tokens each of which is the occupant of a common causal role.

On each of these views, a phrase like "Bill's belief that snow is white" will refer to a particular physical state. On (RFa), this token state will share a common physiological structure with all other token states that constitute an agent's belief that snow is white, and thus all beliefs that snow is white will form a natural kind. On (RFb), Bill's belief that snow is white may not be of the same physiological kind as Bob's belief that snow is white, but each token will occupy a common causal role. All token beliefs that snow is white will form a natural kind by virtue of the fact that each is the occupant of that role. Regardless of which of these options is taken, I will argue that the reference-fixing view has serious problems and must be rejected.

(RFa) gains little over the already rejected associated-beliefs view. In particular, this version of the theory also implies that (E1) will be true. Our folk theory supposedly picks out various things as desires to watch the baseball game; on this version of the reference-fixing account, anything else that is of the same physiological kind is also a desire to watch the game, regardless of its possible failure to satisfy our folk requirements. Hence, the story I told about Ann and her purported desire to watch the baseball game can be told just as well on this theory as it could on the associated-beliefs view. More specifically, it would be coherent to assume that Ann has the neural state picked out by CSP as the desire to watch the baseball game, despite satisfying none of the normal folk criteria. Thus, on the reference-fixing view, it should be coherent to assume that Ann does in fact desire with all her heart to watch the game. Hence, if I am right in my contention that it is *not* in fact coherent to ascribe such a desire to Ann, this story looms as a counterexample to both the associated-beliefs view and the reference-fixing view.

Moreover, any theory that identifies mental types with physiological types also runs into the old problem of multiple realizability. It seems entirely possible that we will encounter creatures with whom we can communicate and to whom we will straightforwardly ascribe ordinary mental states. However, these creatures might have nothing quite like our brain. According to the theory under consideration now, our common-sense beliefs and practices fix the reference of "belief that p" onto whatever natural kind plays the appropriate role. By hypothesis, these new creatures meet the ordinary criteria for having a belief that p, but they have nothing like the neurophysiological kind that plays that role in us. Thus, our common-sense psychology will fail to fix the reference of "belief that p" onto any one natural kind.

The reference-fixing theorist might respond that under these circumstances we would have to conclude that there is more than one kind of belief that p. If the state that occupies the functional role of believing p in the new creatures differs from the state that occupies that role in us, then the creatures' belief is a different kind of belief that p than ours. To evaluate this response, it helps to change the scenario somewhat: Assume not that we run across a new type of creature, but rather that we discover that different types of neurophysiological states can occupy the belief-that-p role in different human beings. Perhaps we even discover that different neurophysiological states can play the same functional role at different times in the life of the same person. The reference-fixing theorist would have to conclude that different normal human beings have different kinds of belief that p, and that even the kind of belief that p that an individual has might change over time. I submit that our practice of ascribing mental states leaves no room for this sort of distinction between kinds of mental states. This purported distinction between kinds of belief, based as it is solely on the physical nature of the occupying state, would have no role within our ordinary practices; the difference in kinds of belief that p would not affect our ascriptions, our intentional explanations, or our attitude toward the agent. It would be like saying that believers of p who were born on a Wednesday, for that reason, have a different kind of belief that p than do the rest of us. (I don't mean to deny the possibility that there could be different kinds of belief; for example, we could distinguish between different *degrees* of belief. However, this is the sort of distinction in kinds of belief that *would* be grounded in the dispositions of the person, whereas the distinction between kinds postulated in the text is, by hypothesis, independent of any behavioral or experiential disposition.)

According to (RFb), the set of token beliefs that p form a natural kind by virtue of the fact that each token occupies a common causal role. Given the motivations for thinking of mental states as natural kinds, this move is a natural response to the apparent constitutive role of our common-sense criteria for mental states and to the possibility of multiple realization. According to this view, we need not admit the coherence of attributing to Ann a strong desire to watch the game, despite the lack of any normally associated behavior; since Ann does not exhibit the functional connections essential to such a desire, she ipso facto has no such desire. Nonetheless, this view still runs into an obstacle.

We first must be more explicit about what it might mean for a token to occupy a causal role. As a first pass, to say that a token state x occupies a causal role is to say that certain events cause x and that x in turn causes other events. Of course, any event that causes x will do so only in a particular set of circumstances; similarly, x will cause a given event only in the right circumstances. For example, assuming the causalist picture, the belief that ice cream has been offered to me may cause me to extend my right arm, but only in the circumstance in which I desire ice cream and in which

I further believe that reaching out my right arm would be a good way of obtaining it. We can thus say that the relevant causal role will be defined by reference to a set of propositions of the following form:

If circumstances C_1 obtain, c_1 causes x.
If circumstances C_2 obtain, c_2 causes x.

.

.

.

If circumstances C_n obtain, x causes e_1.
If circumstances C_{n+1} obtain, x causes e_2.

.

.

.

To say that x occupies the given causal role is to say that all of the above propositions are true of x. However, this claim is still open to varying interpretations, depending on whether we read the conditionals as subjunctive or as merely material conditionals. Suppose for example that the agent is actually in circumstances C_n. If the agent is in token state x, then the claim that x occupies the given causal role at least implies that x will cause e_1. If we read the conditionals definitive of the causal role subjunctively, then it is also implied that if the agent *were* in C_{n+1}, then x would cause e_2. If the conditionals are read materially, there is no such implication about what would happen in non-actual circumstances; since those circumstances don't obtain, the antecedent of each conditional is false and the conditionals as a whole are therefore true.

If we read the conditionals that define the causal role as merely material conditionals, the claim that a token state x occupies a causal role is trivialized. On this reading, the claim that a token state occupies a given causal role commits us only to the claim that the token state will, in the actual circumstances, have the causes or effects that are specified by the given causal role. Causal roles become too cheap on this reading; a given token state will occupy an infinite number of causal roles, for any conditional we like will be true of the state so long as the conditional has a false antecedent—i.e., so long as the conditional talks of circumstances other than those that are actual. Attribution of a mental state (as defined by a particular causal role) to an agent would be no more substantive or significant than attribution of any number of bizarre states defined by other sets of material conditionals.

So it seems that we must read the conditionals subjunctively. However, read this way, it seems that this account implies the possibility of error in attribution of mental states in circumstances where we would not think that such error is possible; in particular, it allows for errors of the sort defined by (E2). Again consider Cheryl, who wants to watch the baseball game on TV. On this account, our attribution to her of that desire implies that there is some brain state Q that will cause her to turn to channel 9 if she believes that the game is being televised on channel 9; our attribution also implies that in the counterfactual circumstance in which the game is on ESPN rather than channel 9 the very same brain state Q will cause Cheryl to turn to ESPN. However, even if Cheryl in fact would have turned to ESPN had she believed that the game was being televised there, the latter implication could still be false. That is to say, it might not be the same brain state that would have done the causing in both circumstances. It might be that in the circumstances in which Cheryl believes that the game is on ESPN a brain state other than Q would have done the work. Suppose that this is the case—that we can't find one brain state that would do the job in both cases. Would we therefore withdraw our attribution of the desire to Cheryl? I contend that we would not. In making attributions of mental states in ordinary life, we indeed care about what Cheryl would do in counterfactual circumstances, but we are not committed to any particular causal story of how the actions would have come about. If we are confident that Cheryl would have tuned to ESPN had she believed the game was televised on ESPN, this serves to confirm our judgment that Cheryl indeed desires to watch the game. The specific causal path by means of which Cheryl would have taken the alternative action is not part of our ordinary criteria for desire attribution.

(RFb) thus overcommits common-sense psychology. (RFb) would require that we withdraw our attribution of a desire to Cheryl on the basis of facts about Cheryl's brain states that are quite irrelevant to our common-sense judgments. Common-sense psychology is not so metaphysically committed. If Cheryl satisfies the ordinary criteria for having a desire to watch the baseball game, we need not worry about which brain state would cause of the appropriate behavior.

I have argued that ordinary mental-state terms do not function as natural-kind terms, and that consequently there is little to be said for viewing CSP as a proto-scientific theory of human behavior. Earlier in the chapter, I also argued that the context sensitivity of CSP attributions and the normative elements in CSP made it look quite unlike a proto-scientific theory of the mind. All of this means trouble for strong naturalism. It is not just that CSP is relatively unsystematic and fails to have laboratories and peer reviewed journals; a reductionist or eliminativist could look past these features and maintain that CSP is nonetheless a rudimentary science. Instead, I have argued that there are substantial and systematic distinctions between CSP and the physical sciences, distinctions that indicate a fundamental difference in kind between the claims of CSP and those of physical science. If this is correct, then one of the central commitments of strong naturalism is false, and strong naturalism must likewise itself be called into question.

As we have seen, a crucial feature of strong naturalism is its emphasis on causation and causal explanation; in particular, according to strong naturalism, CSP explanation of human behavior is a species of causal explanation. On this view, an explanation of the form "Jennifer went to the kitchen because she wanted coffee" is a causal explanation; the explanation implies that Jennifer's desire for coffee caused her behavior of going to the kitchen. This causal construal of common-sense psychological explanation is widely assumed by both strong naturalists and nonreductive materialists. Using some claims by Lynne Rudder Baker as a starting point, I will argue against the causal theory of action explanation.

Baker offers a nonreductive account of the mind in *Explaining Attitudes: A Practical Approach to the Mind* (1995). Although nonreductive materialists deny that mental properties reduce to physical properties, most do claim that each token mental state is identical to (or constituted by, or realized in) a particular brain state. Baker aptly calls this claim of token identity the *Standard View*, for the claim is widely accepted by reductive and nonreductive materialists alike. Baker plausibly suggests that the Standard View is motivated by the following thought, which she calls the "brain explain" thesis:

(BE) If beliefs can causally explain behavior, then beliefs are brain states.

The consequent of this conditional is a slightly abbreviated form of the Standard View. Baker herself puts the principle in what I take to be equivalent terms: "Unless belief states were brain states, they could not causally explain behavior." (1995, p. 17) Baker's own view is distinctive in that she denies the Standard View, although she does maintain that beliefs can causally explain behavior. Since the Standard View follows from (BE) plus the assumption that action explanation is causal, Baker must deny (BE).

Pace Baker, I will argue in section 6.1 that (BE) is true: if beliefs can causally explain behavior, then beliefs are brain states. However, I will argue in section 6.2 that Baker is correct to deny the Standard View, although I will support this claim on grounds largely independent of her text. If (BE) is true but beliefs are not brain states, the obvious consequence is that beliefs do not causally explain behavior. I conclude that the causal theory of action explanation is indeed mistaken. (Although the arguments below will explicitly focus on beliefs, I take them to be equally applicable to desire and other propositional-attitude states.)

6.1 The Case for (BE)

To argue for (BE), I will argue for its contrapositive: If beliefs are not brain states, then beliefs cannot causally explain behavior. Assume, for the sake of argument, that beliefs are not brain states. But if beliefs are not brain states, what are they? In other words, by virtue of what does one have the belief that p? Baker (1995, p.187) suggests that *believing that p* is simply a matter of having certain conditionals true of one:

One has a belief that p by virtue of there being a conjunction of relevant true counterfactuals that mention a range of circumstances in which the believer would perform a range of intentional actions—thinkings, doings, and sayings.

Each of the relevant counterfactuals will presumably be of the form "In circumstances C, the agent will do B." We can abbreviate this as "$C \Rightarrow B$." Thus, each person who believes that p will have this belief by virtue of there being a true conjunction of the form

(1) $(C_1 \rightarrow B_1)$ & $(C_2 \rightarrow B_2)$ & $(C_3 \rightarrow B_3)$ & $(C_4 \rightarrow B_4)$ & . . . .

Baker further suggests that different counterfactuals might be true of two different believers of p. Nonetheless, for each believer of p, some conjunction like (1) will provide a sufficient condition for her having the belief that p.

For example, suppose that Margaret believes that Augusta is the capital of Maine. According to Baker, Margaret believes this by virtue of there being some conjunction like (1) true of her. The relevant circumstances and behavior might include the following:

C_1 = Someone asks her "What is the capital of Maine?"

B_1 = She says "Augusta."

C_2 = She has a meeting with the Governor of Maine in one hour.

B_2 = She drives to Augusta.

.

.

.

The proponent of the Standard View could agree that (1) is a *part* of a sufficient condition for Margaret having the belief that Augusta is the capital of Maine. However, the Standard View adds the claim that there must be a physical state that plays the role specified by (1). By rejecting this requirement, Baker takes a *pure dispositional* view of the nature of mental states: having the right dispositions is sufficient for having the belief that *p*, regardless of what is going on in the brain.

If one denies the Standard View but maintains that beliefs are causes, it seems that one is virtually forced into a pure dispositional view of the nature of mental states. Daniel Dennett's Intentional Systems approach, if it involves a denial of the Standard View, falls into the same category. According to Dennett's approach, "*all there is* to being a true believer is being a system whose behavior is reliably predictable via the intentional strategy" (1987, p.29). The intentional strategy involves treating the object of interest as if it is a rational agent, with the beliefs and desires one would expect of a rational agent in the object's circumstances. Dennett explains further:

... *what it means* to say that someone believes that *p*, is that that person is disposed to behave in certain ways under certain conditions. What ways under what conditions? The ways it would be rational to behave, given the person's other beliefs and desires. (1987, p. 50)

Thus, for the intentional strategy, an individual has the belief that *p* by virtue of there being certain dispositional conditionals true of that agent. Dennett tells us more than Baker about how to determine which conditionals must be true of a given believer of *p* (namely, those that would make the person's behavior rational, given that belief and other beliefs and desires), but it is still an instance of a pure dispositional view.

However, the pure dispositional view of the nature of mental states looks problematic when combined with the claim that beliefs causally explain behavior. Suppose, for example, that Margaret is asked "What is the capital of Maine?" and that she replies "Augusta." Baker would offer the following causal explanation of Margaret's behavior:

(2) Margaret said "Augusta" because she believed that Augusta is the capital of Maine.

However, on the pure dispositional account, (2) looks rather trivial and empty. Margaret believes that Augusta is the capital of Maine by virtue of, inter alia, the fact that she would give the answer "Augusta" to the question "What is the capital of Maine?" Thus, (2) explains the fact that Margaret performs B_1 in C_1 by citing Margaret's disposition to perform B_1 in C_1. This looks perilously similar to explaining salt's dissolving in water by citing the fact that it is water-soluble. The two explanations do differ in this respect: Water-solubility is defined in terms of a single disposition, whereas Margaret's belief is characterized by a number of behavioral dispositions. Since (2) tells us what Margaret was likely to have done in other circumstances, (2) does say more than that Margaret was disposed to act in just the way she did. But this extra information plays no obvious role in *explaining* Margaret's behavior in the circumstances, and hence it does nothing to save (2) from triviality.

Even if we allow for the moment that (2) is not trivial on Baker's account, there will be other objections. First, the pure dispositional account arguably has difficulty with a certain kind of routine scenario: one in which an agent has two or more beliefs that would justify a given piece of behavior, but the agent acts only because of one of the beliefs. Suppose, for example, that Margaret also believes that she will win $1,000 if she says "Augusta" in answer to the next question asked of her, regardless of the question. Once again, someone asks Margaret "What is the capital of Maine?" and she answers "Augusta." Here the appropriate explanation for Margaret's behavior may be this:

(3) Margaret said "Augusta" because she believed that she would win $1,000 if she said "Augusta" to whatever question was asked of her.

Margaret still believes that Augusta is the capital of Maine, but we can coherently suppose that she acted only on the belief mentioned in (3). That is, we can suppose that (3) is true but (2) is false, even though Margaret still has the belief cited in (2).

But it is not clear that Baker can say that (2) is false. On the pure dispositional view, Margaret has the belief mentioned in (3) by virtue of there being a conjunction of counterfactuals true of her—e.g.,

(4) $(C_1 \rightarrow B_1)$ & $(C_8 \rightarrow B_1)$ & $(C_9 \rightarrow B_1)$ & $(C_{10} \rightarrow B_1)$ & ...,

where

C_1 = Someone asks her "What is the capital of Maine?"

B_1 = She says "Augusta."

C_8 = Someone asks her "Who is your Mother?"

.

.

.

Recall that Baker apparently justified explanation (2) above by noting that the conjunction of counterfactuals in (1) was true of Margaret and that, in particular, it was true of Margaret that were she in C_1 she would perform B_1. But all of that is still true in the new case; thus it would seem that Baker must still affirm (2). Of course, a new conjunction of counterfactuals, namely (4), is now also true of Margaret, and that conjunction includes "$C_1 \Rightarrow B_1$." However, this merely means that Baker has grounds for asserting (3); it doesn't follow that her view provides any grounds for denying (2). Baker would appear forced to conclude that both (2) and (3) are true, violating our common-sense intuition that Margaret's belief about the capital of Maine might have had nothing to do with her behavior.

Baker responds to this argument by saying that "further use of counterfactuals will distinguish which belief was the actual cause, or whether [the action] was overdetermined" (unpublished, p. 18). She sets up her own example, in which Jones is set to vote against a school budget and has two beliefs that would be good candidates for explaining his vote: He believes that the budget has misplaced priorities (too much for Latin and Greek and not enough for the football team), and he also believes that the budget would raise taxes on the wealthy (which, as a wealthy landlord, he would like to avoid). Baker tells us that we can determine which of Jones's beliefs explained his vote by asking two questions: "Would Jones have voted against the school budget if he had not believed that it would raise taxes on the wealthy, but still had believed that the school budget had misplaced priorities? Would Jones have voted against the school budget if he had not believed that it had misplaced priorities, but still had believed that it would raise taxes on the wealthy?" (ibid.) And Baker then says:

If the answer to the first question is yes and the second is no, then the explanation of Jones's vote was that he believed that the school budget had misplaced priorities. If the answer to the first was no and the second was yes, then the explanation of his vote was that Jones believed that the school budget would raise taxes on the wealthy. If the answer to both questions was yes, then his vote was overdetermined. (ibid.)

I am dubious about the extent to which this works. It seems to me that the answer to both questions could be answered "Yes," and yet it also be the case that Jones in fact only voted as he did because of one of the two beliefs. Jones might have been so upset about taxes that he wasn't thinking at all about the misplaced priorities; however, if he had *not* believed that the budget would raise taxes on the wealthy, then he would have reflected more on the misplaced priorities, and would have voted against the budget for that reason.

The same point holds for my example. We can, as Baker suggests, ask whether Margaret would have said "Augusta" if she had believed that Augusta was the capital of Maine but had not believed that she would receive $1,000 for answering "Augusta" to whatever question was asked of her next; and we can ask whether she would have said "Augusta" if she believed she would get the $1,000 for answering "Augusta" but not believed that Augusta was the capital of Maine. In each case the answer is "Yes," but this is not enough to show that Margaret's answer was causally overdetermined. She might have been so excited by the prospect of an easy $1,000 that, when asked to name the capital of Maine, she gave no thought at all to whether Augusta was really the capital of Maine. And yet, had she not had the belief about the $1,000 she would have still said "Augusta." So Baker's counterfactuals still provide the practical realist with no obvious way to distinguish between the possible explanations.

Moreover, the situation gets worse for Baker's account. Let us invent a term and say that someone is *shunky* when the following is true of her:

(5) $(C_1 \rightarrow B_1)$ & $(C_{21} \rightarrow B_{22})$ & $(C_{24} \rightarrow B_{25})$,

where

C_1 = Someone asks her "What is the capital of Maine?"

B_1 = She says "Augusta."

C_{21} = Someone asks her "Is the pope Catholic?"

B_{22} = She says "Yes."

C_{24} = Someone asks her "Is the earth bigger than the sun?"

B_{25} = She says "No."

If (5) is true of a person, then that person is shunky. We can stipulate, as seems plausible enough in any event, that these conditionals are true of Margaret. Thus, Margaret is shunky. Now suppose again that Margaret performs B_1 in C_1, and consider the following explanation for her behavior:

(6) Margaret said "Augusta" because she was shunky.

On Baker's story, (6) and (2) have equal claims to explaining Margaret's behavior, for, in each case, being disposed to perform B_1 in C_1 is the sort of behavior that is definitive of the explanans. Both (6) and (2) have an air of triviality about them, but they are both equal on that score. If Baker were to claim that the explanans in (6) is definitionally connected to the explanandum, then she would have to admit that, on her view, are subject to the same objection.

Of course the trick with 'shunky' could be repeated. Simply take any conjunction of counterfactuals that meets these conditions: one of the counterfactuals is "$C_1 \Rightarrow B_1$," and the conjunction as a whole is true of Margaret. With repeated iteration of this trick, we will have indefinitely many bizarrely characterized states, each of which has an equal claim to being the cause of Margaret's behavior.

We can further confirm that these strange results follow from Baker's view by looking at Baker's own test for when one has a causal explanation:

(CT) An occurrence of F in C causally explains an occurrence of G in C if: (i) If an F had not occurred in C, then a G would not have occurred in C; and (ii) given that an F did occur in C, an occurrence of G was inevitable. (1995, p. 122)

First, we should note that ordinary belief explanations arguably fail this test. Even if Margaret had not believed that Augusta was the capital of Maine, she would have said "Augusta" anyway if she believed that she was going to be given $1,000 for doing so. Similarly, the mere fact that she had the relevant belief hardly makes it inevitable that she will answer "Augusta" to the question; had she wanted to mislead the questioner, she might well have said "Portland." Perhaps the test can be patched up by specifying that (i) and (ii) are to be evaluated in "nearby" possible worlds, or by adding an all-purpose *ceteris paribus* clause to each condition. But once (CT) is loosened up in one of these ways, (6) will be quite likely to meet the requirements imposed by (CT) on legitimate causal explanation. In particular, had Margaret not been shunky in the circumstances, then the conditionals in (5) would not be true of her; hence she would not have said "Augusta." Of course she might have said "Augusta" anyway because of some other set of dispositions that were true of her at the time, but this is merely the same problem that we ran into with the ordinary belief explanation in (2). Similarly, given that Margaret was shunky and was thus disposed to perform B_1 in C_1, the occurrence of her saying

"Augusta" was bound to happen; of course, it wasn't truly inevitable in any strong sense, but again this is just the same problem faced by the normal belief explanation. Hence, (6) passes Baker's own test for being a causal explanation at least as well as (2), and we are again stuck with the conclusion that indefinitely many bizarrely characterized states will have equal claim to being the cause of Margaret's behavior.

The conclusion reached here serves to confirm the suggestion (made above) that, on the pure dispositional account, ordinary belief explanations become trivial and empty. We know that (6) is not a meaningful explanation of Margaret's behavior. But the trouble with (6) is not the appearance of a bizarre new term, for we can always introduce and define terms any way we like. The objection is, rather, that (6) is trivial, for it purports to causally explain a behavior in a set of circumstances merely by citing the agent's disposition to perform that behavior in that set of circumstances. But in this respect, on Baker's account, (6) is exactly parallel to (2). Neither (6) nor (2) is as obviously empty as "salt dissolves in water because it is water-soluble," for both (2) and (6) do give the extra information that certain other dispositional conditionals are true of the agent at the time. But this extra information does not save the explanations from triviality, as indicated by the fact that we can, on Baker's approach, multiply indefinitely the number of explanations with equal claim to truth merely by adding different dispositional conditionals to "$C_1 \rightarrow B_1$."[1]

So we have seen that if one denies the Standard View one will naturally affirm a pure dispositional account of the nature of mental states. Baker accepts this much. But we have also seen that, given such an account of the nature of mental states, reason explanations, construed as causal explanations, are trivialized. That is to say, beliefs will not be able to causally explain behavior if one denies the Standard View. Of course it doesn't follow that the Standard View is true. What follows is that *if* beliefs do indeed causally explain behavior, then the Standard View is true. And this just is (BE).

I have argued that if the Standard View is false, then belief explanations, construed as causal explanations, are trivialized. Though not logically necessary to this argument, it is worth noting that the Standard View, at least on one construal, can avoid this problem. The proponent of the Standard View can even agree that an agent will have the belief that Augusta is the capital of Maine only if (1) is true of the agent. But the Standard View would require that some particular physical state of the agent play the causal role specified by counterfactuals in (1). On the Standard View, the dispositional conditionals in (1) serve to specify the physical state that is the belief;

Margaret's belief that Augusta is the capital of Maine just is the physical state (if any) that plays the causal role specified by (1). Accordingly, belief explanations like (2) assert both that there is a physical state that plays the causal role specified by (1) and that the physical state caused the behavior. Far from being trivial, on this construal (2) amounts to a substantial empirical claim. Construed in the same way, the explanation citing shunkiness is quite likely to be false; although Margaret does have all of the dispositions definitive of shunkiness, it is highly unlikely that there is one physical state of Margaret that constitutes the base of each of the dispositional conditionals. Hence the Standard View can avoid the problem of having indefinitely many explanations, each with an equal claim to truth. Moreover, the Standard View, on this version, can choose between competing explanations in a way that Baker's account cannot. If we want to know which of (2) or (3) is the true explanation of Margaret's saying "Augusta," we can look at the brain state that caused the behavior. If that brain state is of the type that plays the causal role defined by (1), then Margaret's behavior was caused by her belief that Augusta is the capital of Maine; if the brain state is of the type that plays the causal role defined by (4), then Margaret's behavior was caused by the belief that she would get $1,000 for saying "Augusta."

On the other hand, there are weak versions of the Standard View that will have the same problem as Baker's account. On one such version, the Standard View also accepts that Margaret will have the belief only if (1) is true of her, but it no longer requires that it be the same kind of physical state that plays the causal role in each case. For example, brain state Q might cause Margaret to perform B_1 in C_1, but brain state R causes B_2 in C_2. The weak version of the Standard View still identifies each mental token with a physical token, but it does not require that different instances of a mental type (even different instances within a single person) be identical to physical tokens of the same type. If a belief that p is said to cause behavior of type B_{15} in circumstances C_{22}, then the weak Standard View is content to identify the token instance of the belief that p with whatever physical state happens to cause B_{15} in C_{22}.

The weak version of the Standard View falls prey to the same objections as the pure dispositional account of mental states. In particular, the weak version of the view would have no way of denying that Margaret is shunky and that her state of being shunky caused her to say "Augusta," nor would the weakened view be able to distinguish between competing explanations. Thus the weakened Standard View is no better able to claim that beliefs causally explain behavior than is the pure dispositional view. I mention this in part because Davidson's anomalous monism can, on one interpretation, be seen as a form of the weak Standard View. If this is right, then anomalous monism cannot consistently maintain that beliefs are causally explanatory.

6.2 The Case against the Standard View

If the Standard View is correct, then each belief token is a brain state. That is to say, if there *are* any mental states, then they are brain states; the Standard View itself should be seen as an account of the commitments of mental-state talk and as not committed in the realism-eliminativism debate. Seen this way, the Standard View might be used by an eliminativist as part of an argument against the existence of mental states:

(1) If the Standard View is true and if there are mental states, then empirical science will ultimately find suitable candidate brain states as the realizers of mental tokens. [premise]
(2) Empirical science will not find suitable candidate brain states as the realizers of mental tokens. [premise]
(3) If the Standard View is true, then there are no mental states. [1,2]
(4) The Standard View is true. [premise]
(5) There are no mental states. [3,4]

In response, of course, the realist could simply deny the second premise and claim that empirical science *will* succeed in finding brain states that realize particular mental states; i.e., the realist will claim that the project of reifying mental states will succeed. The eliminativist argument just presented is flawed, but the flaw is illustrative of a general principle that will show us why we should reject the Standard View. I will diagnose the problem with the eliminativist argument in subsection 6.2.1; I will then present the related argument against the Standard View in subsection 6.2.2.

6.2.1 The Eliminativist Version of the Argument
Let me begin with some methodological observations. According to the familiar Quinean metaphor, our beliefs form an interconnected web. If there is a conflict among the sentences we are inclined to accept—i.e., when there is a defect in the web—then we must make revisions. In principle, revision can strike at any place in the web. However, certain sentences are more privileged than others, in that we are more reluctant to revise those sentences. According to Quine, of course, observation sentences are the paradigmatic case of privileged sentences; rather than reject an observation sentence, we will try to make changes elsewhere in the web. But there are

other theoretical virtues besides that of preserving observation sentences. We aim for a simple theory, and, in the case of conflict within the theory, we strive to revise the theory as little as possible. Accordingly, claims are highly privileged if their rejection would require an unduly complex theory, or if their rejection would require massive revision to our overall home theory. The basic methodological maxim, then, is this: When forced to choose, on pain of contradiction, between two propositions, we should accept higher-privilege claims over lower-privilege claims. This can be put somewhat more abstractly as follows:

(6) If (i) X implies $\sim Y$, and (ii) X is not highly privileged, and (iii) Y is highly privileged, then reject X.

Now consider the instance of (6) in which X is the conjunction of (2) and (4) in the eliminativist's argument—the claim that empirical science will fail to find physical realizers of mental tokens and the claim that the Standard View is true. This yields the following:

(7) If (i) the conjunction of (2) and (4) implies that there are no mental states and (ii) the conjunction of (2) and (4) is not highly privileged and (iii) the claim that there are mental states is highly privileged, then reject the conjunction of (2) and (4).

The eliminativist correctly claims that the Standard View, combined with the assumption that the reification project will fail, implies that there are no mental states. Hence, part (i) of the antecedent of (7) is true. However, unless the assertion that reification will fail can be given a very compelling rationale, it is arguably no more than a speculative hunch about the future results of neuroscience; as such, it can hardly count as a highly privileged claim. If this assertion is not highly privileged, then the conjunction of this assertion and the Standard View is likewise not highly privileged. (I will argue below that the Standard View itself should be viewed as a claim of low privilege, but we don't need to make that claim for the purposes of the present argument.) Thus, part (ii) of the antecedent of (7) is true too. On the other hand, the denial of the existence of mental states would be a truly extraordinary claim. Vast stretches of ordinary discourse presuppose mental states; mental-state attributions are central part to a set of highly successful common-sense practices—practices that are integral to a recognizably human life. That alone should suffice to show that the claim that there are mental states is very highly privileged. The principle of conservativism counsels strongly against accepting claims that would require massive revision of the overall home theory. Thus part (iii) of the antecedent of (7) is true.

Hence the antecedent of (7) as a whole is true, and it follows that we should reject the conjunction of reification's failing and the Standard View. In other words, the sound methodological advice offered by (6) confirms that we should reject the eliminativist argument because we should rather suspect that its premises are false than that its conclusion is true.

6.2.2 The Argument against the Standard View

The argument against the Standard View begins from a related methodological observation. The basic idea behind (6) also applies when there are three propositions involved. Accordingly:

(8) If (i) X, Y and Z, are mutually inconsistent and (ii) X and Y are highly privileged and (iii) Z is not highly privileged, then reject Z.

However, there is an exception to this principle. If it happens that X and Y are inconsistent with each other, then we know that one of them must be false, despite being highly privileged. In this case we don't have any particular reason to suspect the falsity of Z. So the revised principle looks like this:

(9) If (i) X, Y, and Z are mutually inconsistent and (ii) if X and Y are highly privileged and (iii) Z is not highly privileged and (iv) X and Y are not inconsistent with each other, then reject Z.

It will be convenient to explicitly note the following consequence of (9):

(10) If (i) X and Z jointly imply $\sim Y$ and (ii) if X and Y are highly privileged and (iii) Z is not highly privileged and (iv) X alone does not imply $\sim Y$, then reject Z.

Suppose for the sake of argument that we empirically discover that reification fails; i.e., assume that empirical science does not find brain states that are plausible candidates for identification with mental tokens. I will argue that, on this assumption, we should reject Standard View. The strategy will be to instantiate the variables in (10) as follows:

Let X be the proposition that reification fails.

Let Y be the claim that there are mental states.

Let Z be the Standard View.

I will argue that the four conditions in the antecedent hold, and that we are forced to conclude that we should reject the Standard View.

As I noted above when discussing the eliminativist's argument, if the Standard View is true and reification in fact fails, it follows that there are no mental states. Thus condition (i) in (10) is met.

We have assumed for the sake of argument that empirical science fails to find physical realizers for mental tokens. Empirical findings of science are highly privileged claims within the web of belief; thus, the claim that reification fails will be highly privileged. But we have also seen that the claim that there are mental states is integral to the structure of our web of belief and is thus also highly privileged. Thus condition (ii) of (10) is met.

Skipping to condition (iv), there appears to be no reason to think that the failure of reification would, by itself, imply the nonexistence of mental states. On the face of things, whether or not the project of reification succeeds is largely irrelevant to the question of whether mental-state attributions are true or false. By way of analogy, consider poverty. There are a lot of poor people in the world; they are in a state of poverty. We have programs that try to help people in poverty, that try to combat it, and so on. And yet it does not seem likely that we will find some particular physical state and identify it with a poor person's state of poverty. So far as I know, it has never occurred to anyone to try. If someone were to claim that there were no poor people because we can't find any physical state with which to identify token states of poverty, we would not take it seriously. Similarly, even if neuroscience fails to find any physical states identifiable with mental states, this is prima facie irrelevant to the question of whether or not we have beliefs and desires. The claims of common-sense psychology, taken at face value, do not display any obvious dependence on results from neuroscience. In any event, there is certainly no immediate logical implication from the failure of reification to the nonexistence of mental states. Hence condition (iv) of (10) is met.

This leaves condition (iii), the claim that the Standard View is not itself a highly privileged claim. I would suggest that philosophical theories are, in general, of low privilege. Philosophical views allow us to unify and make sense of our experiences in the world. However, philosophical views are by nature somewhat removed from the highly privileged claims of observation, empirical science, and everyday successful practice. Of course, it is possible that a philosophical view can be given a compelling rationale; e.g., certain philosophical claims might follow from claims of high privilege and thus be of high privilege themselves. But, barring an extremely compelling rationale, it is philosophical hubris to think that philosophy can dictate great changes in scientific or common-sense practice. In particular, the

Standard View is a philosophical claim about the commitments of common sense and the nature of mental states. Despite its intuitive appeal to many philosophers, the Standard View must be seen as a claim of low privilege unless it can be given a compelling rationale.

One might think that I have already provided the compelling rationale for the Standard View by arguing in section 6.1 for (BE), the claim that if beliefs can causally explain behavior then beliefs are brain states. The claim that beliefs causally explain behavior is widely held within philosophy of mind. One might well conclude that the causal theory of action explanation and (BE) jointly provide the compelling rationale demanded for the Standard View. But this is wrong, for the causal theory of action is itself a *philosophical construal* of common-sense psychological practice. Thus, the rationale for the Standard View is only as compelling as the grounds for the causal theory of action. The widespread acceptance of the causal theory of action explanation stems apparently from the perceived lack of a developed alternative; indeed, in the landmark article "Actions, Reasons and Causes," Davidson's *only* positive argument for the causal theory is the presumed absence of an alternative account of the explanatory force of the "because" in action explanations. If, as I will try to show in chapter 9, there is a plausible alternative to the causal account, there is no compelling rationale for the causal theory of action. If there is no compelling rationale for the causal theory of action, there are no compelling grounds for the Standard View, and hence condition (iii) of (10) still holds.

Since all four conditions in the antecedent have been met, we can conclude that we should reject Z; i.e., we should reject the Standard View. Of course, this argument was based on the assumption that reification fails— that neuroscience concludes that there are no suitable candidate brain states with which to identify mental states. But it seems quite clear that the truth of the Standard View cannot turn on the empirical question of whether reification fails. The Standard View is the philosophical claim that, if there are any mental states, they can be identified with brain states. This is a claim about the commitments of our common-sense employment of mental-state terminology, and it amounts to the claim that our employment of these terms presupposes that reification is possible. If the Standard View is true at all, it must be true regardless of how the reification question is empirically answered. Otherwise, the Standard View would be the claim that common sense is committed to reification so long as reification turns out to be possible; but that is no commitment at all. Thus, the truth value of the Standard View must remain the same whether or not reification fails.

But we have seen that if reification does fail, we would rightly conclude that the Standard View is false. Hence, we can conclude that the Standard View is false whether or not reification fails.

6.3   Conclusion

Combining this conclusion with the conclusion of section 6.1 (that if the Standard View is false then beliefs do not causally explain behavior), we immediately get the result that beliefs do not causally explain behavior. And without this claim, strong naturalism fails. Of course, this invites the question of how we should construe CSP explanations if not as causal explanations. As one might suspect, a teleological realist views such explanations as teleological rather than causal. I will present the teleological account of action explanation in chapter 9.

7 | Agency and Deviant Causal Chains

7.1 The Problem

When we explain human behavior within common-sense psychology, we do so by citing the agent's *reason* for acting; e.g., we might say "Bill went to the café because he wanted coffee." According to strong naturalism, such explanations will either be entailed or contradicted by physical science. Either way, strong naturalism requires that CSP explanations make the same sort of claim that is made in the physical sciences—if the CSP explanations did not translate into physical science terms, then there could be neither entailment nor contradiction. Thus, the first step for the strong naturalist is to construe CSP explanations as a species of *causal explanation*, for this is what we find in the natural sciences. So, for example, in "Bill went to the café because he wanted coffee," the speaker implies that Bill's desire for coffee caused his behavior. In chapter 6, I argued that this causal construal of reason explanations is a mistake.

Despite the argument of chapter 6, the causal construal of action explanation might have seemed straightforward enough when considering CSP explanations of a certain form, i.e., those that explicitly cite a mental state and use the word 'because'. However, some CSP explanations at least appear to have an overtly noncausal form, and these pose a further problem for strong naturalism. For example, "Joan went to the kitchen in order to get a glass of wine" does not mention a mental state or any antecedent event that might be the cause of the behavior. Instead, the explanation specifies the state of affairs toward which the behavior was directed, namely that Joan obtain a glass of wine. The example in question employs the connective "in order to," but the explanation could have used other connectives with apparently the same sense—e.g., "Joan went to the kitchen for the purpose of getting a glass of wine" or "Joan went to the kitchen to get a glass of wine." All such explanations explain by naming the state of affairs toward which the behavior was directed, and they are referred to as *teleological* explanations (the Greek root 'telos' meaning *goal* or *end*).

Overtly teleological explanations of action pose a special challenge for strong naturalism. Such explanations are central to CSP, for they appear to be intrinsically connected to the very notion of agency. To be an agent is to act for *reasons*; that is, to be an agent is, at least in part, to direct one's behavior toward particular ends or states of affairs. However, there is a prima facie tension between teleological explanation and its concomitant notion of agency on the one hand and the scientific view of human beings as physical objects on the other. Notions like *action* and *goal direction* appear to have no role in purely physical descriptions of the world. Planets, rocks, and elementary particles do not act for reasons, and their behavior is not teleologically explicable. Accordingly, it would seem that the physical science account of the behavior of human beings would not use the language of action and goal direction.

The strong naturalist will try to resolve this tension by assimilating teleological concepts within the causally based perspective of physical science. According to option 2, our common-sense claims about actions and agency will be entailed by the scientific account of the world, given suitable bridge laws, and thus the naturalistically described facts must imply common-sense teleological explanations. For example, if it is true that Joan went to the kitchen in order to get wine, then physical science must imply this fact. Of course, the naturalistically described facts alone will contain no reference to teleological notions. So a purely physical account of Joan's behavior will imply that the behavior was goal directed only if certain naturalistically described facts are *sufficient* for goal direction. Similarly, the physical facts will entail that a piece of behavior is *not* goal directed only if there are *necessary* conditions for goal direction that the behavior fails to satisfy. Thus, for physical science to imply the correct result for each event, there must be naturalistically described conditions that are necessary and sufficient for an event to count as goal directed. Therefore, option 2 requires a causal analysis of teleological explanation. Similar comments apply for the first option: for naturalistic facts to contradict attributions of purposive behavior, there must be necessary conditions for goal direction that are not satisfied. (However, the first option does not require that there be sufficient naturalistic conditions for goal direction. Compare the property of being a witch. Since a witch is taken to be something that is in part supernatural, there will be no list of naturalistic sufficient conditions for being a witch; nonetheless, claims attributing witchhood will contradict naturalistic science, for there are some naturalistically describable necessary conditions for being a witch, e.g., having causal powers of a certain kind, that are manifestly not satisfied by any actual person.) Thus, the naturalist who defends the second option and the naturalist who regards the choice between one and two as an empirical matter must both maintain that there is a reductive analysis of teleological explanation.

A first attempt at a causal analysis might state that A ϕd in order to ψ if and only if

(A1) A had an intention to ψ, and this intention caused her to ϕ.

However, as is well known, such simple analyses are subject to a distinctive kind of counterexample. Here is one from Al Mele's book *Springs of Action*:

A philosopher intends to knock over his glass of water in order to distract his commentator. However, his intention so upsets him that his hand shakes uncontrollably, striking the glass and knocking it to the floor. (1992, p. 182)

In this case, the agent's behavior meets all the requirements of (A1), but the philosopher did not knock over the glass in order to distract his commentator; his behavior was involuntary and so was not directed at any goal at all. Further examples could be cooked up at will. Here is the recipe: suppose that the agent had an intention to ψ by ϕing; then suppose that the agent's having this intention agitates her and thereby brings about some involuntary bodily motion, which, as it happens, ψs by ϕing.

Of course, we are treading on familiar ground. The most sustained treatment of this issue occurs in George Wilson's *The Intentionality of Human Action* (1989). Wilson subjects a variety of purported causal analyses to counterexamples, concluding that "the evidence points to more than infelicity or incompleteness in the various causalist proposals—it points, that is, to a global breakdown in the whole project of reduction" (ibid., p. 258). However, the question must be considered again, for Mele goes on to claim that the "resources presented in chapter 11 [of *Springs of Action*] are ample for handling each of the cases of deviance" advanced by Wilson (Mele 1992, p. 244). Also, a proposal from John Bishop, arising out of work by Christopher Peacocke, is not explicitly considered by Wilson and has yet to receive the close attention it deserves.

In sections 7.2 and 7.3, I will consider the Mele and Bishop-Peacocke strategies for causal analysis of teleology. I will argue that both attempts fail in their aim of reducing teleological explanation to causal explanation. I will then argue that this failure indicates that CSP explanation of human behavior is indeed irreducibly teleological, and that this is highly problematic for the strong naturalist view of mind and agency.

7.2 A Solution Suggested by Mele

It is first worth noting that Mele himself may not be concerned with the problem as I have posed it. Mele's immediate aim is to analyze the concept of *intentional* action, and he appears willing to help himself to the notion of an *action* in the course of analyzing intentional action. In a footnote, he says that "causal accounts of what it is for an action to be intentional (unlike causal accounts of what it is for an event to be an action) cannot be falsified by waywardly caused nonactions" (1992, p. 224). Moreover, in an article co-authored by Paul Moser, Mele's final analysis of intentionally performing an action explicitly includes the requirement that the bodily motion in question be an action (Mele and Moser 1994). More recently yet, Mele (2000) says that he is not offering any analysis of the fundamental notion of *action*.

Since Mele is specifically concerned with analyzing *intentional* action, his comments may not seem to be directly relevant to the task of giving a causal analysis of statements of teleological locutions, for there are behaviors which are purposive and goal directed but which are arguably not intentional. Someone can turn over in her sleep in order to attain a more comfortable position, or a sleepwalker might turn left in order to avoid a wall, but we would presumably hesitate to say that actions performed while asleep are intentional. Hence the analysanda are not equivalent or even coextensive. More important, one might well think that the concept *action* just is the concept of goal-directed behavior. That is, the notion that Mele helps himself to in the course of analyzing intentional action may be the very notion that is in question for the project of reducing teleological explanations to causal explanations.

One even might have qualms about Mele's approach to analyzing intentional action. On some views, for a bit of behavior to be an action is for it to be intentional under some description. (See e.g. Davidson 1980, p. 46.) On such a view, any analysis of intentional action that presupposes the notion of an action would be circular, for the notion of *action* is in turn to be analyzed in terms of the notion of *intentional action*. Moreover, Mele's overall project is to provide a "causal theory of the explanation of intentional action" (1992, p. vii); I take it that this is conceived of as a part of the naturalistic project of subsuming talk of reasons and agency within the realm of causation and causal laws. If I have this right, then it would be of grave concern to Mele if the notion to which he helps himself, viz. voluntary action, was in fact irreducibly teleological.

Whatever Mele's precise intentions, his account in *Springs of Action* does suggest some ways of improving on (A1). The recipe for generating counterexamples called for the intention to cause some state of nervousness or agitation which in turn causes the bodily motion. For example, in the case of the philosopher spilling the drink, the causal chain would look roughly like this:

(C1) Intention to spill → state of agitation → bodily motions.

Mele's basic response is to insist that in genuine cases of intentional action the intention is a *proximate* cause of the behavior. In other words, a state of intention-inspired nervousness may not "fill a causal gap between intention and action" (1992, p. 243). Hence, on the new analysis,[1] A φd in order to ψ iff

(A2) A had an intention to ψ, and this intention proximately caused her to φ.

At first, (A2) looks way too strong. Suppose that Peter goes to the kitchen in order to wash his hands, and that his going to the kitchen is constituted by a certain set of bodily motions; (A2) would require the following causal chain to have been in place:

(C2) Intention to wash his hands → appropriate bodily motions.

On Mele's account, Peter's intention is realized in some brain state. However, this brain state clearly does not *proximately* cause Peter's bodily motions. At bare minimum, some sort of signal must travel from Peter's brain to his limbs; thus, various physiological events occur that are not parts of Peter's intention or his bodily motions. So the causal chain must look like this:

(C3) Intention to wash his hands → physiological events x, y and z → bodily motions.

Hence there appears to be a causal gap between intentions and actions even in ordinary cases of goal-directed behavior.

Mele responds by including the intervening physiological events as a part of the action that is being explained: "Since the causal route from intention acquisition to overt bodily movement in beings like us involves a causal chain initiated in the brain, the suggestion that the acquisition of a proximal intention must proximately initiate the action requires that the action begin in the brain, too" (1992, p. 202). Of course,

Mele does not claim to know which precise physiological events will link the intention to the bodily motions. Offhand, the idea seems to be this: Whatever the precise intervening events are, we should simply include anything that is to the right of the first causal arrow in (C3) as a part of the action.

But now we have a new problem. If Mele can save (A2) by claiming that Peter's action includes all of the physiological events (whatever they are) that causally link the intention to the bodily motion, then why shouldn't we make the same move in the allegedly deviant cases? In the case of the philosopher's deviantly caused water spilling, the full causal chain is presumably something like this:

(C4) Intention to spill → state of agitation → physiological events v and w → bodily motions.

On Mele's account the state of agitation itself will be realized by some physiological state, so we could also put the causal chain in this form:

(C5) Intention to spill → physiological events u, v and w → bodily motions.

(C5) is now parallel to (C3); if in (C3) the intention to wash his hands is a proximate cause of Peter's action (now construed as including both the bodily motions and physiological events x, y, and z), then why shouldn't we likewise say that the philosopher's intention to spill the water is a proximate cause of the action of spilling the drink (now construed as including both the bodily motions and physiological events u, v, and w)?

Mele owes us an account of the relevant difference between (C3) and (C5): Why does the physiological state of agitation *not* count as part of the philosopher's action when unknown physiological states x, y, and z do count as parts of Peter's action? The answer one might like to give is that physiological states cannot count as parts of the action when they bring it about that the agent no longer *guides* or *controls* the bodily motion (and Mele suggests this very answer at pp. 202–203); but, as I will argue below, *guidance* and *control* appear to be teleological notions themselves. Alternatively, one might suggest that the physiological events that count as parts of an action are those that are *normally* involved in the causal chain leading to such motions. Of course, 'normally' cannot here mean the same as "in those cases where the behavior is a genuine goal-directed action," lest the analysis be circular. I take it, then, that 'normal' refers to statistical normality. On this approach, the analysis of teleology would be hostage to an extremely strong empirical assumption: that there is a specific set of physiological states that links the intention to the bodily motion in all and only those cases of goal-directed action. Given the enormous complexity of the human body and the wide variety of circumstances in which one can intentionally perform any given action, I would find this assumption dubious at best. And even if it happens to be true, it is hard to see why it would be a *necessary* condition for goal direction; the CSP practice of identifying behaviors as goal directed does not seem to be committed to such an empirical hypothesis.

There is a further objection to (A2). With a little ingenuity, we can construct a case without any obvious causal gap between intention and action but in which the behavior is nonetheless involuntary. Go back to the philosopher who intended to distract his commentator by spilling a glass of water. There is no need to suppose that there is a causal gap between the intention and the behavior: the philosopher intends to spill the water; his having this intention makes him so agitated that his hand shakes involuntarily and he knocks over the water; however, we can assume that the intention remains in existence and still causes some small portion of the philosopher's arm motion, though the intention is not by itself causally sufficient to bring about a spilling of the water. This can be represented schematically as shown in figure 7.1. Here I think we still want to say that the spilling was involuntary, since the shaking hand motions were not sufficiently under the control of the agent. But it should count as voluntary according to (A2), for the intention was still *a* proximate cause of the bodily motions.

One might try to revamp (A2) accordingly, saying that A φd in order to ψ iff

(A3) A had an intention to ψ, and this intention was a *sufficient* and proximate cause of A's φing.

More narrowly, one might specifically rule out actions whose etiology essentially includes a state of nervousness or agitation:

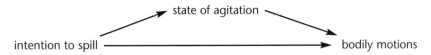

Figure 7.1

(A4) *A* had an intention to ψ, this intention proximately caused her to φ, and it is not the case that a necessary causal role was played by a state of nervousness or agitation.

However, an example offered by George Wilson shows that both (A3) and (A4) would be too strong and would exclude too much:

> . . . it should not be forgotten, on the other hand, that intentions cause states of nervous agitation that positively *enable* the agent to perform the type of action intended. A weight lifter, competing before a huge crowd at an important event, may firmly believe that he can lift the enormous barbell before him and, when he makes the attempt, he succeeds. However, it may also be that his intention to lift the weight then caused a rush of nervous excitement that was, in fact, necessary for him to budge the great weight even slightly from the floor. Hence, the intention caused nervousness that helped cause the intentional lifting of the weight. (1989, p. 252)

In this example, a state of nervous agitation is causally necessary, but it doesn't detract from our conclusion that the weight lifter lifted the weight intentionally. There is an important moral to be drawn from this example: It is not nervousness or agitation per se that is creating the deviance in the deviant causal chains. Nervousness is simply cited as one state that might plausibly lead an agent to lose control over certain of bodily motions; the agent is no longer *directing* those movements, and the movements are not done *for* any purpose. Of course, these remarks of no help in refining the causal analysis, for they employ explicitly teleological language.

So far, it seems that the requirement of proximate causation does not save the attempted causal analysis of teleological explanation. However, Mele offers a further suggestion that can be read as supplementing the proximate-causation account. Returning again to the philosopher who knocked over the glass of water, Mele suggests that the causal chain is deviant because the philosopher's "intention to knock over the glass did not *guide* the movements involved in his hand's striking the glass" (1992, p. 182). Mele also maintains that in true cases of intentional action the "causal role of the prior intention extends through the completion of the bodily movement" (ibid.). This would presumably yield the proposal that *A* φd in order to ψ iff

(A5) *A* had an intention to ψ, this intention proximately caused her to φ, and the intention guided and sustained her φing.

I see two flaws in this analysis. First, it seems too strong to require that the actual state of intention guide and sustain the entire bodily movement. A typist forms an intention to type a paragraph of text; on Mele's account, this intention will be some brain state, call it brain state Q. Admitting for the sake of argument that Q causes the typist to begin typing the passage, is it really a necessary condition that the very same brain state remain in existence, causally guiding each movement of the typist's hands? Of course, skillful typing presumably requires complicated brain states and complex interaction between the brain, the visual system, and the typist's hands. But it seems dubious to require specifically that the typist's original intention must do the work. Suppose for example that Q does cease to function, and that the typist just rolls along; it would be quite unnatural to claim that the typist's skilled job was in fact done unintentionally or that it was not goal-directed behavior. The second flaw is more fundamental. The requirement that the intention guide or control the behavior sounds perilously close, if not identical, to the teleological notions we are attempting to analyze. The causalist is attempting to analyze the notion of *goal-directed* behavior, and 'guide' and 'direct' appear, in this context, to be synonyms. When an agent φs in order to ψ, she *directs* her behavior toward that outcome; i.e., she *guides* it in accordance with the given purpose. Although Mele says at one point that "guidance" is a causal notion (1992, p. 207), this claim is surely as contentious as the original claim that teleological explanations are analyzable causally. If *guidance* truly is a causal notion, then one ought to be able to give a purely causal analysis of what it means for an agent or intention to guide behavior. One might suggest, for example, that an intention guides behavior if and only if the intention had constant and continuing causal influence on the behavior. But Mele himself admits that this is insufficient, for an intention could continually "contribute to the generation and sustaining of the nervousness" that (deviantly) causes some bit of bodily behavior (1992, p. 203). What one perhaps wants to say is that an intention guides behavior if it causes it in the right way. But then, of course, one would need to spell out "in the right way" in purely causal terms. By now the sense of déjà vu should be pretty strong.

7.3 Bishop and Peacocke's Attempted Solution

John Bishop (1989), building on work by Christopher Peacocke (1979), employs what he calls the *sensitivity strategy* for analyzing intentional behavior. In a sense, the Bishop-Peacocke strategy can be seen as picking up where Mele left off, for their account offers some promise of accounting for the idea that intentions *guide* actions. The central claim is that intentional behavior must show a certain kind of sensitivity to the content of the intention that causes it, and that the requisite sensitivity is not present in deviant cases. Bishop considers two different ways of spelling out the sensitivity requirement. On the first, which Bishop ultimately rejects,[2] the behavior is sensitive to the content of the intention if a certain range of counterfactual conditionals is true of the agent. The second is Peacocke's idea that in nondeviant cases the intention will *differentially explain* the behavior. The proposal, then, is that A φd in order to ψ iff

(A6) A had an intention to ψ, the intention caused her φing, and the intention differentially explains her φing.

In what he calls the "final breakthrough," Bishop essentially adopts this analysis, but adds to it a condition meant to rule out certain tricky cases in which the causal chain from intention to behavior passes through another agent's intentions (1989, p. 171). Even apart from such cases, I will argue that Peacocke's notion of differential explanation is of no help and that (A6) and its derivatives are inadequate as analyses of teleology.

Bishop never fully explains Peacocke's notion of differential explanation; we will have to turn back to Peacocke's *Holistic Explanation* for that. That one fact or event causes another does not guarantee that the first differentially explains the second. Whether a cause differentially explains an effect depends on the nature of the causal law backing the singular causal claim. Peacocke (1979, p. 66) tells us that in the simplest case of differential explanation the law will have the form

$$(\forall x)(\forall n)(\forall t)(Fxt \ \& \ Gxnt \supset Hxk(n)(t + \delta t)),$$

where n ranges over numbers, t ranges over times, and $k(\ )$ is a numerical function. For example, suppose we have an ordinary scale that registers up to 240 pounds. The downward force upon the scale will differentially explain the reading, where the reading is determined by how far a dial is rotated counterclockwise. This will fit the above form if we let "F" be "x is a scale at t," let "G" be "x has a downward force of n pounds upon it at t" and let "H" be "x has a dial that moves counterclockwise $k(n)$ degrees at $t +$ δt." We then define the function: $k(n) = 3n/2$. (Thus if a force of 120 pounds is exerted on the scale at t, the law tells us that the dial will move 180° counterclockwise, corresponding to a reading of 120 pounds.)

More generally, Peacocke says that "x's being φ differentially explains y's being ψ iff x's being φ is a nonredundant part of the explanation of y's being ψ, and according to the principles of explanation (laws) invoked in this explanation, there are functions (such as k in the above example) specified in these laws such that y's being ψ is fixed by these functions from x's being φ" (1979, p. 66). Thus, differential explanation requires that in the backing laws there be functions that specify the nature of the end result from the nature of the cause. Peacocke notes that the functions need not be numerical but may also be defined over "colours, chemical elements, compounds, shapes and so forth" (p. 67). For example, Peacocke says that when an ordinary camera takes a picture, the distribution of light in the scene before the camera differentially explains the distribution of colors in the picture. The subsuming laws in such a case would presumably be rather complex, but it is reasonably plausible that the laws will involve a function defined over colors: for each element in the domain (patches of light of particular intensities and colors), the function will correlate a unique element in the range (patches of photographic paper that reflect light of particular colors).

In regard to the matter at hand, Peacocke claims that "for a chain from the intention to φ to a bodily movement believed to be φing to be nondeviant, the agent's possession of the intention to φ must differentially explain his bodily movement of a kind believed by him to be a φing" (1979, p. 69). Thus, for an intention to differentially explain an agent's φing, there must be functions specified in the subsuming law such that the agent's φing is fixed by these functions from some feature of the intention to φ. Peacocke tells us very little about how such functions might look. One can surmise, along with Bishop, that the functions' domain will consist of possible intentions—i.e., intentions with slightly differing contents—and that the range will consist of possible behaviors. For example, suppose I intend to go get coffee at 9:30 this morning, and that when 9:30 arrives I indeed rise from my desk and leave my office. The suggestion might be that the covering law subsuming this (alleged) causal interaction will look (in relevant part) something like

$$(\forall x)(\forall t)(\ldots \& \, Cxt \supset \ldots Rxk(t) \ldots),$$

where "Cxt" is "x intends to get coffee at time t" and "$R\,xk(t)$" is "x rises from his desk at $k(t)$." Presumably the function will simply be $k(t) = t$, meaning that I rise at the intended time. But it could easily be otherwise. Perhaps $k(t) = t + 5$, implying that no matter what time I intend to go get coffee, I will in fact rise to do so five minutes later than the intended time. Of course, there could be other functions involved. Perhaps the bodily motions I use in executing my intention will be a function of the motions I intended to employ. On this reading, the relevant function is from certain features of the *content* of the intention to certain features of the behavior. That is, the function takes as input some variable feature of the content of the relevant sort of intention, such as the time or manner in which the behavior is intended; the function then yields as output correspondingly different behaviors. However, there is textual evidence that Peacocke himself does not think that the relevant function will be a function of the content of the intention. Instead, Peacocke says that the intention is realized in a physiological state, and he apparently claims that the function takes as input non-intentionally specified features of the physical realization of the intention. My objections will concentrate first and foremost on the first version of the theory, in which we are concerned with functions of the content of the intention. After arguing that this account does not provide the tools for a successful analysis of teleological locutions, I will briefly consider Peacocke's own favored version, and I will argue that it too is inadequate.

Peacocke has surprisingly little to say about why his criterion would rule out deviant cases. He tells us that in the deviant cases in which the agent acts out of nervousness the bodily movement is "differentially explained not by the physiological realization of his intention but by the physiological states with which the nervousness interacts to produce a bodily movement that may just happen to match his original intention" (1979, p. 70). However, he gives no argument for this, and it is not obviously true. First we should note that there is nothing in the notion of differential explanation that precludes the possibility of more than one state differentially explaining another; indeed Peacocke himself tells us that the notion of differential explanation is transitive. Hence, even if the state of nervousness differentially explains the behavior, this is consistent with the behavior also being differentially explained by the intention.

So why does Peacocke think that the intention will not differentially explain the behavior in deviant cases? His intuition is perhaps that if the intention causes nervousness and involuntary shaking or the like, then the specific manner in which the behavior is intended will not matter to the result—the motion will be the same involuntary shaking. For example, if the philosopher's intention to spill the water so agitates him that his hand shakes and he involuntarily spills the water, then he would have been equally agitated, and the same result would have ensued regardless of minor differences in the content of the intention (e.g., small differences in the precise manner in which he intended to knock over the glass). But even if this is granted, it doesn't follow that the philosopher's intention fails to differentially explain his hand motion. There will still be a function from the possible variations in intention to the bodily movement. For example, suppose that the philosopher involuntarily knocks over the glass with a hand motion of trajectory x, and that he would have done so regardless of small differences in the content of the intention; then it will be true that, had the philosopher intended to knock over the glass in manner n, he would have knocked it over in manner $k(n)$, where $k(n) = x$ for all values of n. The point is that functions are cheap and plentiful, requiring only a unique assignment from the range for each assignment from the domain. If the resulting movement does not vary with the content of the intention, then so be it: the required function will simply be a constant function. So far, the notion of differential explanation does nothing to rule out deviant cases.

Despite his earlier flat assertion that differential explanation is enough to eliminate deviance cases from nervousness, ultimately Peacocke does recognize the problem I have just raised, and he responds to it by substantially adding to his account. He says that "p *strongly* differentially explains q if p differentially explains q in the sense already explained, and given the initial conditions the explanation (of q) other than p, together with the fact that q is the explanandum, one can recover (work out) the condition p" (1979, pp. 79-80). As described above, if p differentially explains q, then there must be a function from possible p-like causes to effects; i.e., for each element in the domain of p-like causes there must be a unique effect, though more than one cause could have the same effect. In essence, for the notion of *strong* differential explanation, Peacocke adds the requirement that each element in the range is correlated with a unique element in the domain; in other words, the function must be one-to-one.

In the case of the philosopher who spilled the drink, we supposed that his motion in knocking over the glass would have been the same for a wide range of specific intentions he might have had; if he had intended to knock over the glass in any number of precise ways, the intention would have caused nervousness and the same bodily motion as in the actual case. This means that if we knew the initial conditions, and we knew the bodily motion that resulted, we would not be able thereby to determine which of the precise intentions the philosopher had; i.e., we would not be able to "recover" the explanans from the explanandum. Hence the function would not be one-to-one, and the philosopher's intention does not strongly differentially explain his motion.

The revised analysis of teleological explanation, based on this account, would be that an agent, A, ϕd in order to ψ iff

(A7) A had an intention to ψ, and this intention strongly differentially explains her ϕing.

Accordingly, since the philosopher's intention did not strongly differentially explain his behavior, then he did not spill the drink in order to distract his commentator, and this is the result we would want. Despite the fact that (A7) gives the right result in this case, I will argue that it provides neither necessary nor sufficient conditions for teleological explanation, and that hence the sensitivity strategy leaves us no better off than we were before.

(A7) succeeds in ruling out as deviant the case of the philosopher whose intention-inspired nervousness causes him to knock over the water, on the assumption that other variations on the same intention would have had the same result, for on that assumption the relevant function would not be one-to-one. However, it seems that we can construct a deviant case in which the function is one-to-one and thus in which the intention strongly differentially explains the movement, even though the movement was involuntary. We can do this by making a relatively minor modification to the philosopher case; we need merely suppose that function embodied in the covering law(s) is such that, for each of the possible intentions the philosopher might have had, his bodily movement would have been somewhat different. Perhaps in each such case the movement would have still been an involuntary jerking motion of his hand, but the differing intentions would have inspired the nervous twitch in slightly different ways, such that, given the precise trajectory of the twitch, one could recover the precise intention that caused it. I am not suggesting that each of the involuntary twitches would match the content of the intention that caused it—if they did so, one might reconsider whether the action was truly involuntary. Rather, each of the involuntary jerks presumably fails to match the content of the intention, *except* in the actual case, where the involuntary movement does happen to match the content of the intention. This would still be enough for the intention to strongly differentially explain the involuntary jerk, and hence enough to make the philosopher's involuntary behavior count as goal directed. Note that (A7) and the notion of strong differential explanation do not require that in the counterfactual cases the behavior match the content of the intentions the agent had in those circumstances. Nor would we want to add this as a requirement, for it would be too strong and would rule out many cases of truly intentional action (e.g., suppose I intend to pick up my coffee mug with my right hand and successfully and voluntarily do so; my action is then intentional even if, had I intended to pick it up with my left hand, I would have clumsily knocked it over.)

I also claim that (A7) is not a *necessary* condition for truly goal-directed action: recoverability is too strong a condition and would rule out many cases of truly intentional action. Suppose we have a baseball pitcher who is practicing her delivery; she has with her a coach who is operating a radar gun by means of which they can gauge the speed with which the pitcher's arm moves during the critical part of her pitching motion. They are trying to determine the arm speed at which her curveball is most effective. In the course of this session, she throws many pitches, each time intending to move her arm at a particular speed. After some practice, her actual arm speed comes to be a function of her intended arm speed; roughly, if she intends to move her arm at velocity v, then her arm moves at velocity v. The presence of such a function would allow Peacocke to say that her intention differentially explains her arm motion. However, *strong* differential explanation requires that the function be one-to-one. This condition will fail for at least two sorts of reasons.

First, there will be limitations on how precisely the pitcher's arm speed matches her intention. Suppose that her arm speed matches (within the accuracy range of the radar gun) her intended arm speed about 80 percent of the time. Now suppose that she makes a pitching motion of a certain kind in which her arm speed reaches 70 miles per hour when her intention was to move her arm at 70 mph. Can we, from the explanandum and other conditions, recover the explanans (namely, her intention to throw at 70 mph)? It would seem not; she might have had exactly the same motion when she intended to throw at 69 mph or 71 mph. So her intention to move her arm at 70 mph does not strongly differentially explain her actual arm motion; and hence on (A7), she did not direct her behavior toward the goal of moving her arm at 70 mph. That seems wrong; she consciously formulated that objective, she was clearly trying to move her arm at that speed, and she even succeeded in doing so. What more could we ask?

Second, suppose that the pitcher's maximum arm speed is in fact 75 mph. Hence, roughly speaking, for any intention to move her arm at a speed greater than 75 mph, her actual arm speed will in fact be 75 mph. Now suppose that she intends to move her arm at 75 mph (not knowing that this is as fast as she is capable of in any event), and that she succeeds in doing so. Again, we will not be able to recover the explanans from the explanandum; the explanandum in question would have, by hypothesis, resulted from any number of different intentions. Once again, the function from intention to behavior is not one-to-one; but that does not and should not affect our intuitive judgment that her behavior was directed at moving her arm at 75 mph. Thus, with respect to both necessity and sufficiency, (A7) and the notion of strong differential explanation fail to provide an analysis of teleological locutions.

As was noted above, I have been assuming that the functions we are concerned with are functions from the content of the intention to aspects of the resulting behavior. Peacocke himself does not seem to see the functions in this way. When he first begins to apply his account of differential explanation to intentions and action, he notes that "it is not obvious what it might mean to talk of something's being a function of an intention, according to the operative principles of explanation" (1979, p. 69). In the next two sentences, he says:

> I shall take for granted in this section a principle the content of and evidence for which I shall consider in a later chapter, viz. the principle that every psychological state in which a given person is at some given time, is realized for that person at that time by some physical state. Now for differential explanation in nondeviant action chains, a bodily movement of a kind believed to be a ϕing is differentially explained (under its bodily movement description) by the neurophysiological state that realizes for the given agent at the given time his psychological state of intending to make a bodily movement of a kind he takes to be a ϕing in the circumstances. (1979, pp. 69–70)

So, I take it, the action is differentially explained by the intention *under its neurophysiological description*. And indeed Peacocke goes on to say that the laws in which such functions appear "will often be . . . stated at the electrochemical level" (1979, p. 70). The revised analysis would claim that A ϕd in order to ψ iff

(A8) A had an intention to ψ that was realized in brain state Q, and brain state Q strongly differentially explains her ϕing.

Now Peacocke might be supposing that the relevant features of the neurophysiological state will neatly mirror features of the content of the intention. For example, let "Lct" represent my intention to lift my coffee cup at time t. For different values of t, the content of my intention will change slightly. Now let "Fxy" represent the predicate "neuron x is firing at rate y," and let us wildly oversimplify the physiological picture by supposing that my intention to lift my coffee cup is realized in the neurophysiological state "Fab." One way the physiological state could neatly mirror the content of the intention would be if there were a neat correlation between values for y in "Fxy" and values for t in "Lct." Moreover, Peacocke's picture might be this: The brain state Fab differentially explains the behavior of lifting my coffee cup precisely because the relevant covering law states that the time of my lifting the cup is a function of *y* in "*Fxy*." On these suppositions about the relation between brain states and intentions, then the claim that it is the brain states rather than the intentions that differentially explain behavior matters little to the above discussion. On this picture, the counterexamples presented above to (A7) will work equally well against (A8); we would simply need to perform the relevant transformation from talk of content of the intentions to talk of physiological aspects of the realizing brain state. If the mirroring relationships like that described here actually hold, then such transformation would pose no problems.

However, Peacocke may not be supposing the existence of any neat mirroring relationship between the content of the intention and physical features of the realizing brain state. Though this makes the picture a bit more complicated, there is still no reason to think that (A8) provides a necessary condition for goal-directed action. Consider our water-spilling philosopher again. We have supposed that he has an intention to distract his commentator by spilling his water, and that having this intention so agitates him that his hand involuntarily shakes, knocking over the water and distracting his commentator. We now further suppose that the philosopher's intention is realized in brain state *Q*. To rule this causal chain as deviant, Peacocke needs to show that it is not the case that *Q* strongly differentially explains the philosopher's involuntary handshaking. In other words, he needs to show that the covering law does *not* include a one-to-one function of the physiological aspects of *Q* to the philosopher's behavior. There would be such a function so long as for each distinct behavior of the philosopher there was a physiological difference in the intention that would have caused it. But Peacocke gives us no reason to think that such a situation is impossible. That is to say, it seems entirely possible that the following conditions could obtain:

(i) Brain state *Q* caused an involuntary hand motion that knocked over the water.

(ii) The relevant covering law includes a one-to-one function with a domain of possible brain states and a range of possible behaviors.

If both (i) and (ii) obtain, then brain state *Q* strongly differentially explains the involuntary motion and (A8) fails. The combination of (i) and (ii) would have to be *impossible* for (A8) to succeed in providing necessary and sufficient conditions; I can see no reason at all for thinking that this combination is impossible.

Furthermore, even apart from this problem, Peacocke's favored picture would give us an epistemological mystery. Let us introduce a new notion of a behavior being *goal directed*, and we simply stipulate that a behavior is *goal directed* iff the conditions of (A8) are met. In practice, how could we possibly have any idea of whether a piece of behavior is *goal directed*? If the covering laws and functions involved the *content* of the intention, then we might think that we could start to formulate a rough version of the covering law by drawing on our common-sense psychological knowledge, and we might think that we could thereby have some idea of whether a one-to-one function was involved. But if the law and the functions it involves are purely physiological, then, given our complete ignorance of even the purported realizing state let alone the covering law, it is hard to see how we could have any idea of whether the brain state strongly differentially explains the behavior. In particular, without the assumption that content is mirrored in physiological structure, we could not draw on our common-sense psychological knowledge, and we would be left with no practical basis at all to determine whether an action was *goal directed*. Since we do in fact have some ability to distinguish goal-directed behavior from bodily movements that are not goal directed, this strongly suggests that *goal directed* and *goal directed* are not equivalent concepts; moreover, given our complete ignorance about when behavior is *goal directed*, we would have no reason whatsoever for thinking that the two concepts are even roughly coextensive. I conclude that moving away from content and to purely "electrochemical" laws and functions does not help to make Peacocke's analysis any more plausible.

7.4 Conclusion

I have argued that two sophisticated strategies for causally analyzing teleological locutions are inadequate. Of course, the failure of extant analyses does not demonstrate the irreducibility of teleological explanations. Nonetheless, I think we have reason to echo George Wilson's conclusion: ". . . the evidence points to more than infelicity or incompleteness in the various causalist proposals—it points, that is, to a global breakdown in the whole project of reduction" (1989, p. 258). But the enticement of a naturalistic reduction of mind and agency is strong, and I suspect that there will be further attempts at reduction. Perhaps there will also continue to be a sentiment among philosophers that there *must* be a reductive solution to the "problem" of deviant causal chains. Strong naturalist views of the mind and agency rely on the assumption that a causal analysis of teleology is possible, and a great deal of creative and interesting philosophical work has implicitly assumed this possibility. Of course, such programmatic considerations do not amount to an argument unless one simply assumes that the strong naturalists about mind and agency are correct. The persistent troubles encountered by the reductive project suggest that this assumption should be called into question. Moreover, at minimum, these troubles suggest that we start looking seriously at nonreductive approaches.

III

8   Supervenience without Reduction: Option 3 without the Supernatural

In part I, the mind-body problem was formulated as a question about the logical relationship between common-sense psychology, or CSP, and physical science. According to option 1, CSP and physical science are inconsistent and CSP is to be rejected. According to option 2, the propositions of CSP are ultimately entailed by those of physical science; as explained in chapter 4, option-2 accounts, including functionalism, count as reductionist views. Rather than commit to either option 1 or option 2, one might more cautiously say that the choice between option 1 and option 2 will be made on empirical grounds. On this view, which I called *strong naturalism*, CSP is indeed in the same territory as physical science, and its claims will either be shown false or vindicated and subsumed within physical science.

In part II, I presented a number of arguments against strong naturalism. In chapters 5–7, I presented reasons for thinking that CSP is not competing with physical science; I argued that CSP does not have the characteristics of a science or proto-science, and, in particular, I argued that CSP explanations of behavior are not a species of causal explanation.

The drift has been clear: By attempting to undermine the foundation of strong naturalism, I have been preparing the way for the third option, according to which CSP and physical science are independent of one another. In part III, I will lay out a positive option-3 account. The linchpin will be the account of reason explanation and agency; that will come in the next chapter. First, however, I will explore the question of whether it is even possible to have an option-3 account without collapsing all the way back into substance dualism, a view rejected back in chapter 2. The substance dualist would be well placed to defend option 3, for the subject matter of CSP would be the immaterial mind, and this immaterial mind would be out of the reach of physical science. So CSP and physical science would be independent by virtue of having quite different subject matters. The question is whether there is any other way of defending option 3, or whether any nonreductionist option-3 account inevitably falls back on something quite like the substance dualist picture.

To avoid the charge of introducing something immaterial or otherwise supernatural, nonreductionist philosophers sometimes claim that although the mental cannot be *reduced* to the physical, nonetheless, the mental does *supervene* on the physical. The doctrine of *supervenience* is thus meant to serve as an expression of weak naturalism or physicalism, while not committing to reductionism or strong naturalism. The purpose of this chapter is to see whether this is tenable—to see whether there is even logical space for supervenience without reduction.

8.1 Definition of 'Supervenience'

'Supervenience' is used in a number of different ways; in fact, many who use the term specify several different types of supervenience. Supervenience is a relation between sets of properties or facts. For example, one might well claim that the aesthetic properties of paintings supervene on their physical properties; we could also put this as the claim that the aesthetic facts about paintings supervene on the physical facts about those paintings. As a first pass, this means that there could be no change in the aesthetic properties of the painting without some sort of change in its physical properties. The painting could not, for example, change from beautiful to ugly while its physical properties remained exactly the same. To put it in different words, any two physically identical paintings would have the same aesthetic properties. Someone might, of course, deny that the aesthetic supervenes on the physical; one might suggest, for example, that the beauty of a painting is merely in the eye of the beholder; since the beholder's opinions could change while the painting remains the same, the painting's status as beautiful could change without any physical alteration in the painting itself. Alternatively, one might deny supervenience by suggesting that two physically identical paintings might have different aesthetic properties if, say, one was a forgery of the other.

These last examples bring out a feature on which differing definitions of supervenience could diverge. In suggesting that aesthetic properties supervene on physical properties, I have been assuming that we are talking about the nonrelational properties of an individual painting. Following the literature, we can call this idea *local supervenience*. Instead, one might talk of the aesthetic and physical properties of the world as a whole, yielding the concept of *global supervenience*. Saying that the aesthetic globally supervenes on the physical would mean that there can be no change in the aesthetic properties in the world without a change in the physical properties. Thus, if a painting is beautiful in one world and not beautiful in another, there must be some physical difference between the worlds; however, in contrast with local supervenience, the physical difference need not lie in the paintings themselves. So, for example, even if a forged *Mona Lisa* would not have the same aesthetic properties as the genuine *Mona Lisa,* this is still consistent with the global supervenience of the aesthetic on the physical. A world in which the painting sitting in the Louvre is forged is going to be a world whose history has various physical differences from our world. In the actual world, the painting sitting in the Louvre has a physical history that includes being touched by the brushes of Leonardo Da Vinci; in the possible world in which the painting in the Louvre is a forgery, that painting has a different physical history.

We can formulate a definition of global supervenience as follows: *M* facts supervene on *P* facts if and only if any two worlds that differ in their *M* facts also differ in their *P* facts. In symbolic terms, this becomes

$$(\forall w_1)(\forall w_2)(M_1 \neq M_2 \supset P_1 \neq P_2),$$

where "M_1" denotes the mental facts in world w_1 and so on. If we let *M* facts be the mental facts and the *P* facts be the physical facts, this serves as a characterization of the claim that the mental supervenes on the physical.

However, unless we qualify this supervenience claim it will be pretty obviously false. Even if we assume that all rational beings in the actual world are entirely constituted by physical particles, surely it is *possible* that there could be worlds in which there are purely immaterial beings. For example, consider two possible worlds. In world w_a, physical facts are as in the actual world, but there is also an immaterial being named Gabriel; at time *t*, Gabriel is thinking "Goldbach's conjecture is true." In world w_b, physical facts are as in the actual world, but there is also an immaterial being named Gabriel; at time *t*, Gabriel is thinking "Goldbach's conjecture is false." These two worlds have the same physical facts as our world, but differ from our world (and from each other) in mental facts. Since worlds like w_a and w_b are possible, it follows from our definition that the mental does not supervene on the physical. On the other hand, no naturalist should be particularly worried about the mere logical possibility of immaterial beings, so this merely points to a need to refine our definition of supervenience.

The simplest way around this seems to be as follows: Instead of claiming that the mental facts *in general* supervene on the physical facts, we can say that the mental facts *about actual human beings* supervene on the physical facts. Accordingly, the supervenience thesis would be this: any world that differs from the actual world in its mental facts about human beings also differs in its physical facts. Symbolically, this would be written as

$(\forall w_2)(M_A \neq M_2 \supset P_A \neq P_2)$,

where M_A denotes the mental facts about human agents in our world and M_2 denotes the mental facts about their counterparts in the other world. This would allow for the existence of immaterial agents in other worlds so long as they are not human beings. I will take this claim to be an expression of weak naturalism.

Even this characterization of weak naturalism might seem flawed. Since Hilary Putnam's paper "The Meaning of 'Meaning'" (1975) it has become apparent to most philosophers that the content of our thoughts is determined in part by the nature of the thing about which we are thinking. Water-thoughts differ from twater-thoughts because H_2O is different from XYZ, even if the thinker is not aware of those differences. For example, suppose that in one possible world ghosts exist, Harry has thoughts about them, and the ghosts are composed (in some sense) of an immaterial substance we will call *ectoplasm*. In another possible world, the same situation obtains, but ghosts are made of a distinct kind of immaterial substance we will call *mitoplasm*. By Putnam-style considerations, we can maintain that, even if the two possible worlds are *physically* indistinguishable, the content of Harry's thoughts differ. So it seems that supervenience can fail because of the possibility of immaterial objects, even if the immaterial objects are merely the object of thought, rather than the thinking things; and thus it would seem that supervenience cannot serve as an adequate of expression of weak naturalism.[1]

However, I think that the flaw is merely apparent. I contend that the supervenience claim described above still holds, even granting that there are possible worlds in which immaterial objects exist and are the objects of human thoughts. I am assuming, as a part of my weak naturalism, that we do not live in a world in which there are immaterial beings that are objects of our thought. So if the actual Harry has any thoughts about ghosts, the content of these thoughts is not determined by causal contact with immaterial objects; rather, the content of his ghost thoughts will presumably be determined by properties he attributes to ghosts. Now there presumably is a possible world in which ghosts exist and in which the content of Harry's thoughts is determined by causal contact with ghosts. The mental facts in this world would be different from those of the actual world, since the content of ghost thoughts would, by Putnam-style considerations, be determined by the actual nature of ghosts (whether they are ectoplasm or mitoplasm, etc.). However, the supervenience claim is not endangered, for there is bound to be a physical difference between the worlds. If the content of ghost thoughts in the possible world is determined by causal contact with ghosts, this causal contact must result in some physical difference from the actual world. Of course, there are possible worlds in which ghosts exist but have no causal contact with human beings, and these worlds could have the same physical facts as our world. However, in this case I would say that the mental facts are the same as in our world; without the causal contact between us and the ghosts, the Putnam considerations will not apply and human thoughts about ghosts will have the same content in both worlds.

8.2   Does Supervenience Matter?

Jaegwon Kim has done more than any other philosopher to explain and clarify the notion of supervenience; moreover, he has been central in bringing philosophical attention to the notion. However, Kim doubts that the notion is particularly important for philosophy of mind:

Supervenience is not a metaphysically deep, explanatory relation; it is merely a phenomenological relation about patterns of property covariation. Mind-body supervenience, therefore, *states* the mind-body problem—it is not a solution to it. (1998a, p. 10)

Kim provides two reasons for this negative conclusion. First, he argues that supervenience "is consistent with a host of classic positions on the mind-body problem," including not only straight identity theories but also functionalism, emergentism, epiphenomenalism, and even certain forms of Cartesian substance dualism. He then says that "if mind-body supervenience is a commitment of each of these conflicting approaches to the mind-body problem, it cannot itself be a position on this issue alongside these classic alternatives" (1998a, p. 9). Second, and related to the first point, Kim says that "the mere fact (assuming it is a fact) of mind-body supervenience leaves open the question of what *grounds* or *accounts* for it— that is, why the supervenience relation obtains between the mental and the physical" (1998a, p. 9).

I will say more about the second point later in the chapter, but some comments about the first are in order here. While Kim is right that certain forms of substance dualism might be compatible with supervenience, there are other forms of substance dualism that are not compatible with supervenience. Basic Cartesian dualism maintains that my beliefs and desires are determined by soul states and that beliefs and desires have no essential connection to the brain. If this form of dualism were correct, my beliefs and desires could presumably change without any physical change in the world; thus Cartesian dualism is incompatible with supervenience. Indeed, it would be a rather odd form of substance dualism that would be compatible with mind-body supervenience. I would speculate that most of those who believe substance dualism are motivated, like Descartes, by the apparent possibility that one can exist without one's body. This possibility is explicitly affirmed within common religious doctrines, according to which people can survive their bodily deaths in a condition that is utterly independent of their decomposing body. The belief that one can exist without one's body clearly presupposes that mental properties do not supervene on physical properties; thus the standard motivation for substance dualism is inconsistent with supervenience. Indeed, it is hard to see how one could motivate a form of substance dualism that was compatible with supervenience: Once one grants primacy to the physical in the way that supervenience would appear to do, I don't know what would motivate the view that there is also a separate immaterial substance of which minds are composed.

Thus, the doctrine of mind-body supervenience is a fairly precise way of characterizing that which Descartes (and the typical layperson dualist) denies. Since substance dualism is not considered a live option by most philosophers, supervenience will still appear to be a very weak claim. Nonetheless, I think it is rather useful to have a precise formulation of a denial of typical substance dualist views. Kim ultimately agrees with this: ". . . our considerations indicate that mind-body supervenience captures a commitment common to all positions on the nature of mentality that are basically physicalistic" (1998b, p. 14). An affirmation of supervenience would appear to be enough to rule out anything obviously supernatural—ghosts, spirits, and the like. Accordingly, one might identify supervenience with weak (as opposed to strong) naturalism.

This conclusion gives us ample reason to consider supervenience in some more detail, for we will want to know whether one can affirm supervenience (and reject dualism) without thereby being forced into a reductionist or option-2 view. Many have assumed that one can have supervenience without reduction; others have questioned the existence of a stable middle ground here. Kim reports that "much of the discussion that followed the introduction of the supervenience idea into the mind-body debate was over the question whether supervenience was indeed free of reductionist implications" (1998a, p. 8). Kim goes on to report that this "question is unsettled" (ibid.). Later in the same paper, however, Kim seems to take a different position on the question of supervenience and reduction:

> There has been much scepticism about the viability of a functionalist account of intentionality; in particular, Hilary Putnam, the father of functionalism, has recently mounted sustained attacks on the causal/functionalist accounts of content and reference, and John Searle has also vigorously resisted the functionalization of intentionality. However, I remain unconvinced by these arguments; I don't see unsurmountable obstacles to a causal/functional account of intentionality. Let me just say here that it seems to me inconceivable that a possible world exists that is an exact duplicate of this world but lacking wholly in intentionality. Such a world must be identical with ours in all intentional-psychological respects. (1998a, p. 19, footnotes omitted; see also Kim 1998b, p. 101)

Though his words are susceptible of more than one interpretation, Kim appears to justify functionalism by appealing to his conviction that two physically identical worlds would have identical intentional properties. This latter conviction just is the claim that the mental globally supervenes on the physical; thus Kim defends functionalism by appealing to the plausibility of supervenience. On the other hand, Kim correctly views functionalist accounts of intentionality as reductionist. (See Kim 1998a, pp. 16–17, where he presents a model of reduction that follows functionalist lines.) So Kim infers a form of reductionism on the basis of supervenience; that is, he assumes that supervenience entails reduction. In contrast, I would like to affirm supervenience while denying reductionism. I think it can be shown that this is not inconsistent; that is the intent of the next section.

8.3 Supervenience Does Not Entail Reduction: Three Proofs

I will present three arguments for the conclusion that, in principle, one set of facts can supervene on another set of facts without it being the case that the first set of facts is reducible to the second set of facts. That is, for some sets of facts M and P, it can be the case that the M facts supervene on the P facts, whereas it is not the case that the M facts reduce to the P facts. I will conclude from this that one can consistently maintain that the mental facts supervene on the physical facts while denying that the mental facts are reducible to the physical facts. The arguments will work by characterizing a set of M facts and a set of P facts, where the nature of these facts and the way they are distributed will guarantee that the M facts supervene on the P facts but where it will also be guaranteed that there is no bridge law B such that the conjunction of B and P suffices to entail M.

8.3.1 First Proof

Definitions

Supervenience   The M facts supervene on P facts if and only if any two possible worlds that differ in their M facts also differ in their P facts. We can write this as $(\forall w_1)(\forall w_2)(Mw_1 \neq Mw_2 \supset Pw_1 \neq Pw_2)$.

Reduction   The M facts *reduce to* the P facts iff there is some statement B such that from the conjunction of B and the P facts, one can deduce the M facts. Note that this notion of reduction is far broader than the notion characterized in chapter 3. B functions as the bridge law, but here there are no constraints placed on B. For the philosophical notion of *reduction*, one would normally require that B at least be *true*, and one would presumably place other constraints in addition. (See chapter 3.) Such details will not matter for my purposes here, for the argument will show that even with no constraints whatsoever placed on B (other than being stateable), the reducibility of the M facts to the P facts does not follow from the supervenience of the M facts on the P facts.

Noncomputable number   A number is *noncomputable* iff there is no algorithm that can compute a decimal expansion of the number to an arbitrarily high degree of accuracy.

Of course, all rational numbers are computable: one can easily compute the decimal expansion of 3/7, or any other ratio, to an arbitrarily high degree of accuracy. And, as John Winnie explains, many irrationals, including π and $\sqrt{2}$, are computable, for "there are algorithms that allow their computation to arbitrarily high degrees of accuracy" (1992, p. 263). "Still," Winnie goes on to explain, "since there must be a Turing machine for any computable number, and there are only a countable infinity of such machines, the set of computable numbers is countable and hence of measure zero. In this sense, 'most' of the irrationals are noncomputable numbers." (1992, p. 263–264)[2]

The M Facts and the P Facts

Stipulate that each object in each world has an M value; that an object has a given M value at a given time is an M fact about that world. Similarly with P values and P facts.

Let q be some noncomputable number.

Assume the following: The M value of every object in every world at every time is equal to q. The P value of every object in every world at every time is equal to 0.

The Argument

Claim 1   The M facts supervene on the P facts; i.e., any two worlds with different M facts have different P facts.

First consider all pairs of worlds that contain the same individuals (or, to put it differently, each object in the first has a counterpart in the second, and vice versa) and in which each individual exists for the same periods of time as its counterpart. Since each individual has the same M value across all the possible worlds in which it exists, pairs of worlds that each contain the same individuals will have the same M facts. That is, such pairs of worlds will not have different M facts, so the claim holds for them.

Next consider all those pairs of worlds where either (i) the worlds do not contain the same individuals or (ii) the worlds contain the same individuals but in at least some cases the individuals exist for different periods of time in the two worlds. In either case, such pairs of worlds will have different P facts, for one of the worlds will have a P fact of the form "X has P value k at time t" that does not hold in the other world, because X will not exist at t in the other world. So the claim holds for these worlds too.

Since these cases exhaust all the pairs of possible worlds, the claim holds for all possible worlds.

Claim 2   The M facts do not reduce to the P facts.

Suppose that the M facts reduce to the P facts. That is, suppose that there is a bridge statement B such that B in conjunction with the P facts (in our world) formally implies the M facts (in our world). But since first-order logic is complete, that means that there is a mechanical derivation of M facts about individuals. But since the M facts are each of the form "object X has M value q at time t," this means that we can derive a statement of the value of q. But this would mean that q is computable, which is contrary to our hypothesis. Thus it must not be the case that the M facts reduce to the P facts.

One might object that this argument fails if the bridge law B contains noncomputable information. Of course, the bridge law can't simply state or have as a logical consequence that a given M value is q (where q is a noncomputable number), nor can the bridge law provide any mechanical way of computing a noncomputable number such as q. But one might argue that B could nonetheless provide a way of approaching q. For example, suppose that there is some physical parameter that is identical to q, say the mass of a certain object. This would allow the bridge law to refer to q, and even give us a way of specifying q within the limits of our ability to measure the mass of the object. In this way, B might provide a back-door method for learning the M values in question. For practical purposes, the M facts would be reducible to the P facts, even if one could not literally derive the entire decimal expansion of q. In response, I'm willing to grant for the sake of argument that there are measurable physical parameters with noncomputable values, and that if the M value in question happened to be one of these numbers then a sort of practical reduction would be possible. But it also seems simple enough to stipulate that our particular number q is not the measure of any physical parameter. Between any two numbers there are nondenumerably many noncomputable numbers, so it seems reasonable to conclude that there are vastly more noncomputable numbers than there are physical parameters. We can stipulate that, in the argument in the text, q is a noncomputable number that is not tied to a measurable physical parameter.

Comments

Technically, I think this argument works to show that, in principle, supervenience does not entail reduction. However, the particular way in which the proof works might make it seem to make its scope quite limited. In the argument as it stands, I stipulate a class of facts that are in principle unstateable (or, at least, cannot be stated with arbitrarily high degree of precision). Reduction does fail in this case, but it fails because the M facts themselves are unstateable. Thus, even if the argument technically shows that one can have supervenience without reduction, it shows this only in a case where the facts that supervene but are not reduced are unstateable facts. That is presumably of no comfort to the nonreductionist about the mental, since mental facts are eminently stateable.

However, by making the argument somewhat more complex, we can produce a proof in which a set of M facts supervenes on but is not reducible to the P facts, but where the M facts are themselves stateable.

8.3.2 Second Proof

Definitions
Same as in the first proof.

The M Facts and the P Facts
Stipulate that each object in each world has an M value; the fact that an object has a given M value is an M fact about that world. Similarly with P values and P facts.

Let q be some noncomputable number such that $1 < q < 10$.

Stipulate that nearly all objects in all worlds have an M value of 0. However, suppose that there is one object, x, that has, for a very short period of time, a nonzero M value. Moreover, during that short interval x's M value increases in a certain way, a way correlated with the decimal expansion of q. During a one-second interval beginning with time t, the M value of x increases in accord with the following pattern: At t the M value of x is equal to the first digit in the decimal expansion of q; at $t + 0.9$, the M value is equal to the first two digits in the decimal expansion of q; at $t + 0.99$, the M value is equal to the first three digits in the decimal expansion of q; and so on. If we suppose, for example, that the first seven digits in the decimal expansion of q are 5.428949, the M value of x proceeds as shown in table 8.1. Assume that this assignation of M values applies to all possible worlds in which the given individual x exists. Assume also that x does exist over that time interval in the actual world.

For the P values, assume that each object in each world has a P value of 0.

The Argument

Claim 1 The M facts supervene on the P facts; i.e., any two worlds with different M facts have different P facts.

First consider all those pairs of worlds that contain the same individuals and in which each individual exists for the same periods of time as its counterpart. Such pairs of worlds will have the same M facts, so the claim holds for them.

Next consider all pairs of worlds where either (i) the worlds do not contain the same individuals or (ii) the worlds contain the same individuals but

Table 8.1

Time	M value of x
t	5
$t + 0.9$	5.4
$t + 0.99$	5.42
$t + 0.999$	5.428
$t + 0.9999$	5.4289
$t + 0.99999$	5.42894
$t + 0.999999$	5.428949
.	.
.	.
.	.
$t + 1$	0

in at least some cases the individuals exist for different periods of time in the two worlds. In either case, such pairs of worlds will have different P facts, for one of the worlds will have a P fact of the form "X has P value k at time t" that does not hold in the other world (because X will not exist at t in the other world). So the claim holds for these worlds as well.

Since these cases exhaust all the pairs of possible worlds, the claim holds for all possible worlds.

Claim 2 The M facts do not reduce to the P facts.
Suppose that the M facts reduce to the P facts. That is, suppose that there is a bridge statement B such that B in conjunction with the P facts (in our world) formally implies the M facts (in our world). But, since first-order logic is complete, that means that there is a mechanical derivation of M facts about individuals given the P facts and B. Thus, the P facts plus B will allow us to derive, for example, x's M value at $t + 0.99999$, or at $t + 0.9999999$, or at any other time. (Indeed, a finite subset of the M facts will suffice, given the Compactness Theorem for first-order logic.) But if we can derive these facts in first-order logic, there is an algorithm for stating such facts. We thus would have an algorithm for computing, to arbitrary degree of accuracy, the decimal expansion of q. Thus it would follow that q is computable, contrary to our hypothesis.

Comments
This line of argument should be enough to shake any a priori faith that the supervenience of the mental must entail that the mental reduces to the physical. However, one might still argue that this proof relies on very specific features of the M facts, and that, since these features are not shared by mental facts, the proof has little direct relevance to the mental and physical facts. In particular, in both proofs the M values were assigned such that any given individual had the same M values in all possible worlds in which that individual exists. This was in fact crucial to establishing the supervenience claim in each of the above arguments; by assuming that the M values remained constant across possible worlds in this way, we were able to directly infer that any two worlds with the same individuals across the same times would be identical in their M facts. This made the supervenience claim rather trivial. However, to assume that the M values are assigned in this way is, in effect, to assume that the M values are *necessary* or *essential* properties of any individual; for if there are any properties that an individual has across all possible worlds, these will ipso facto be the essential properties of that individual. Accordingly, one might object that the proof is not

relevant to the mental properties, since these are not typically essential properties of an individual—while it may be an essential property of me that I have a mind, it is presumably not an essential property of me that I have all of the specific beliefs and desires that I have in the actual world. In fact, however, we can rework the proof one more time such that it does not rely on the claim that the M values are essential properties of the objects.

8.3.3 Third Proof

Definitions
Same as in the first proof.

The M Facts and the P Facts
Each object in each world has an M value; that an object has a given M value is an M fact about that world. Similarly with P values and P facts.

Let q be some noncomputable number such that $1 < q < 10$.

Some objects in some worlds have nonzero M values. Whenever any given object has a nonzero M value, it has this nonzero value for an interval of one second (and it has an M value of 0 immediately preceding and succeeding each such interval); during that one-second interval, its M value increases in accord with the same pattern described in the second proof.

Whenever an object has a nonzero M value, its P value is 1; otherwise its P value is zero.

Suppose further that there is at least one object in the actual world that has nonzero M values for at least one second of its existence.

The Argument

Claim 1 The M facts supervene on the P facts; i.e., any two worlds with different M facts have different P facts.
Consider any pair of worlds with different M facts.

First consider all pairs of worlds that contain the same individuals (or, to put it differently, each object in the first has a counterpart in the second, and vice versa) and in which each individual exists for the same periods of time as its counterpart.

(subcase 1) Some object x has M value 0 in one of the worlds and a nonzero M value in the other.

In such cases, x will have different P values at that time, for it will have a P value of 0 in the first world and a P value of 1 in the second. Hence, the two worlds will have different P facts, and the claim holds.

(subcase 2) Some object x has nonzero M values in both worlds, but the values are unequal.

In such cases, in the first world, x at t has an M value that is equal to the first n places in the decimal expansion of q, for some number n; in the second world, x at t has an M value that is equal to the first m places in the decimal expansion of q, for some number m, and $n \neq m$.

The two objects will have identical P values at t, but there will be a time at which their P values differ; one or the other will be first to have its M value revert back to 0, and at that time it will have a P value of 0 while the other will still have a P value of 1.

Second, consider all pairs of worlds in which either (i) the worlds do not contain the same individuals or (ii) the worlds contain the same individuals but in at least some cases the individuals exist for different periods of time in the two worlds. In either case, such pairs of worlds will have different P facts, for one of the worlds will have a P fact of the form "X has P value k at time t" that does not hold in the other world (because X will not exist at t in the other world). So the claim holds for these worlds too.

Since these cases exhaust all the pairs of possible worlds, the claim holds for all possible worlds.

Claim 2 The M facts do not reduce to the P facts.
Suppose that the M facts reduce to the P facts. That is, suppose that there is a bridge statement B such that B in conjunction with the P facts (in our world) formally implies the M facts (in our world). But, since first-order logic is complete, that means that there is a mechanical derivation of M facts about individuals given the P facts and B. If x is an object in the actual world that has nonzero M values from t to $t + 1$, then a finite subset of the P facts (see note 1) plus B will allow us to derive x's M value at $t + 0.99999$, at $t + 0.9999999$, or at any other time. But if we can derive these facts in first-order logic, there is an algorithm for stating such facts. We thus would have an algorithm for computing, to arbitrary degree of accuracy, the decimal expansion of q. Thus it would follow that q is computable, contrary to our hypothesis.

8.4 Application to Mind-Body Supervenience

At the most general level, the above arguments show that one set of properties can supervene on another set of properties without reducing to the other set of properties. The arguments show that two sets of properties can covary in the way required by supervenience without having the kind of systematic relationship that would allow for reduction. In each of the above scenarios, the *M* and *P* properties exhibit the required pattern of covariance, but they lack the kind of systematic relationship required by reduction. The application to mind-body supervenience is this: Mental and physical properties might covary in the way required by supervenience without the sort of systematic relationship that would allow for reduction.

Perhaps the true situation regarding supervenience and reduction can be seen more clearly if it is contrasted with the position taken by David Chalmers. Chalmers claims that supervenience does entail reduction; specifically, he says that a natural phenomenon "is reductively explainable in terms of physical properties—or simply 'reductively explainable'—when it is logically supervenient on the physical" (1997, p. 48). He argues for this by claiming that "if a phenomenon *M* supervenes logically on some lower-level properties, then given an account of the lower-level facts associated with an instance of *M*, the exemplification of *M* is a logical consequence" (ibid.).[3] Thus, if the *M* facts supervene on the *P* facts, Chalmers thinks that a complete account of the (lower-level) *P* facts will automatically entail the *M* facts. However, he then notes that this might seem problematic:

. . . such an explanation can sometimes seem unsatisfactory, for two reasons. First, the lower-level facts might be a vast hotchpotch of arbitrary-seeming details without any clear explanatory unity. An account of all the molecular motions underlying an instance of learning might be like this, for example. Second, it is possible that different instances of *P* might be accompanied by very different sets of low-level facts, so that explanations of particular instances do not yield an explanation of the phenomenon as a type. (ibid.)

Chalmers's reply to the problem is to distinguish between reductive explanation simpliciter and illuminating explanation. He insists that logical supervenience is necessary and sufficient for reductive explanation, but he suggests that "a reductive explanation is not necessarily an illuminating explanation" (ibid.). Thus, according to Chalmers, "logical supervenience implies that there is a reductive explanation in principle, although perhaps one that only a superbeing could understand" ((ibid., p. 49). However, the above proofs show that supervenience does not guarantee reduction, even if we allow a reduction to be an unilluminating and "vast hotchpotch of arbitrary seeming details." The artificial cases spelled out in the proofs show that there can be supervenience without any reduction at all, illuminating or otherwise. In each of those cases, not even God could reductively explain the *M* properties via the *P* properties.

Of course, the arguments above do not show that the mental facts are not reducible to physical facts. Rather, I have merely argued that it is possible for one set of properties to supervene on another without reducing to the other. I have shown this by setting up arbitrary and artificial examples, but the point was to deny any strong conceptual link between supervenience and reduction.

One might still object that the proofs are not applicable to the case of mind-body supervenience, because the proofs rely on specific features of the M and P properties that presumably are not shared by mental and physical properties. In the proofs, the M and P values were arranged such that a contradiction would result if reduction were possible: A noncomputable number would be computable. This result was guaranteed in the first proof by making the M values themselves noncomputable. It was arranged in the second and third proofs by assigning M values so that one would be able to compute a non-computable number if one could deduce *all* of the M facts. (If one had a general procedure for deducing arbitrarily many M facts, one would be able to get arbitrarily close to the noncomputable number.) Thus the proofs relied on a very special arrangement of M and P properties. One might then infer that the reasoning applies to the mind-body case only if either (i) mental properties themselves are somehow noncomputable or (ii) mental properties are arranged such that a general procedure for deducing them would entail the computability of a noncomputable number. Since we have no reason to think that either of these conditions holds, we have no reason to think that the reasoning behind the proofs applies to the case of mind-body supervenience.

But this would misread the aim of the argument. I am not claiming that a noncomputable number would be computable if the mental were reducible to the physical. Rather, my point is to show that, as a general matter, supervenience does not entail reduction; it is perfectly possible for there to be sets of facts such that reduction is impossible but the sets of facts still covary in a way that yields supervenience. There are more facts than there are deducible facts. In light of the general argument that supervenience does not entail reduction, I suggest that it is incumbent on my opponent to show why supervenience of the mental on the physical entails the reducibility of the mental to the physical.

In any event, it is worth keeping in mind that the argument allowed for a ridiculously weak notion of *reduction*. For the M facts to reduce to the P facts, the proofs above require only that there be some statement B such that the P facts conjoined with B imply the M facts. In fact, if we were to have a reduction of the M facts to the P facts, we would need much more than this. Not only must the bridge laws be stateable; they must also be true, and, as was discussed above, they must be commitments of practitioners of CSP about CSP—claims to which practitioners are committed to regardless of their commitment to the existence of mental states. Viewed from this perspective, the above proofs are excessive. So, even granting that the mental facts supervene on the physical facts, it should not be taken as *obvious* that there will be bridge laws that meet the constraints and which, in combination with the P facts, suffice to imply the mental facts.

8.5 Explanations for Supervenience

8.5.1 The Challenge

As was mentioned earlier, Kim has a second reason for saying that supervenience "is not a metaphysically deep, explanatory relation" (1998a, p. 10). He argues that "the mere fact (assuming it is a fact) of mind-body supervenience leaves open the question of what *grounds* or *accounts* for it—that is, why the supervenience relation obtains between the mental and the physical" (p. 10). Kim is not alone in making this demand; Horgan (1993, 1994) makes it too. This is a strong challenge to those who maintain that the mental supervenes on the physical without being reducible to the physical. If mind-body supervenience holds, there can be no difference in mental properties without a difference in physical properties—i.e., any two worlds that differ in their mental properties also differ in their physical properties. If that is true, then why is it true? And if there is no explanation for why supervenience holds, then we have no reason to believe that it does hold.

An example far from the mind-body case might make the demand for explanation clearer. Suppose that someone claimed that the economic properties of the United States supervene on the economic properties of Pakistan. According to this claim, there could be no change any aspect of the United States economy without some sort of change in Pakistan's economy as well; in any possible situation in which the US economy was different than it actually is, the Pakistani economy would be different too. This would be a quite remarkable, and implausible, claim, for there would seem to be no reason for such a systematic covariation in the two sets of properties. Admittedly, national economies are becoming ever more interconnected, but it would be incredible to think that there could be no change, no matter how small, in the US economy without some sort of change in the Pakistani economy. (To take a simple example, it seems that there could be a possible world in which, while I was at the grocery store, I bought a candy bar, but in which everything about Pakistan and the Pakistani economy remains exactly the same.) Of course, both the US economy and the Pakistani economy are constantly changing, so there is never any period of time during which there has been a change in the actual US economy while there was no change at all in economic facts about Pakistan—so it is not as if we can see empirically that the supervenience claim is false. Nonetheless, we would need much more than this to be convinced of the supervenience claim. We would need to know what could possibly *explain* the supervenience relationship; we would need to see, for example, some sort of necessary link between economic transactions in the United States and transactions in Pakistan. In this case, any such link would have to be far-fetched—e.g., if one were to claim that there is a direct causal link between the behavior of US citizens and Pakistani citizens, such that US citizens are not autonomous beings at all but are completely controlled via the behavior of Pakistani citizens. If we have no such explanation, we have no reason to believe that the supervenience relationship holds.

So, to take the contrapositive of this last claim, if we *do* have reason to believe that supervenience holds, then we must have some explanation for its holding. The reductionist has no worries here; if reductionism is right, then each mental fact is entailed by the physical facts plus appropriate bridge laws. That is, for a given mental fact M, some physical facts P, and the bridge laws B,

$$P \mathbin{\&} B \to M.$$

Since this is a logical entailment, if follows that if M did not hold then the conjunction of P and B would be false; but B just reflects our commitments about CSP apart from any commitment to CSP, and there is thus no reason to think that B would be falsified by falsity of M. Hence, if M failed to hold, it would follow that P is false. Thus any change in the mental facts would entail a change in the physical facts, and thus supervenience holds. Thus the reductionist has an explanation for why supervenience holds: the mental facts are entailed by the physical facts and are thus themselves, in a sense, a species of physical fact.

Kim's and Horgan's point is that things are less clear for the nonreductionist about the mind. The nonreductionist wants to maintain mind-body supervenience; but if there are no reductive laws connecting the mental to the physical, then what could possibly explain why supervenience holds? And if reductionists have no such explanation, what reason do they have for believing that supervenience does hold? Clearly this is a challenge to which the nonreductionist must respond. On the other hand, a fairly obvious response does seem to be available: The fact that mental properties supervene on physical properties is explained by the fact that the agents to whom we ascribe mental properties are ultimately *constituted by* physical particles. This is a clear difference between mind-body supervenience and the alleged supervenience of the US economy on the Pakistani economy. Persons are entirely composed of material particles, whereas it is not the case that all economic changes in the United States are constituted by (or otherwise intrinsically linked to) changes in the Pakistani economy. In the absence of reduction, supervenience without composition indeed seems miraculous; but, because we are composed of physical particles, supervenience is no longer mysterious. In fact, it seems obvious to me that the supervenience of the mental on the physical can be explained by the fact that we are composed of physical particles. However, I gather that this is not so obvious to everyone, at least not to Kim and Horgan. So I will endeavor to make explicit an argument for thinking that composition explains supervenience.

8.5.2 The Answer: Why Composition Explains Supervenience

First I will explore an example in which chess boards and pixels on computer screens take the place of human beings and physical particles. When one plays chess on a computer, the board and pieces are displayed on the computer screen. Viewed from the standpoint of chess, the computer screen depicts a position with a canonical description (e.g., white pawn on e2, white king on e1, etc.). The board in question is composed entirely of the pixels that make up the computer screen—my own screen is set at 800×600 = 480,000 pixels. My monitor control panel tells me that each of these pixels can be one of millions of colors, making for a rather enormous number of possible displays on the screen (somewhere above $10^{6,000,000}$ by my calculation), far more than enough to represent all of the possible positions on a chess board (a large but finite number less than 10^{68}). Naturally, each possible chess position could be represented by a huge number of different configurations of pixels, for the size, shape, and color of the pieces and board could have many different variations. Nonetheless, given a particular screen, it seems clear that we could say that the chess facts of the depiction supervene on the pixel facts. That is, there could be no change in the depicted chess position without some change in the pixels on the screen— e.g., the black king's position could not switch from one square to another without some change in the pixels on the computer screen. To put it another way, there cannot be two screens that depict different positions in a game of chess but which are exactly alike in their pixel configuration. The supervenience of the chess properties on the pixel properties does not seem particularly mysterious, for the chess board is *composed* of pixels. Its properties cannot change without some change in the parts that compose it, and those parts are the pixels on the screen.

Now with the example as stated, the chess properties of the chess boards also arguably *reduce* to the pixel properties, at least with the weak notion of reduction operative in this chapter. In principle, there could be a bridge law B such that B conjoined with a description of the pixel configuration on the screen will tell us all of the chess properties of the board. We know that there could be such a bridge law, in principle, because there are only a finite number of pixel configurations, and, for that matter, a finite number of possible chess positions. The bridge law could simply consist of a list of all the possible pixel configurations along with the chess position (if any) that the configuration depicts. (The "in principle" is important here, obviously.)

However, we can change the example so that we get supervenience without reduction, and this will help make it clear that the supervenience is explained by the composition rather than the possibility of reduction. Suppose that the screen can be infinitely large. And suppose that we the screens depict not chess but a game we will call chessplus. Chessplus is like chess, but played on a board with eight rows and infinitely many columns. Accordingly, on the second row at the outset of each of game of chess plus is an infinite row of pawns (equal in number to the integers); somewhere on the first row will be a white king on a black square and a white queen to its left, and arrayed out from the king and queen will be a bishop, a knight, and a rook, then another bishop, knight, and rook, and so on. For the chessplus facts to be reducible to the pixel facts, each chessplus fact must be entailed by some set of pixel facts plus some bridge law B. But since first-order logic is complete, this means that there will be a deduction of each chessplus fact. However, we can show that there are nondenumerably many chessplus positions.[4] Since there are only denumerably many logical proofs or deductions, that means that there are multitudes of chessplus facts that cannot be deduced at all, and thus the chessplus facts do not reduce to the pixel facts.

Despite the impossibility of reducing chessplus facts to pixel facts, it still seems clear that the chess positions will supervene on the pixel configurations. If two screens differ in the chess positions depicted on them, there will be some difference in the configuration of pixels on those screens; or, in other words, there could not be two screens with identical pixel configurations but which depicted boards with different chess properties. Despite the lack of reduction, the supervenience here seems unmysterious: the chess boards are composed of the pixels, so it seems quite natural that if two entire pixel configurations were identical they would have identical chess positions.

So we have seen in this artificial example that one need not have reduction to explain supervenience. The analogy to the mind-body case is reasonably clear: Just as the chess positions were constituted by the pixels, so too are we constituted by elementary physical particles, and hence it should be unsurprising that our mental properties supervene on physical properties. However, the analogy between us and the chessplus screens is not perfect. The chessplus properties of the board do not depend on anything external to the screen, so the screen's constitution by pixels is enough to explain the supervenience of chessplus facts on pixel facts. By contrast, we know that the content of our mental states can depend on things external to our skin, so the mere fact that *we* are constituted by physical particles is not enough by itself to make the supervenience unmysterious. If we could say that the entire world is composed of physical particles, we would be back in business; the physical constitution of the world as a whole would explain the global supervenience of mental properties on physical properties. However, it is dubious to claim that everything is constituted by physical particles: Numbers and many other abstract objects seem firmly a part of our ontology and yet are not constituted by physical particles. However, even if the world as a whole is not entirely physical, I will argue that everything relevant to the determination of mental content is in fact composed of physical particles, and thus the analogy still succeeds.

In his 1975 article, Putnam argues that when we think about water, the content of those thoughts is determined, at least in part, by the nature of water itself. Of course, water is composed of physical particles. So, even though meanings "ain't in the head," that upon which meaning depends is still composed of physical particles. The point appears to generalize to other examples of externally determined content. In the original Putnam case, the people on Twin Earth had never had any contact with water (i.e., H_2O), and this fueled the intuition that the Twin-Earthians could not be having thoughts about water. Thus, the content of our water thoughts differs from the contents of our twins' thoughts precisely because we have been in contact with completely distinct substances. To put the point more generally, when things external to the skin help to determine the contents of our mental states, they do so because we have been in causal contact with them. (Or, to allow for what Putnam calls the linguistic division of labor, at least some of us have been in causal contact with them.)

What about thoughts concerning abstract objects, say the number *e*? Here, I think we should say that the content of our thoughts is not actually determined by the number itself. Rather, in cases like this, the content of our thoughts is determined by the descriptions that we are able to give, descriptions that suffice to pick out the referent of the term *e*. That is not to say that one must know the formula that defines *e*; it is enough that there are mathematically sophisticated types around who know the formula, and that the rest of us have the right sort of connection to those people. But the point is that with abstract objects, particularly mathematical ones, one could not run a Putnam-style thought experiment; there is no possible Twin Earth where everyone's characterizations or descriptions of the number e are the same as their twins on Earth, but where the number e is different.

If all of this is correct, any external object that determines the content of my mental states is capable of having effects. But anything that is capable of having effects is composed of physical particles. So, given also that everything inside the skin is composed of physical particles, it follows that everything capable of determining the content of mental states is composed of physical particles. So the analogy to chessplus can work after all; everything that determines the content of mental states (including, especially, everything happening within our brains) is constituted by physical particles. So, just as the constitution of the chessplus boards by pixels *explains* the supervenience of chessplus properties on pixel properties, the supervenience of the mental on the physical is explained by constitution.

8.6 Conclusion

On the face of things, this chapter has been concerned with what can appear to be technical minutiae: whether supervenience entails reduction and whether a nonreductionist can provide any explanation for the claimed supervenience of the mental on the physical. But what is at stake was the conceptual possibility of an option-3 view that does not collapse back into substance dualism—i.e., whether it is possible to exclude supernatural ghostlike immaterial minds without thereby committing oneself to strong naturalism. Having argued that weak naturalism is a genuine possibility, I now turn to presenting the positive side of teleological realism.

9 | Agency and Teleological Explanation

I have framed the mind-body problem as a question about the logical relationship between the truths of physical science and the claims of common-sense psychology. There were three options: that CSP and physical science are inconsistent, that physical science ultimately implies CSP, and that CSP and physical science are independent of one another. Strong naturalism was the view that either the first or the second option is correct, with the results of physical science determining which. Teleological realism instead goes for option 3, according to which the claims of CSP and physical science are logically independent of one another. Of course, it is not enough simply to assert the logical independence of CSP and physical science. On the face of things, CSP and science would appear to share a subject matter, and they both offer explanations of human behavior. One might well think that these explanations cannot be logically independent of one another, for either they will agree and hence imply each other or they will disagree and hence contradict each other.

The cornerstone of teleological realism is its account of action explanation; this account is also the key move in the attempt to show the logical independence of CSP and physical science. In place of the causal theory of action explanation, the teleological realist suggests, naturally enough, that action explanation is teleological.

9.1 The Form of Teleological Explanation

Teleological explanations typically employ connectives such as "in order to," "for the purpose of," or "to"; for example, we might say "Joan went to the kitchen in order to get a glass of wine" or "Russ bunted to move the runner to second base." Teleological explanations explain the behavior by citing the state of affairs toward which the behavior was directed: getting a glass of wine and moving the runner to second base, in the above examples.

Some ordinary explanations of action do not explicitly employ teleological connectives, e.g.,

Ann went outside because she wanted to see a comet.

Here the connective is 'because' rather than one of the more explicitly teleological formulations. However, I will still construe this as a teleological explanation. The cited propositional attitude serves to describe the state of affairs at which the agent's behavior is directed. However, we must take some care here; clearly we cannot simply replace 'because' with "in order to," for this would yield

Ann went outside in order to want to see a comet.

This is, of course, false, for Ann's purpose was to see the comet; she was not trying to *want* to see the comet. Ann desired that a certain state of affairs come to pass, namely one in which she is observing a comet, and it was toward this state of affairs that she was directing her behavior. Thus the original explanation can be construed in more explicitly teleological language as follows:

Ann went outside in order to bring it about that she see a comet in the way she desired.

Action explanations that cite beliefs rather than desires work similarly. Suppose that an agent ϕs because she believes that she can ψ by ϕing. This explanation of her behavior can be construed in more explicitly teleological form as follows: "The agent ϕd in order to bring about the state of affairs (namely, ψ) that she believed could be brought about by ϕing."[1]

Although I have said a bit about the form of teleological explanations, their distinguishing characteristic lies in their function rather than their form. First some background. Explanations are, I take it, answers to certain kinds of questions. (See Bromberger 1965; van Fraassen 1980; Achinstein 1983.) Such questions typically begin with the word 'why'. However, when we ask why an agent performed a given action, we might be asking one of several distinct questions: What brain state caused the behavior? What sensory stimulus prompted the behavior? To what end was the agent's behavior directed? Each question may be perfectly appropriate given a certain context and set of interests. Teleological explanations are presented in answer to the last sort of question: They tell us the state of affairs toward which the behavior was directed.

It might help to consider an example in more depth. Jackie is at a picnic, and she sees someone holding a beer; she decides she would like one too, so she walks in the direction of the cooler. Obviously, she believes that beer can be obtained at the cooler, and she is walking toward the cooler because she wants a beer. According to the causal theory of action explanation, Jackie's desire and belief are the causes of her walking. The teleological realist agrees that Jackie went to the cooler because she wanted a beer. But the use of 'because' in that explanation simply signifies that the desire for beer *explains* her going to the cooler, and, as has just been suggested, there can be more than one explanation of that behavior, depending on the question we want to answer. The implicit question, according to the teleological realist, concerns the purpose of Jackie's action. If we are asking the teleological question, then we want to know the goal, if any, toward which her behavior was directed. And the answer is that she walked to the cooler in order to obtain a beer; i.e., her goal was the state of affairs in which she has a beer. It was toward that state of affairs that she directed her behavior. By mentioning her desire for beer in the explanation, we do two things. First, by specifying the *content* of the desire (that she get a beer), we specify the state of affairs toward which she was directing her behavior. Second, by saying that she *desired* that state of affairs, we say something about the way in which the state of affairs was valuable to her. Having a beer was of value because she *wanted* to drink it, and not, for example, because of a felt obligation to hold a beer at a picnic despite hating the stuff.

Naturally, one could also ask about the cause of Jackie's behavior. Here we can surmise that a sensory stimulus triggered a chain of events in her brain and nervous system, with the ultimate result that she walked to the cooler. The lesson of the arguments of chapter 6 is that CSP is not committed to the claim that Jackie's desire for beer can be aptly identified with one of the physical states in this chain. But that is not to deny that her behavior has a perfectly good causal explanation.

What does it mean to say that she was *directing* her behavior at that state of affairs? I have already argued in part II that one cannot define or reduce the concept of goal direction to purely causal notions. In fact, I doubt that there is *any* reductive analysis of *goal direction*, just as there is arguably no reductive analysis of what it means to say that one event *caused* another. Nonetheless, even if we cannot analyze teleology in causal terms, we need some account of how we identify and justify teleological explanations. We might characterize what is needed as the epistemology of teleological explanation. That is the project of sections 9.2 and 9.3.

9.2 The Rationality Principle

9.2.1 Simplicity and Rationality

How do we make teleological judgments? This will depend in part on the exact question we are asking. There are several possibilities: Is the thing before us an agent? Is the behavior goal directed? To what end is the behavior directed? We might consider only the second and third of these questions if we take it for granted that the thing before us (e.g., a person) is an agent. Or we might ask only the third question if we are already sure that the agent is engaged in goal-directed behavior. Finally, we might know one or more goals toward which the behavior is clearly directed and still want to know what further objective the behavior has. For example, if I see someone get up and walk toward the door of the living room I may assume that she is leaving the room, but I may want to know what further goal is served by leaving the room. Such assumptions are defeasible; we stand ready to withdraw the claim that the behavior is goal directed and even the assumption that we are dealing with an agent at all.

So how do we go about answering these questions? Starting with the first, how do we determine whether the thing before us is an agent? I suggest that an agent is someone to whom the norms of rationality apply; an agent is someone about whom we can give a theory according to which the agent is rational, in a very broad sense of that word. This would appear to put theories of agents into a different category from physical theories about inanimate objects. As I suggested in chapter 2, in physical science our theorizing is governed at least in part by a principle of simplicity:

(S) Given two theories, it is unreasonable to believe the one that leaves significantly more unexplained mysteries.

Thus, as our physical theory of the world improves, it gradually leaves fewer and fewer unexplained mysteries. Something is mysterious, roughly speaking, when it is unexpected; we explain apparently mysterious events by giving a theory according to which events of that kind would be expected. Within physical science, there is no further requirement that events be justified or make rational sense. For example, if we can explain a tornado's occurrence in terms of general laws and existing meteorological conditions, we don't ask what justifiable purpose it served. The tornado serves no justifiable or reasonable purpose, but this fact does not count as an unexplained mystery for our meteorological theory.

When our subject matter includes agents and their behavior, things are different. When theorizing about an agent, we aim for a theory according to which the agent is rational and her behavior makes sense. In the course of constructing such a theory, we will be guided by the simplicity principle, but we will also be guided by an additional maxim:

(R) Given two theories of an agent, it is unreasonable to believe the one according to which the agent is significantly less rational.

As Donald Davidson puts it, when we are dealing with an agent, "in our need to make him make sense, we will try for a theory that finds him consistent, a believer of truths, and a lover of the good (all by our own lights, it goes without saying" (1980, p. 222).

(R) by itself does not provide much guidance on exactly how to do this, for (R) is phrased quite generally, and it is not immediately obvious how it applies to individual items of behavior. Indeed, by the very nature of the principle, it cannot simply be applied, in a vacuum, to a single piece of behavior, for we determine the purpose of behavior against the background of a more general theory of the agent. So we will need to explore further to see what sorts of explanation make better sense of a behavior. But we can note a couple of points at the outset. First, the idea behind (R) is that agents are basically rational. To quote Davidson again: "Global confusion, like universal mistake, is unthinkable, not because imagination boggles, but because too much confusion leaves nothing to be confused about and massive error erodes the background of true belief against which alone failure can be construed." (1980, p. 221) Second, in the context of explaining behavior, the rationality of a piece of behavior can be measured along two axes: the extent to which the behavior is appropriate for achieving the agent's goal, and the extent to which the goal itself is of value from the agent's perspective. If an agent is ineffective at achieving her goals, then she is, to that extent, not rational; but an agent is also irrational insofar as her goals themselves have no value. Accordingly, built into (R) is the expectation that agents will be effective in achieving their goals and that their goals will be of value. Of course, we do not expect perfect efficiency or an ideal set of goals. Instead, the twin expectations built into (R) will be something like the following:

(R$_1$) Agents act in ways that are appropriate for achieving their goals, given the agent's circumstances, epistemic situation, and intentional states.

(R$_2$) Agents have goals that are of value, given the agent's circumstances, epistemic situation, and intentional states.

I should emphasize that the notion of *value* involved in (R₂) is weaker than other notions involving the same word. We sometimes speak of an agent as *valuing* certain things, or we speak of an agent's *values*; in this sense of the word, values are the things upon which a person places the greatest importance. Valuing friendship means more than simply desiring friendship or having friendship serve one's interests. According to one famous line of thought, what we value is what we desire to desire. (Something like this is suggested in Frankfurt 1988 and more explicitly advocated in Lewis 1989.) In this strong sense of 'value', there could be human beings or animals that clearly have desires and interests but which do not have values. Very young children, for example, presumably have desires and interests, but may lack the reflective capacity for second-order desires. In saying that a goal must be *of value* to the agent, I do not mean to imply that an agent must have the capacity for second-order desires, nor do I mean to imply that an agent's goals must be among her values, in the strong sense of that word. Saying that something is *of* value to a person is far weaker than that. Watching a mindless sitcom can be of value to me at times, but it is not one of my values. What is required for something to be of value to an agent? I don't have any reductive explication to offer, and so I will operate with fairly intuitive ideas. Something is of value, for example, if it is pleasant for the agent, or if it serves the agent's interests, or if it satisfies the agent's desires, or if it is a good thing and the agent is able to appreciate that goodness.

Before going further with the details of applying (R), I will first consider what would appear to be an obvious objection.

9.2.2 Objection: People Can Be Irrational

When we explain an individual piece of behavior, we thereby contribute to our overall theory of an agent; so, in accord with (R), we will generally aim for explanations according to which the behavior is as rational as possible. This might seem problematic. (R) apparently forces us to see agents as always rational, but we know that agents are sometimes not rational. In reply, we should first note that (R) does not say that people are perfectly rational. Rather, given the person's behavior and everything one knows about the person, and given a choice between two overall theories, the principle tells us not to believe a theory on which the person is significantly less rational. Moreover, our theory of the person and the person's behavior will be evaluated in the context of an overall theory of the world, which will be constrained by the simplicity principle. Given this, we will often be forced to ascribe various false beliefs or mistaken inferences, for the only available alternative theories might make the agent even more irrational or might create large mysteries in our theory of the rest of the world.

Consider a simple example. Someone at a dinner table takes a small bowl of salt at the table and spoons some of it into her coffee. What explanation of the agent's behavior will make her out to be the most rational? Of course, the obvious explanation is that the agent mistakenly thought that the salt was sugar, yielding

(1) *A* put the salt in her coffee in order to bring it about that her coffee was sweetened.

This explanation makes our agent less than completely rational, since it attributes to her a false belief. So (1) is not ideal as far as (R) is concerned, but it is doubtful that we could come up with any other explanation that would do any better. We could propose a different explanation:

(2) *A* put salt in her coffee in order to make her coffee taste salty.

This would make *A*'s action appropriate to its goal, and if she likes salty coffee, then the goal would have intelligible value from her perspective. But suppose that, after drinking a sip of the coffee, *A* contorts her face, goes to the kitchen, and pours the coffee down the sink. In that case, it would be implausible to say that she was aiming at making her coffee taste salty, for her subsequent behavior would not look reasonable. And if *A* accompanies these subsequent actions with "Oops, I thought that was sugar," a theory including (2) would fail even more obviously in making sense of her behavior.

All things being equal, *A* would be much more rational if we could adopt the following:

(3) *A* put sugar in her coffee in order to bring it about that her coffee was sweetened.

But our theory of the agent cannot be considered in isolation from our theory of the world as a whole. If I put some of the substance from the same bowl onto my potatoes, and I know that it tasted like salt, and if the bowl has remained on the table throughout dinner, then it is not credible at all to say that *A* put sugar in her coffee. The assertion that there was sugar in the bowl would create quite a number of mysteries for the theory, for it would be, on the face of things, inconsistent with what I experienced earlier about the contents of the bowl. Of course, we could add to our theory the claim that the salt magically transformed into sugar, but this would be even more mysterious. So, on simplicity grounds, we are constrained to say that the substance in the bowl was salt, and thus (3) is ruled out despite the fact that it would see the agent as more rational.

Going back to (1), it is true that the overall theory of which (1) is a part attributes a false belief to *A*, and thus makes her, to that extent, less than perfectly rational (though even here, there might be some reasonable explanation of *why* the agent had that belief). One might think that the rationality principle requires us to choose a theory that does not attribute to the person this false belief. But the available alternative theories would, on the whole, make the agent even more irrational. Our best overall theory of the world may well have to make the agent less than perfectly rational. And that's fine—there is no violation of (R). This is analogous to the point that our overall physical theory of the world will still leave some things unexplained. We don't create the world when we theorize about it (Nelson Goodman notwithstanding). Our theorizing is in response to our perceptions of the world, and if we ignore those perceptions we introduce even bigger mysteries. Similarly, our theorizing about agents, besides also taking place in the context of our overall theory of the world, is in response to the behavior we actually see. Given the totality of that behavior, and given the rest of our overall theory of the world, our claims about any particular person will perhaps inevitably involve attributing some degree of irrationality. So there is no conflict between our occasional foibles and the truth of (R).

9.3 Applying the Rationality Principle

9.3.1 Dawkins and Reverse Engineering

I will approach the question of how we apply (R) via a related discussion by the biologist Richard Dawkins.[2] Suppose you come upon an unknown object, and you want to determine the purpose (if any) for which the object was designed. Dawkins says that you will employ reverse engineering:

You are an engineer, confronted with an artifact you have found and do not understand. You make the working assumption that it was designed for some purpose. You dissect and analyze the object with a view to working out what problem it would be good at solving: "If I had wanted to make a machine to do so and so, would I have made it like this? Or is the object better explained as a machine designed to do such and such?" (1995, p. 82)

The technique of reverse engineering assumes, as a working hypothesis, that the object was well designed for achieving some end. To determine what end, we ascertain the object's *utility function*, meaning that which is maximized or optimized by the operation of the object. Roughly speaking, we then assume that the utility function is the object's intended purpose. For example, if someone unfamiliar with baseball saw a catcher's mask, he might be initially puzzled. But upon examining the straps, the metal bars in front, and the padding around the edges of the bars, he might quickly infer that this would be a good device for fitting over a person's head and protecting the face from baseball-size objects. Dawkins's specific question is whether living bodies are the result of intelligent design. He argues that "the true utility function of life, that which is being maximized in the natural world, is DNA survival" (1995, p. 83). Thus, the utility function of living bodies is not the good of the individual or the welfare of the species; even when those goods happen to be served, this is a secondary consequence of the primary function of DNA survival. As Dawkins puts it: "Nature is neither kind nor unkind. She is neither against suffering nor for it. Nature is not interested in suffering one way or the other unless it affects the survival of DNA." (ibid., p. 85) Here Dawkins talks as if Nature is a designing agent, albeit an agent that is interested only in survival of DNA and is indifferent to suffering. But Dawkins suggests that this supposed indifference to suffering actually shows that living bodies are not the products of intelligent design at all: "In a universe of electrons and selfish genes, blind physical forces and genetic replication, some people are going to get hurt, other people are going to get lucky, and you won't find any rhyme or reason in it, nor any justice. The universe that we observe has precisely the properties we should expect if there is, at bottom, no design, no purpose, no evil and no good, nothing but pitiless indifference." (ibid., p. 85)

Dawkins's point is this: If we are to vindicate the working assumption that a thing was designed for a purpose, it is not enough to show that the object *has* a utility function; in addition, the utility function must be of the right sort. In particular, we should conclude that the thing has a purpose only if the utility function exhibits rhyme, reason, or justice. That is to say, the utility function must be of some sort of intelligible value. Note also that Dawkins is hereby making a distinction between explanations citing genuine design on the one hand and evolutionary explanations on the other.

To summarize: On Dawkins's account, when we attempt to ascertain whether and what purpose an object has, we presuppose two principles.

If an object has an intended purpose, then its purpose is its utility function.

An object has an intended purpose only if its utility function has rhyme and reason.

9.3.2 The Principles Underlying Teleological Explanation

Of course, the question of whether an object was *designed* is different from the question of whether something is an agent, and it is also different from the question of whether a bodily motion was directed by an agent. Nonetheless similar considerations are involved. We apply something like the reverse engineering approach, but instead of deciding whether the object itself was designed, we look to see whether the object's behavior is "designed"—i.e., directed—and, if so, to what end. If we were to apply Dawkins's account directly to this task, we would assume the following two principles:

(D_1) If a behavior is directed to a goal, then its goal is its utility function.

(D_2) A behavior is directed toward a goal only if the utility function of the behavior has intelligible value.

These principles constrain what can count as the goal of a piece of behavior; (D_1) tells us that the goal, if there is one, has to be the utility function of the behavior, and, according to (D_2), for the utility function to be a goal, it must have intelligible value. (D_1) and (D_2) have a fairly obvious correlation with the two axes of rationality noted above in (R_1) and (R_2). According to (R_1), agents act in ways that are appropriate to achieving their goals, modulo the agent's circumstances and epistemic situation; (D_1) takes this somewhat further by specifying that the goal of a behavior is precisely that which the behavior is most effective at obtaining. (R_2) says that agents have goals that are of value from their perspective, and the correlation between this and (D_2) is even more direct. There is, I claim, something importantly correct about (D_1) and (D_2); however, the account will require some refinement before it accurately reflects our practice of giving teleological explanations.

To see the need for refinement, it will help to consider another example. During the course of a commencement speech, Ben, who has never seen or heard of American Sign Language, notices someone standing to the side of a podium making (to his mind) strange gesticulations, and he wonders what the person is doing. The person's behavior would be good for accomplishing any number of aims: Signing is a good way of burning a certain number of calories per hour, a good way of demonstrating one's ability for certain kinds of hand and arm motions, and a good way of displacing a certain number of air molecules. Ben quite rightly does not consider such possible objectives, for he would find it hard to imagine that these goals would have any particular value for the agent in these circumstances. Ben might notice that the signer's hand motions have a certain correspondence to the speaker's words: When the speaker pauses, the hand motions cease soon thereafter, and when the speaker resumes, the hand motions begin again. Unlike the case of a conductor waving her arms in front of a choir, there is no reason here to think that the signer is directing the speaker's words in any way, for the speaker pays no attention to the signer. The signer could be responding to the speaker's words in the way that a dancer responds to music, but this would rightly strike Ben as a goal that would be of dubious value in the circumstances. Ben might hit upon the idea that if the hand motions are used as symbols, they might be a good way of expressing the speaker's words. Why would this be of value? It would not benefit those who can already clearly hear the speaker's words, but it could help the hearing-impaired members of the audience. Ben tentatively concludes that this is the goal of the behavior. Further investigation could then serve to confirm this hypothesis.

I have belabored this rather obvious example in order to highlight a number of points about how teleological interpretation works. First, while we do ascertain what the behavior would be good for, we do not assume that its goal is the one state of affairs that the behavior is best suited to achieve. In the case of the person signing, the behavior would be an effective means for bringing about any number of states of affairs, and it is not at all clear that there is *one* state of affairs for which the behavior is most appropriate. And the point is quite general: Given any piece of behavior, we can postulate any number of outcome states for which the behavior is well suited. Items of behavior do not typically have any *one* utility function. Many possible goals are ruled out (or never even brought into consideration) if they have no obvious value in the circumstances. So we might try revising (D_1) by saying that if a behavior is directed to a goal, then the behavior must be *optimal* for achieving that goal, where this leaves open the possibility that a given behavior could be optimal for achieving any number of goals. We would then rely on (D_2) to exclude those candidate goals that have no intelligible value.

However, we will have to revise (D_1) and (D_2) even further, for in fact we do not assume that a piece of behavior must be optimal for achieving its goal; indeed, we don't necessarily assume that the behavior is even effective at all. The person making the hand motions might be an incompetent signer, and hence might not be communicating anything to anyone. Or consider a different example: A car owner installs a new battery in his car and then attaches the red cable to the negative terminal and the black cable to the positive terminal. This behavior would be well suited to frying the cable wires, but that is not the goal toward which it was directed. The car owner was attempting to replace the battery and get the car in working order again, but his behavior was in fact optimally suited to damaging the car rather than restoring it to operation. The lesson is this: When ascertaining the purpose of a behavior, we will allow for various failings on the part of the agent, especially mistaken beliefs and failures of execution.

So if we are to explain the agent's φing by saying that it was directed at ψing, we need not claim that φing would be optimal for ψing; however, φing still must be *appropriate* for the goal of ψing. Behavior can be appropriate, even if it is not effective, if it is at least a reasonable sort of thing to try given the agent's situation. Given that the car owner thought that the terminals on the new battery would have the same relative position as the terminals on the old battery, his actual hand motions in attaching the cables were appropriate for the goal of restoring the car to working order. His mistake is at least comprehensible. And the point here is general. We improve the intelligibility of a teleological explanation to the extent that the behavior is appropriate to achieving the hypothesized goal state, modulo the agent's epistemic circumstances and intentional states.

We can summarize this as follows. In trying to find a teleological explanation according to which an agent φd in order to ψ, we do the following:

(I_1) Find a ψ such that φing is optimally appropriate for ψing, given a viable theory of the agent's intentional states and circumstances.

In the limit case, where φing is not even the right sort of thing to try, the purported explanation loses sense altogether. If an ordinary car owner were to bludgeon the engine of her car repeatedly with a sledgehammer, then, in the absence of a compelling story, it would simply make no sense to suggest that she was doing this in order to restore the car to working order. Similarly, in the sign language example above, Ben never considers the possibility that the agent is making the hand motions in order to fly to the moon. In the course of teleological interpretation, we restrict our attention to outcome states for which the behavior would be a reasonable or comprehensible means.

In one sense, (I_1) is less restrictive than the Dawkins-inspired (D_1), for the goal need not be that which the behavior is best suited to accomplish. If the agent falsely believes that φing will be very appropriate for ψing, the requirements of (I_1) could be met even if φing fails miserably at ψing. On the other hand, (I_1) is intended to include an idea that may be stronger than

Dawkins's corresponding formulation: There should not be another action that would have been obviously more appropriate for ψing. In most circumstances we will want to go beyond finding a goal for which the behavior is minimally appropriate. For example, suppose a carpenter attaches a piece of nosing to a cabinet top; she uses glue and very small nails which she taps in below the surface of the wood and covers with tiny bits of wood fill. This complex behavior is effective at attaching the nosing to the cabinet, but this behavior is not optimally appropriate if the goal were *simply* to attach the nosing. If that were the goal, we would want to know why the carpenter did not take the easier and equally effective course of simply driving a few reasonably large nails in. Given the availability of a much simpler way of attaching the nosing, the carpenter's complex and painstaking behavior would not be highly appropriate for that goal. Instead, we would conclude that the carpenter was directing her behavior at some goal beyond that of attaching the nosing: The behavior was also directed at the goal of making the final result aesthetically pleasing. Since most people would think that visible nails in a finished piece of furniture are ugly, the carpenter's added effort is highly appropriate to the more complex goal of attaching the nosing in an aesthetically pleasing fashion. Put in general terms, even if ψing is the state of affairs that is best accomplished by ϕing, ϕing would not be optimally appropriate if there were some other action that would be obviously more effective at ψing (given a viable theory of the agent's intentional states and circumstances).

As was the case with (D_1), (I_1) by itself would seriously underdetermine teleological explanation; as we saw in the case of Ben and the person communicating in American Sign Language, there are any number of conceivable goals for which the signers hand motions would be quite appropriate. However, Ben will rightly fail to consider possible goals that would be of no intelligible value. Accordingly, we will need an analogue to (D_2) that also makes it explicit that we are operating within the context of an overall theory of the agent. Specifically, when trying to find a teleological explanation according to which an agent ϕd in order to ψ,

(I_2) Find a ψ such that ψing is the most valuable state of affairs toward which ϕing could be directed, given a viable theory of the agent's intentional states and circumstances.

Thus, in explaining behavior, we do the best we can in jointly satisfying instructions (I_1) and (I_2). When Ben saw the person translating the commencement speech into American Sign Language, he tried to determine what the arm motions might accomplish that would also be of intelligible value. We adopt the same approach in utterly routine cases as well; if I see a student raise her hand in my class, I understand that this behavior is likely to be directed at indicating that she has something she wishes to say. Given the circumstances, including accepted conventions, raising her hand would be a highly appropriate means of achieving that end, and doing so is likely the most valuable goal she could achieve by that behavior under the circumstances. Of course, there is room for error. If she had nothing that she wished to say, and her head itched, then scratching her head might have been the most valuable thing that could be accomplished by moving her hand at that time. Further inquiry would presumably settle the matter.

There are times, of course, when no explanation seems to be in accord with the instructions. If I see a student suddenly collapse into a motionless heap while walking out of class, no teleological explanation leaps to mind. Such behavior would be a good way of inciting a certain amount of attention and inquiry from bystanders, but the sort of attention received would be valuable only given a rather odd set of intentional states. Attributing these states to the agent might be the best interpretation, but, without specific evidence in favor of such a theory, it does not seem likely. In a case like this, we might well conclude that there is no ψ such that, given a viable account of the agent's intentional states and circumstances, (i) the observed behavior is appropriate for ψing and (ii) ψing would have intelligible value. That is to say, there is no ψ that would allow us to satisfy both (I_1) and (I_2) in anything beyond a degenerate way. In such cases we would conclude, at least provisionally, that the behavior was involuntary and was not goal directed at all.

9.4 The Nature of Reasons

According to Davidson, a reason for action must consist of a pro-attitude of the agent toward actions with a certain property, along with a belief that the action has that property (1980, p. 5). 'Pro-attitude' is a broad term meant to encompass desires, wishes, urges, and the like. So according to Davidson, any reason for action must include a desire-like state of some sort. Other causalists about action explanation, including Mele (2003), have largely agreed with Davidson on this point. As I will argue in chapter 11, the teleological realist need not insist that a desire figure into every reason explanation. Some noncausalists, including Dancy (2000) and Schueler (2003), have gone even further in disagreeing with Davidson about desires. Dancy claims that if psychological states are reasons at all, then beliefs but not desires would be a necessary part of what motivates (2000, p. 77). However, Dancy ultimately says that "no reasons at all, neither motivating nor normative, are psychological states of the agent" (p. 100); instead, reasons will be the facts or states of affairs in light of which the agent acts. Schueler likewise claims that it will be facts or states of affairs that explain action rather than desires or beliefs (2003, p. 112).

As set up by Dancy and Schueler, the question is whether reasons are desires or states of affairs. However, from the standpoint of teleological realism, this question itself looks somewhat confused. The paradigmatic form of a teleological explanation is

A ϕd in order to ψ.

Given this form of explanation, what is *the reason* for action? The behavior is directed toward the state of affairs ψ, so we might say that the reason is ψ. But this doesn't look as if it can be right. If Vera goes to the kitchen to get tea, she is directing her behavior toward a state of affairs in which she has tea. But the state of affairs is not itself her reason. Rather, we would say that her reason was *to get tea*; i.e., her reason was *to bring about* that state of affairs. So, on the face of things, neither a fact nor a desire will be *the reason* for an agent's behavior. But that is not because there is some other kind of entity that does serve as the reason. Rather, it is a mistake to look for a *thing* that is the agent's reason for ϕing, whether the thing be a state of affairs, fact, or psychological state. There is a perfectly good answer to the question "What was her reason for doing that?" However, the answer is not some reified state, psychological or otherwise.

However, there is another way of looking at the question of whether a desire can be a reason. On my account, explanations of action imply that the state of affairs toward which the agent directed her behavior had some apparent value from the perspective of the agent. The question about desires and reasons might arise again in this context. In particular, if the agent ϕd in order to ψ, then we might say that the agent's reason for ϕing was whatever made ψ valuable from the agent's perspective. In other words, the agent's reason will be whatever explains the value of ψ. Then the question will be whether a desire for ψ can be a reason in this sense of the term. The two extreme positions on this question would be as follows:

The value of ψing is *always* to be explained in terms of the agent's desires or similar psychological states.

The value of ψing is *never* to be explained in terms of the agent's psychological states.

According to the first alternative, the agent must have a desire (or other pro-attitude) toward ψ; the agent could have an intrinsic desire for ψ or could desire ψ instrumentally as a means to some other state of affairs that the agent desires intrinsically. The second alternative is in the spirit of Dancy's account, for Dancy says that a desire to ψ cannot give us any normative justification for doing something that ψs. I take it that Schueler would agree with Dancy here.

I find either of the alternatives too extreme. The first would be a version of the Humean account of motivation, which I will address in chapter 11. Dancy appears to agree with the second, claiming that a desire to ψ by itself provides no reason for the agent to ψ. He argues that if ψing is "silly or even just not very sensible" the fact that the agent might desire it "does not make it less silly or a bit more sensible" (2000, p. 32). By way of argument, he alludes to a case in which he has every reason avoid ψing but nonetheless has a desire to ψ:

I hesitate to give an example of this, but the sort of one that springs to mind is some shameful act that would immediately bring my career and marriage to an end, but which I still have some desire to do. All agree that I have no reason to do this act, and every reason not to do it. (2000, p. 37)

I don't agree that Dancy has *no* reason to do the act. I will be somewhat more explicit and assume that Dancy, in the purely hypothetical example, is contemplating an extramarital affair with a female student. I readily grant that he has overwhelming reason against this course of action; one might even put this, as Dancy does, by saying that he has no reason to do it and every reason not to do it. But this seems to be hyperbole. Even if, on balance, it would be an enormously stupid thing to do and would be the subject of intense regret, surely his attraction to the student and his desire for the affair gives him *some* reason to go through with it. Given his desire, it is not as if the action would be utterly unintelligible. By way of comparison, suppose that the hypothetical Dancy has a gay colleague who is in a committed long-term relationship and thus has some of the same reasons *not* to have an affair with that female student. However, we can also plausibly suppose that the colleague has no desire to have the affair in the first place. On Dancy's view, he and his colleague would be in exactly the same position with respect to the contemplated action: Each would have no reason to do it. Thus, presumably, it would be equally unintelligible for either one to perform the action. But this seems clearly wrong.

We need not look to such dramatic cases to see that Dancy's view of desires and reasons is problematic. Mele cites the example of "a currently cheerful person's wholly intrinsic desire to sing a certain cheerful tune" and plausibly suggests that "such a desire is a reason for singing that tune" (2003, p. 82). Other examples that come to mind have to do with hobbies and special interests. I play bluegrass guitar, and I have a colleague who collects old fountain pens; our differing desires give us reasons to do very different things with our time and money. In contrast, Dancy holds that "desires are held for reasons, which they can transmit but to which they cannot add" (p. 39). Accordingly, if Dancy agrees that my colleague and I have different reasons for action, he must claim that our differing reasons do not have their source in differing desires, but rather that we have differing desires because we see the reasons differently. Similarly, Mele's cheerful person who desires to sing a particular tune must have a reason upon which the desire is based, rather than the other way around. But none of this is plausible. My colleague and I differ not in our evaluation of objective reasons but in what we like. This is not to say that our differing predilections are utterly inexplicable; various events have something to do with how I have come to like and play bluegrass music, and there will be a different story concerning my colleague's interest in fountain pens. Moreover, in very general terms, each of us can understand something of what is desirable about the other's hobby. I can acknowledge that fountain pens have beauty, elegance, and historical value. But I'm still not interested in collecting them, and my lack of interest does not mean that I am failing to appreciate properly some reason that my colleague understands; nor is my colleague misjudging the reasons for playing bluegrass guitar. Rather, our desires are simply different, and they lead to different reasons for action.

Thus, although I will claim in chapter 11 that desires are not *required* to ground reasons for action, it is also not the case that desires *never* ground good reasons. In some cases it makes sense to explain an action without citing (even implicitly) a desire of the agent, and in some cases it does make sense to explain an action by citing the agent's desires. The extreme alternatives to this common-sense view are motivated, I think, by the misguided search for some identifiable thing or state that can be the reason for an action.

9.5 Observations about the Account

I will close the chapter by briefly noting some implications of the account just given.

First, I take (R_1) and (R_2) to imply the truth of various counterfactual conditionals. Joan goes to the kitchen in order to get wine, which is to say that she has the goal of getting wine. According to (R_1), agents act in ways that are appropriate for achieving their goals, given their epistemic situation. So, if Joan had not had the goal of getting wine, she presumably would not have walked to the kitchen, unless walking to the kitchen would have served some other goal she had. On the other hand, suppose that Joan had the goal of getting wine, but that the wine had been in the dining room instead of the kitchen. Assuming that Joan was aware of the location of the wine, then (R_1) implies that she would have walked to the dining room. Put more generally, if the circumstances had required a slightly different action to achieve her goal, then Joan would have performed the required action. Thus, in saying that an agent's bodily motions are appropriate to her goals, we are also including consideration of what would happen in counterfactual situations. And, very roughly speaking, we can say that (R_1) implies that Joan would have done whatever it took to obtain wine. Of course, this is highly defeasible. If obtaining wine required a trip to the liquor store, the effort required might have conflicted with other desires Joan had at the time (continuing her conversation with family members, relaxing after a long day, and so on). The fact that teleological explanations support counterfactuals will play a critical role in defusing some objections to teleological realism, so I will return to this topic in the next chapter.

Second, it is worth noting that teleological explanations as characterized here are quite different from evolutionary explanations of the existence of traits. On the face of things, the two sorts of explanations look similar, for many biological explanations appear to have a teleological form:

Tyrannosaurus rex had sharp teeth for eating meat.

Flowers have bright colors to attract bees.

Most animals have eyes in order to see.

In these cases, the general form is this: Species K has trait T for purpose G. Explanations of this form gesture at a familiar evolutionary story: At some point, an ancestor of the current members of K developed trait T through a genetic mutation, or a series of genetic mutations, and this trait was passed to its offspring. The trait T in turn helped those animals with it to attain G, and G was, under the circumstances, favorable for the survival and reproduction of those organisms. Given survival pressures, the favorability of G, and the heritability of the trait T, trait T came to dominate the relevant population. One might argue about the precise details of how to reduce selectional explanations to purely causal terms, but clearly the beauty of Darwinian evolutionary theory is that biological explanation no longer involves anything above and beyond the mechanistic principles of physical science. It is fine to use the shorthand version that sounds teleological, but the teleological version is a stand in for the longer story wherein there is no agent who *did* something for the sake of achieving G. There is no *genuine* purpose involved anymore. We could put this another way: When making evolutionary explanations, any appeal to the rationality principle is merely heuristic and can be spelled out in purely causal terms. Teleological realism claims that no such reductive story can be told concerning the typical teleological explanations of CSP. When we say that Joan went to the kitchen in order to get wine, this will not reduce to a story about the survival value of some genetic propensity on Joan's part. Of course, human beings are the product of evolution, and we can give evolutionary explanations of many of our traits and dispositions. That is to say, we can ask and answer causal questions about how we came to have certain characteristics. But when we give a genuinely teleological explanation of a piece of behavior, we are simply not asking that sort of question and we are not looking for that sort of explanation; rather, we are seeking to know the state of affairs toward which the agent's behavior was directed. (For a positive attempt to encompass CSP within evolutionary modes of explanation, see Millikan 1984.)

Finally, (R_1) and (R_2) as stated might be a bit misleading, for they might convey the impression that I am trying to reduce agency to facts about circumstances, epistemic states, intentional states, and appropriateness. This is not the aim of the account. I don't mean to reduce agency to some other kind of facts, even if those facts are themselves not reducible to the facts of physical science. Facts about agency belong in a circle of concepts that include intentional facts, epistemic facts, facts about appropriateness, rationality, reasonableness, and value. But the point is not to *define* agency in terms of other facts in this circle. Thus, (R_1) and (R_2) are meant to state truths about agents, but they are not meant to give a reductive set of necessary and sufficient conditions for being an agent.

10 | Objections to the Teleological Account

In the previous chapter, I gave an account of how we make teleological explanations. Before investigating some possible objections, I will summarize the principal elements. The account begins with a general principle that governs our theorizing about agents:

(R) Given two theories of an agent, it is unreasonable to believe one according to which the agent is significantly less rational.

In cashing out this principle, I noted that the rationality of a piece of behavior can be assessed along two axes, and that built into (R) is the expectation that agents will be rational in both ways:

(R_1) Agents act in ways that are appropriate for achieving their goals, given the agent's circumstances, epistemic situation, and intentional states.

(R_2) Agents have goals that are of value, given the agent's circumstances, epistemic situation, and intentional states.

I then argued that, in trying to find a teleological explanation according to which an agent ϕd in order to ψ, we operate the axes suggested by (R_1) and (R_2) by doing the following:

(I_1) Find a ψ such that ϕing is optimally appropriate for ψing, given a viable theory of the agent's intentional states and circumstances.

(I_2) Find a ψ such that ψing is the most valuable state of affairs toward which ϕing could be directed, given a viable theory of the agent's intentional states and circumstances.

In determining the correct teleological explanation of a piece of behavior, we do our best to jointly satisfy (I_1) and (I_2).

In this chapter, I will canvass various possible objections to this account.

10.1 Davidson's Challenge

Donald Davidson's landmark article "Actions, Reasons and Causes" (1963) convinced most of the philosophical world that action explanation is a species of causal explanation. Of course, Davidson's attack was not aimed at the details of the present account, but it will be worthwhile to explore his critique from this vantage point.

On the face of things, Davidson simply poses a challenge to noncausalist approaches:

> If, as Melden claims, causal explanations are "wholly irrelevant to the understanding we seek" of human action then we are without an analysis of the 'because' in "He did it because . . . ," where we go on to name a reason. . . . I would urge that, failing a satisfactory alternative, the best argument for [a causal account] is that it alone promises to give an account of the "mysterious connection" between reasons and actions. (ibid., p. 11)

Davidson asks for an alternative to a causal construal of the 'because' in action explanation. But even apart from the details of the above account, it seems that a teleological construal should have been obvious: we can read "Vera went to the café because she wanted coffee" as claiming that Vera went to the café in order to satisfy her desire for coffee. So why has this alternative view of action been so widely ignored by philosophers since Davidson? The answer here has to do, in part, with the state of philosophy of action in the years immediately preceding Davidson's article. Many Wittgenstein-inspired authors thought that reasons couldn't be causes, although such authors were not very explicit in saying what reason explanation was if not causal. Davidson rightly exposed the inadequacy of their arguments against the causal construal; then, in that context, he placed on the table his challenge for an alternative reading of the 'because' in action explanations. This gave his question substantial rhetorical force.

Davidson also discussed a type of case that is handled well by causal theories, but which would seem to pose more difficulty for a noncausal account:

> . . . a person can have a reason for an action, and perform the action, and yet this reason not be the reason why he did it. Central to the relation between a reason and an action it explains is the idea that the agent performed the action because he had the reason. Of course, we can include this idea too in justification; but then the notion of justification becomes as dark as the notion of reason until we can account for the force of that 'because'. (ibid., p. 9)

If one simply claims that reason explanations justify the behavior, Davidson's challenge has some force. But it is not clear that his argument has any bite against teleological realism. Briefly put, teleological explanations support certain counterfactual conditionals, and this will allow us to distinguish the reason for which an agent acted from other nonmotivating reasons.

For example, suppose that Sally is faced with a sad situation: Her elderly father is terminally ill and comatose, and the doctors say that there is no hope that he will ever revive. He can be kept alive by machines, or Sally can decide to end the life support and he will die naturally. Sally desires that her father be allowed to die with dignity, and she believes that withdrawing life support will allow him to do that. At the same time, Sally wants to buy a new boat, and she will be able to do that if she pulls the plug on her father, for she will then be relieved of the enormous hospital bills. Thus, Sally has two reasons that would justify ending the life support: allowing her father to die with dignity and enabling herself to buy a new boat. She decides to withdraw the life support. However, as Davidson notes, we can coherently suppose that Sally acted for only one of those reasons, even though both were served by the action. For the proponent of the causal theory of action, this simply means that only one of the two desires played a causal role in the production of the behavior. Davidson's challenge would be as follows: How can the teleological realist make sense of the idea that Sally acted because of only one of the two reasons?

However, the teleological realist can answer Davidson's challenge. According to (R_1), agents act in ways that are appropriate for achieving their goals, given the agents' circumstances, epistemic situations, and intentional states. As was noted in the last chapter, this means that a wide variety of counterfactual conditionals will hold of an agent. Suppose that Sally withdrew life support only because she wanted her father to die with dignity, and not because this would help her to buy a new boat. (To put it in more directly teleological terms, suppose she was directing her behavior only at the goal of allowing her father to die with dignity and not toward the state of affairs in which she has a new boat.) If this is true of Sally, we would expect that, had the circumstances been altered, her behavior would have remained appropriate to allowing her father to die with dignity, but would not have necessarily remained appropriate for buying a boat. For example, suppose that the hospital charged a large fee for withdrawing life support, such that this course of action was actually more expensive for Sally than allowing her father to stay on the machines.

In this case, withdrawing life support would still have served the goal of allowing her father to die with dignity, but it would have been detrimental to her ability to buy a new boat. If in those circumstances Sally still would have withdrawn life support, that is good evidence that in the actual circumstances she was directing her behavior only toward allowing her father to die with dignity. Thus, although she had a standing desire to buy a new boat, and although withdrawing the life support promoted the satisfaction of that desire, her behavior was not directed toward the goal of buying a boat. On the other hand, suppose that a well-endowed anti-euthanasia group offered to pay for the father's continued hospitalization. If, given this turn of events, Sally would have decided to keep her father on life support while eagerly going to the boat yard, we would conclude that Sally's actual behavior (withdrawing life support) was directed, at least in large part, toward the goal of buying a boat.

In more general and abstract terms, the picture is as follows. If an agent has a desire for X and a desire for Y, each of which would be served by behavior the agent performs, then we have two candidate teleological explanations:

A φd in order to achieve X.

A φd in order to achieve Y.

When we are determining which of these is true, we can look at a variety of counterfactual situations. We will ask questions like the following: Would A still have φd if circumstances were such that φing would achieve X but would be detrimental to achieving Y? If circumstances were such that achieving X would have required a different action, ψ, but ψing would have been detrimental to achieving Y, what would the agent have done? Basically speaking, we look at the agent's behavior in the counterfactual situations and determine the goal or goals for which her behavior would have been appropriate. We will have to restrict which counterfactual circumstances we look at in some ways—excluding, for example, counterfactual situation in which the agent's φing would serve some new goal that had not been on the table before. The general point is that we are looking at counterfactual situations to see what account of the agent's behavior makes the most rational sense. Thus, the sort of case that Davidson proposes is not enough to undermine the teleological alternative to causalism.

However, support of counterfactuals is a feature one associates with causal explanations; if teleological explanations are said to support counterfactuals as well, then one might see this as renewed grounds for seeing teleological explanations as little more than causal explanations in disguise. In other words, the very fact that teleological explanations support counterfactuals might seem to suggest that there must ultimately be some successful analysis. However, the objection can be answered, for it turns out that causal explanations do not support the same sort of counterfactual conditionals as are supported by teleological explanations. To see this, it will help to proceed slowly.

We have a teleological explanation of the form

(1) A ϕd in order to ψ.

The causal construal of (1) would presumably look something like

(2) A's desire for ψ caused her to ϕ.

On the basis of (R_1), the teleological realist claims that teleological explanations of the form of (1) support counterfactuals of the following forms:

(3) Ceteris paribus, if ψing had required πing, A would have πd.

(4) Ceteris paribus, if A had not had the goal of ψing, A would not have ϕd.

And it was this sort of counterfactual support that raised the accusation that the teleological explanation must ultimately be reducible to the causal explanation, for support of counterfactual conditionals is the hallmark of causal explanation. But causal explanations do not support the same counterfactuals. We typically assume that an explanation of the form

(5) C caused E

supports counterfactuals of the form

(6) Ceteris paribus, had it not been for C, E would not have occurred.

Thus, (2) would support

(7) Ceteris paribus, if A had not desired ψ, then A would not have ϕd.

There is much similarity between (7) and (4); be that as it may, the teleological explanation (1) also supports (3), and (3) is different from (7). Now, (3) says that A would have done whatever it took to ψ, while (7) says that A would not have ϕd if A had not desired to ψ. The causal explanation in (2) does not support anything quite like (3). So teleological explanations and causal explanations do not support the same counterfactuals, and thus there is no evidence here to support the claim that teleological explanations must be reducible to causal explanations. Quite the contrary; the fact that teleological explanations support a form of counterfactual not supported by causal explanation strongly suggests that teleological explanation is not reducible to causal explanation.

I am not claiming that the causalist is utterly unable to account for the truth of (3). Given an appropriate account of the nature of mental states, (3) will be a likely consequence. However, it will be the theory of the nature of mental states, rather than the causal construal of action explanation, that does the work in supporting (3). Thus the fact that the teleological explanation in (1) supports (3) yields no reason for thinking that (1) must be a causal explanation in disguise.

10.2 Obscurity and the Spectrum of Cases

One might have a second, relatively independent concern about teleological explanation. One can construct a spectrum of cases which indicates that it is unclear just when teleological explanations do and do not apply. Consider the following events:

(1) A rock remains motionless on the ground.

(2) A marble rolls down the inside edge of a bowl.

(3) A heat-seeking missile turns toward the north.

(4) A plant turns toward the sun.

(5) A spider runs across the web.

(6) A cat climbs up a tree.

(7) Jackie goes to the kitchen.

For each of these events, one might put forward the following explanations, each of which has an apparently teleological form:

(1a) The rock remained motionless in order to maintain a constant velocity.

(2a) The marble rolled down the inside edge of the bowl in order to reach the bottom of the bowl.

(3a) The heat-seeking missile turned toward the north in order to destroy the target.

(4a) The plant turned toward the sun in order to maximize its exposure to sunlight.

(5a) The spider ran across the web in order to collect the trapped prey.

(6a) The cat climbed up a tree in order to avoid the dog.

(7a) Jackie went the kitchen in order to get a glass of wine.

The seven explanations vary in their degrees of plausibility. The event described in (7) is a paradigmatic case of teleologically explicable behavior, and the corresponding explanation seems perfectly ordinary. We are also normally willing to put forward explanations like (6a) and maybe (5a), though some might claim that these are merely "as if" explanations and are not true teleological explanations. Explanation (4a) sounds more strained; we are not comfortable with its apparent suggestion that we view the plant as an agent aiming for a particular goal. Explanation (3a) sounds odder yet; we want to add that, really, the missile is controlled by a feedback mechanism such that it is caused to turn in the direction of a hot object; we would want to resist any attribution of agency to the missile. Explanation (2a) seems even further off the mark; the marble is simply the subject of gravitational force and is in no way aiming for the bottom of the bowl. (This particular example is from Bedau 1992.) Similarly, the rock maintains its constant velocity because the forces on it at that moment are approximately equal; no one would suggest that it has the goal or object of so doing.

This spectrum of cases might be taken to indicate that we are not always clear on when or how to use teleological language. While our intuitions are relatively clear concerning the ends of the spectrum, the cases in the middle are more difficult. Moreover, in all seven cases, the behavior of the object exhibits plasticity, which has often been taken (see e.g. Collins 1987) to be the prime hallmark of teleologically explicable behavior. In each of the above cases, the object indeed manifests a certain degree of plasticity with respect to the claimed goal. For example, in the face of a large number of perturbations, the marble will ultimately arrive back at the bottom of the bowl. And the rock will maintain a constant velocity in a very large array of possible circumstances. Thus, the spectrum of cases appears to show not only that we are unclear on the applicability conditions of teleological explanation but also that this particular range of cases indicates that at least one trademark of teleology is, by itself, unhelpful in distinguishing genuinely goal-directed behavior from non-goal-directed behavior.

The apparent obscurity might be thought to indicate that teleological explanation, if legitimate at all, must be reducible to causal explanation. If we knew that each of the explanations (1a)–(7a) amounted to a particular kind of causal explanation, then, by ascertaining the truth of the corresponding causal explanation, we could determine the aptness of the teleological locutions. This might require that we gather further evidence, but all difficulties would in principle be resolvable. Without a causal analysis, it will be alleged that the obscurity problem is insoluble, and that this indicates that teleological explanations are not to be taken seriously.

The spectrum of cases thus places several demands on an account of teleological explanation. First, the account must square with our clear intuitions, e.g., about the rock, the marble, and the person. (An account based solely on plasticity would fail even this test.) Second, the account must clarify and systematize our less clear intuitions. That is, it should tell us what to say about the unclear cases, or at least provide some idea of what further facts would be relevant to deciding them. Moreover, the account should explain why our intuitions are fuzzy in these cases.

However, I think that the account given in the previous chapter can answer these concerns. I'll start with a couple of general observations about the account, and then apply them to the spectrum of cases. First, according to (R_2), agents have goals that are of value, given the agent's circumstances and intentional states. Thus, if an agent directs her behavior toward a goal, that goal must have some intelligible value. However, isolated states of affairs cannot simply be of value to an agent. As Anscombe points out, the question "What's the good of it?" is "something that can be asked until a desirability characterisation has been reached and made intelligible" (1957, p. 74). As an example of the point, she asks what would happen if someone announced "I want a saucer of mud":

He is likely to be asked what for; to which let him reply that he does not want it for anything, he just wants it. It is likely that the other will then perceive that a philosophical example is all that is in question, and will pursue the matter not further; but supposing that he did not realise this, and yet did not dismiss our man as a dull babbling loon, would he not try to find out in what aspect the object desired is desirable? Does it serve as a symbol? Is there something delightful about it? Does the man want to have something to call his own and no more? (1957, p. 70)

The point I want to take from the example is this: The state of affairs toward which an agent directs her behavior will be of value for the agent because it exemplifies some general feature whose desirability is intelligible. But this means that other states of affairs that exemplify the same general feature will also, to that extent, be of value to the agent in question. That is to say, once a system is within the realm of genuine agents for whom states of affairs have value and disvalue in certain respects, many different states of affairs will be of value or disvalue to the agent.

I would suggest further that if a state of affairs has value for an agent insofar as the state of affairs exhibits some general property, then states of affairs must also have value (either negative or positive) for the agent, insofar as they exhibit *other* general properties. A system would not truly be an agent if its behavior were plastic and persistent with respect to states of affairs with just one property in common. For example, whereas it is perfectly natural to act for the welfare of one's children, one cannot imagine a genuine agent whose only goal is the welfare of his or her children. (One might even give overriding importance to the welfare of one's children, but this is quite different from having no other goals that are of value.) The notion of value is much more complex. Roughly speaking, states of affairs have value given a life into which they fit. For a genuine agent, many different kinds of states of affairs will have value and disvalue. The agent will direct its behavior toward those states of affairs with value (from its perspective) and away from those with disvalue. Thus, the account of teleological explanation indicates that a genuine agent will have a system of goals toward which it directs its behavior in various circumstances.

With these reflections in hand, we can see that the teleological account of action explanation accords with our clear intuitions in cases (1)–(3). (R_2) requires that agents have goals that are of value; i.e., genuine agents are the sort of thing for which states of affairs can have value. The motionless rock indeed exhibits some degree of plasticity with respect to the claimed goal of maintaining a constant velocity. But the rock is not the sort of thing for which states of affairs have value. Nothing about the rock gives us any reason to believe that the rock feels pleasure, satisfaction, or pain, so it would be hard to get a grip on the idea that there are states of affairs that are of value to the rock. Moreover, before we can say that the rock is an agent we must be able to attribute to the rock a relatively complex system of goals. But in any such candidate system, the rock would be a manifest failure at achieving these goals, for the rock's repertoire of behavior is simply not rich enough for us to interpret the rock as directing its behavior toward a complex system of goals. Any theory of the rock as an agent would make the rock highly irrational. And, as has been discussed in the context of the rationality principle (R), if all candidate theories make a putative agent massively irrational, we should conclude that we are not dealing with an agent at all. This reasoning clearly rules out the motionless rock, the marble in a bowl, and the heat-seeking missile; these are not systems for which states of affairs have value, and hence they are not agents that exhibit goal-directed behavior.

The requirement that agents have systems of goals also implies that plants are not agents. As was noted in (4), certain plants slowly move in a way that keeps them facing the sunlight. Many plants also have a behavioral repertoire that is more complex than that of a rock; they grow, produce seeds, shed leaves in the winter, and so forth. Nonetheless, it is difficult to imagine attributing to a plant even a moderately complex system of goals such that the plant's behavior is flexible and persistent with respect to attaining those goals. Since plants are rooted to the ground, they will exhibit a range of behavior that is far less complex than that of animals. "If you root yourself to the ground," Patricia Churchland memorably noted, "you can afford to be stupid." (1986, p. 13) For any complex system of goals that we might contemplate attributing to a plant, the plant would come out as notably irrational, for its behavior would be limited and not effective at achieving many of those goals. Thus, plants do not count as genuine agents, and explanations like (4a) are not genuine teleological explanations.

Even though (4a) cannot be counted as a genuine teleological explanation, we often speak in such terms, even in scientific contexts. For example: "Stomatal openings are necessary to admit carbon dioxide to the leaf interior and to allow oxygen to escape during photosynthesis, hence transpiration has been considered by some authorities to be merely an unavoidable phenomenon that accompanies the real functions of the stomates." ("Transpiration," Encyclopaedia Britannica Online) On the surface, this appears to be a discussion of teleological purpose of transpiration in trees. However, I take this to be a form of biological, functional explanation discussed briefly in the last chapter. The function of the stomates is not a genuine teleological purpose. As I suggested in chapter 9, functional explanations in biology typically have something like the following form: Species K has trait T for purpose G. To say that the plant has stomates for purpose G is to say that ancestors of the plant developed stomates through some series of genetic mutations, and that the stomates in turn helped those plants to attain G, and G was favorable for the survival and reproduction of those plants. Any appeal to the rationality principle in such explanations is merely heuristic. Of course there is nothing wrong with explaining plant traits in apparently teleological terms, so long as we keep in mind that this is a metaphorical stand-in for the selectional explanation.

The case of the spider is a bit more complicated. We routinely explain spider behavior with the likes of (5a). Indeed, the particular example is taken, in only slightly paraphrased form, from a *Scientific American* article on the behavior of spiders (Vollrath 1992). The actual quote runs as follows: "The spider runs about on top of the sheet to collect prey that have fallen or jumped on board." The author makes no apology for the teleological language, and it is certainly true that the behavior of spiders and similar creatures can appear to be genuinely goal directed.

However, when one probes a bit more deeply, the initial appearances can look deceiving. Here is a famous description of some interesting wasp behavior:

> When the time comes for egg laying, the wasp Sphex builds a burrow for the purpose and seeks out a cricket which she stings in such a way as to paralyze but not kill it. She drags the cricket into the burrow, lays her eggs alongside, closes the burrow, then flies away, never to return. In due course, the eggs hatch and the wasp grubs feed off the paralyzed cricket, which has not decayed, having been kept in the wasp equivalent of deep freeze. . . . The Wasp's routine is to bring the paralyzed cricket to the burrow, leave it on the threshold, go inside to see that all is well, emerge, and then drag the cricket in. (Wooldridge 1963, p. 82, quoted in Dennett 1984, p. 11)

Checking the burrow seems a good idea, since the wasp might discover a centipede or another wasp inside the burrow, and either of these would pose a danger (Brockman et al. 1979); the wasp would presumably be more vulnerable to such dangers when trying to drag a paralyzed cricket into the burrow. So we are tempted to say that the wasp dropped the cricket before checking the burrow in order to preserve its own safety.

However, Wooldridge writes,

> If the cricket is moved a few inches away while the wasp is inside making her preliminary inspection, the wasp, on emerging from her burrow, will bring the cricket back to the threshold, but not inside, and will then repeat the preparatory procedure of entering the burrow to see that everything is all right. If again the cricket is removed a few inches while the wasp is inside, once again she will move the cricket up to the threshold and re-enter the burrow for a final check. The wasp never thinks of pulling the cricket straight in. On one occasion this procedure was repeated forty times, always with the same result. (1963, p. 82)

According to (R_1), we presuppose that agents act in ways that are appropriate for achieving their goals, and this holds for the agent's behavior in both actual and counterfactual circumstances. In the actual circumstances, the wasp drops the cricket and moves into the burrow, and this seems appropriate to the alleged goal of preserving itself from predators. On the other hand, we know from the experiment that if the cricket is moved a few inches, the wasp will repeat the whole maneuver. But this behavior is not appropriate to the goal of preserving the wasp's safety; repeatedly checking the burrow provides no new evidence of its being free from predators, wastes effort, exposes the wasp to danger, and makes it more likely that its cricket will be stolen. The optimal behavior for the wasp would be to get on with it and go into the burrow. Thus, the wasp, in the experimental circumstances, is clearly not optimal or reasonable with respect to the claimed goal of preserving its safety. Since the wasp we see in the actual circumstances would act the same way as the wasp in the experiment in those circumstances, we conclude that the wasp is not rationally directing its behavior.

Of course, the wasp's actual behavior does help to preserve its safety and its ability to have offspring, and this is no mere coincidence. The wasp's disposition to drop the cricket and check the burrow presumably has an evolutionary explanation. But the experiment shows that if you take the wasp ever so slightly out of its evolutionary niche, it will no longer behave in an optimal or appropriate way. Evolution has given the wasp dispositions toward behaviors that will tend to propagate its DNA under the right circumstances. (That is true of us humans too, of course.) But if we tried to consider the wasp as a rational agent seeking that end, the wasp would turn out to be woefully inadequate. If the experiment with the wasp Sphex is at all indicative, it seems highly unlikely that we can construct a successful theory according to which the wasp has a system of values and directs its behavior (in both actual and counterfactual circumstances) to achieving appropriate goals. The wasp is not an agent directing its behavior. Or so it would appear, but I stand ready to be corrected if wasp behavior turns out to be much more subtle and complex than I have reason to believe.

I reach the same conclusion regarding the spider, though I hasten to admit that I know even less about spider behavior than about wasp behavior. Nonetheless, my strong suspicion is that we would be unable to construct even a minimally successful theory of a spider as a rational agent, especially if we take into account nearby counterfactual situations. Our intuitions are a little fuzzy in this case for two reasons. First, the fact that the spider has been "designed" by evolution to promote its DNA survival can give it dispositions to behave in ways that look intelligent with respect to goals such as eating and ensuring the well being of its offspring, so long as the spider stays within circumstances very similar to those of its ancestors. Second, most of us have only limited knowledge of spider behavior.

When we reach the explanation of the cat's behavior ("the cat climbed up a tree in order to avoid the dog") we may be on firmer ground. Although we cannot attribute to cats a system of goals with anything like the complexity of the goals attributable to human beings, cat behavior seems sufficiently rich and sophisticated to warrant attribution of a relatively complex set of goals. Moreover, we can get a grip on the idea that various kinds of states of affairs are of value from the cat's perspective: eating, being fed, being let outside, being let back inside, having its belly scratched, etc. Thus, it seems reasonably clear that teleological explanations of cat behavior are at least sometimes warranted, though perhaps with a somewhat attenuated force.

The objection had been that the applicability conditions of teleological explanation are hopelessly obscure unless teleological explanations are reducible to causal explanations. The account above attempts to meet this objection by drawing attention to some of the factors that are relevant in reaching teleological judgments. Although the account still leaves us far short of a mechanical decision procedure for determining the truth of teleological claims, the account does, I hope, make teleological explanation less mysterious.

10.3 Mele's Challenge

Mele (2000) has defended the causal theory of action explanation and has argued against teleological accounts of action explanation. The heart of Mele's argument is an example involving a man named Norm and some powerful Martians:

[The Martians'] aim was to make it seem to [Norm] that he is acting while preventing him from even trying to act by selectively shutting down portions of his brain. To move his body, they zap him in the belly with M rays that control the relevant muscles and joints. When they intervene, they wait for Norm to begin a routine activity, read his mind to make sure that he plans to do what they think he is doing . . . and then zap him for a while—unless the mind-reading team seems him abandon or modify his plan. When the team notices something of this sort, the Martians stop interfering and control immediately reverts to Norm.

A while ago, Norm started climbing a ladder to fetch his hat. When he reached the midway point, the Martians took over. Although they controlled Norm's next several movements while preventing him from trying to do anything, they would have relinquished control to him if his plan had changed (e.g., in light of a belief that the location of his hat had changed). (2000, p. 284–285)

In this case, Norm intends to move up the ladder and thinks he is directing his behavior. He is aware of what he is doing, and his behavior is even sensitive to changes in his plans—if his intentions change, the Martians will relinquish control and Norm will act in accord with his new plan. Norm seems to meet the requirements that teleological realists have typically put forward as indicative of goal-directed activity. And yet, Mele says, it is clear that Norm was not acting at all, for the Martians were in complete control of his body and prevented him from even trying to fetch his hat. Mele's suggestion is that the causalist, but not the teleological realist, can explain why Norm's motion up the ladder fails to be a goal-directed action.

It is not trivial for a causalist to explain why Norm's behavior fails to count as an action. After all, by hypothesis, Norm's intention did cause his bodily motion—albeit via an indirect route involving Martians. The causalist will have to say that in this case the desire did not cause the bodily motion "in the right way." And that can land the causalist in a long debate. (See chapter 7.) However, I will accept, for the sake of argument, that the causalist can accommodate this case.

I will make some general comments about the case of Norm, then look at it in relation to the account of teleological explanation given in chapter 9. First, given the small amount of information we have about the case, it is not obvious that Norm's behavior fails to be an action. Suppose that instead of fetching his hat, Norm is doing something of grave moral concern: shooting his philosophy professor. At the moment when Norm is picking up the gun and about to shoot it, the Martians take over his body and make it carry out the dirty deed. However, they make it seem to Norm as if he is acting, and if Norm had changed his mind and decided to put the gun down, the Martians would have immediately relinquished control, and Norm would not have committed the murder. Now, at his murder trial, it comes out that the Martians controlled Norm's body at the time of the shooting. Does this completely absolve Norm of responsibility for shooting his professor? Should the district attorney only charge Norm with having a plan to commit murder, and drop the actual murder charge? It is not obvious to me how to answer these questions. Accordingly, even in the routine case of going up the ladder, I take it not to be obvious that Norm failed to act.

What we say about such examples might depend on further details about the supposedly controlling agent. What if it were God, instead of Martians? And suppose God never relinquished control but always moved our bodies exactly in accord with our intentions and plans? This would look like a variety of occasionalism, and I would lose any strong intuition that we would fail to be agents of our behavior.

I am willing to grant Mele that Norm's behavior is not an action, but I think that these observations shed light on the oddness of the example. (And I don't mean the M rays or the Martians; for better or worse, we philosophers are used to that sort of oddness.) What is odd about the case is the motivation of the Martians. They periodically take control of Norm's body, but only to make him do exactly what he planned to do anyway. Why? What's in it for the Martians? One senses that the Martians are giving a benign demonstration of a powerful technology that could easily be put to much more nefarious use. And in this implicit feature of the example lies the reason we are inclined to think that Norm's behavior was not an action. Mele stipulates that the Martians are going to make Norm's body do exactly what Norm planned to do anyway. If this were an ironclad promise from the Martians, or, better yet, something that followed necessarily from their good nature, then we would be back at something very like occasionalism, and I have little problem saying that Norm is still acting, despite the fact that the causal chain involved is an unusual one. If he commits a murder under these circumstances, we will definitely not let him off.

However, since Mele uses Martians rather than God, he thereby suggests that their plan—to relinquish control if Norm changes his mind—is a contingent one. The Martians have chosen not to disrupt Norm's plans on this occasion, but there are no guarantees that they will always use their powerful technology in such a benign manner. If the desires and intentions of the Martians had been different, then Norm's body would have moved very differently. For example, if the Martians had decided to make Norm's body jump off of the ladder's top rung, then that is what would have happened. How Norm's body moves at the time is completely at the whim of the Martians. For a wide range of counterfactual situations, namely those involving different desires on the part of the Martians, Norm's behavior will be far from appropriate for achieving his goals.

In terms of my account of the epistemology of teleology, this means that, at the moment in question, Norm fails to satisfy the condition imposed by (R_1). His behavior is ultimately appropriate to the goals and values of the Martians, rather than his own. As it happens, Norm's body does move in accord with his goals, but this is only because of the happy fact that the Martians made that decision. The Martians also happen to have made the decision that if Norm's plans change, they will stop the M rays, and Norm will be back to normal. But again, so long as these are just decision that the Martians happen to have made (for no especially compelling reason), then there are plenty of very nearby counterfactual circumstances in which Norm's behavior is not appropriate to achieving his goals. Since Norm fails, at that time, to satisfy the condition imposed by (R_1), his behavior does not count as goal directed on my account of the epistemology of teleology. And thus my account is in accord with the intuitions the case is meant to engender.

One might reply by trying to seal off those counterfactual possibilities; for example, one might stipulate that it is in the Martians' nature that they only want to see Norm's plans fulfilled. In that case, (R_1) is still true of Norm, and it looks as if I have to say that his behavior is goal directed. However, with this revision to the example, it seems to me that this is the right thing to say, for I lose the intuition that Norm's behavior was a non-action. If the Martians are Godlike in their intentions and effectiveness, then the situation looks again like a temporary occasionalism, and I would suggest that Norm's agency is intuitively still intact. Thus, with either version of the example, teleological realism gives an intuitively acceptable diagnosis of the case of Norm and the Martians.

Mele's objection had been that the teleological realist's account was too liberal—the criteria given would count Norm as genuinely acting when our intuitive judgment is that he was not acting. I argued that this is mistaken, and that the teleological realist is able to accommodate our intuition that Norm is not acting. One might fear that I have gone too far in the other direction, and that my account is now too restrictive, in that it will fail to count as goal directed some behaviors that are, intuitively speaking, goal directed. Consider Sally, who is about to pull the trigger of a gun, thereby murdering her philosophy professor. Sally has an odd neurological disorder, such that when she attempts to make a finger-pulling motion of the required sort, it is very often the case that her finger becomes paralyzed, and instead of the finger pulling motion, her body goes through any number of other random motions. However, as things happen, she pulls the trigger successfully, and murders the professor. Intuitively, it seems reasonably clear that Sally's behavior counts as a goal-directed action.

I argued that Norm's motion is not that of an agent, because in a range of nearby counterfactual situations his behavior is not appropriate to his goals. Specifically, in all those situations in which the Martians simply change their mind about what they want to have Norm's body do, Norm's body will do something quite different. Suppose that whether Sally's finger makes the intended motion or instead becomes paralyzed depends on some random events in her nervous system. Had those events gone differently, her behavior would not have been appropriate to her goals. The suggestion is that, like Norm, Sally fails to satisfy the condition imposed by (R_1) and thus teleological realism should not count her as a genuine agent at the time in question.[1]

However, I think that the teleological realist can distinguish between the cases of Norm and Sally. Norm's behavior fails to be appropriate to his goals in a much wider array of nearby counterfactual situations than is true of Sally's behavior. For example, if the Martians had decided to make Norm's body leap off the ladder, that is what Norm's body would have done, regardless of Norm's intentions or desires. In other words, depending on the whim of the Martians, Norm's bodily motions might have no connection to his desires and intentions. In Sally's case, given that she decides to make a

trigger-pulling motion with her finger, there are a number of nearby counterfactual situations in which her body does something else, for we have
assumed that Sally has a strange neurological disorder that leads to random
bodily motions much of the time when she starts to pull her finger.
However, we are also assuming that her behavior is subject to these flukes
only when it involves a finger pulling. If Sally had decided not to shoot the
gun, to put it down, to do a jumping jack, or to scream, her behavior presumably would have been appropriate to her goals. Thus, given the scenario
as described, her behavior is generally very sensitive to her goals. So Sally,
unlike Norm, satisfies the condition imposed by (R₁) well enough to make
her an agent at the time in question.

One could alter the example by making Sally's neurological disorder
much more general, such that she rarely does what she intends; but with
that revision, my own intuitions about the case grow flimsy. I'm not sure
what to say about her agency in such a case, and I'm not too troubled by
the conclusion that she is not exhibiting genuine goal-directed behavior at
any particular moment.

10.4 Simplicity Challenge

Naturalistic explanations make essential use only of the concepts of physical science; in particular, naturalistic explanations will not employ normative, intentional or teleological terminology. Insofar as teleological
explanation is merely metaphorical or is reducible to naturalistic explanation, then it too makes essential use only of the concepts of physical science. However, the teleological realist claims that genuine teleological
explanations are irreducible. This can seem rather mysterious. When discussing the rock's motion (case (1) above), all the explanation we want or
need can be provided without any essential use of teleological locutions. I
suggested that the same holds for cases (2)–(5). However, all seven of the
systems in question, from the rock to the human being, are material things
equally subject to the laws of nature. So what justification can there be for
thinking that somewhere along the spectrum of cases a non-naturalistic
mode of explanation mysteriously kicks in? Is this not just a vain attempt
to put human beings, and maybe some other high-level animals, outside
the reach of natural science? It seems incumbent on the teleological realist
to provide reasonable answers to these questions.

The naturalist's worry can be given a sharper form if we put it in terms
of simplicity. We seek theories of the world that are as simple as possible,
and that means, at least in part, that we seek theories that leave us with the

fewest irreducible mysteries. Any theory of the world will presumably postulate some brute facts that are left unexplained: for example, physics has no explanation for the fact that a top quark weighs 40,200 times as much as an up quark or for the fact that the electromagnetic force is 10^{42} times the gravitational force. (These examples are from Greene 1999.) However, if a theory's irreducible mysteries are fully explained by an alternative theory, this is surely a significant embarrassment. (Hence, if string theory can explain the above facts, then, ceteris paribus, this would be a significant advantage for string theory over standard modern physics.) Applying this to the case at hand, if teleology is irreducible, then we have no explanation for why teleological explanation works, and in particular we have no explanation for why it works so well for some systems (e.g., human beings) but does not work for others (e.g., rocks). If we had a causal analysis of teleology, we would be able to answer these questions. In particular, we would expect that cognitive science would find the causal story underlying the cognition of humans and other animals, and that this causal story would explain the applicability and legitimacy of teleological concepts.

This objection poses a deep challenge for teleological realism. The quick answer is this: From the standpoint of simplicity, it would indeed be nice if teleological explanations were reducible to causal explanations. But no such reduction seems to be possible, and so we must ultimately accept teleology as irreducible. However, there is much more to be said about this objection, and I will return to it in chapter 13.

10.5 A Final Objection

Lastly, I turn to an objection that some readers may think I should have replied to long ago. The first version of the objection goes something like "Isn't it just overwhelmingly obvious that mental states cause behavior?" Jerry Fodor gives voice to something like this thought in characteristic fashion:

> . . . if it isn't literally true that my wanting is causally responsible for my reaching, and my itching is causally responsible for my scratching, and my believing is causally responsible for my saying . . . , if none of that is literally true, then practically everything I believe about anything is false and it's the end of the world. (1990, p. 156; second ellipsis in original)

At another point, Fodor refers to the causal account of action as the "common-sense view" (1990, p. 5). However, Fodor also admits that, as far as the Man on the Clapham Omnibus is concerned, "it is untendentious that people regularly account for the voluntary behavior by citing beliefs and desires," but he notes that it requires a "philosophical gloss" before we can read these explanations as causal (1990, p. 4). And that, in essence, is my response to the first version of the objection: It is indeed obvious that mental states often *explain* behavior, but it is far from *obvious* that these explanations are causal. Pre-philosophical common sense is committed to the former claim but not the latter.

This leads to a second form of the objection: Isn't it obvious that many of our explanatory locutions are most reasonably taken as causal? One might start with the word 'because' itself. It appears as the connective in many reason explanations, and, perhaps because it contains the word 'cause' as a proper part, the word might be thought to suggest that causal explanation is at work. In response, I suggest that 'because' signals that the explanatory factor is about to be named but gives us no particular insight into the nature of the explanation. It should also be noted that the word 'cause' itself does not always connote anything like the efficient causation of the physical sciences. We speak of someone's acting "with cause," or of someone's "having cause," and here 'cause' means something like *justifying reason*. Moreover, the etymology of 'because' suggests that the word implies nothing more than the *justifying reason* sense. According to the *Oxford English Dictionary*, 'because' entered the language in the form of the two-word phrase "by cause," usually followed by 'that' or 'why', followed by a subordinate clause. The subordinate clause would then express the relevant reason or purpose. I would not lean hard on etymology as a source of insight about the best philosophical reading of common-sense claims, but perhaps a little etymology can serve as an antidote to the claim that 'because' *must* be given a causal construal.

However, even granting that the word 'because' should not automatically be taken as causal, reason explanations use other connectives that might seem to invite a causal reading. For example:

(1) His overwhelming desire to win motivated him to cheat.

(2) His pity for the child moved him to action.

(3) Prompted by her desire for coffee, she went to the café.

(4) Her desire for fame caused her to audition for the part.

The word 'motivated' as it occurs in (1) might sound overtly causal to some, but to my ear it doesn't. 'Motivate' is just the verbal form of 'motive', which is another word for 'reason'; indeed, 'motive' comes from the French 'motif'.

Thus, as with 'because', the connective is far less causal than it might at first appear to be.

The word 'moved' in (2) sounds more causal, especially in contexts like "the wind moved his hat off the bench." However, when we speak of one's emotions' being moved, or of a moving performance by a musician, it is less clear that there are any directly causal implications. Construed as a teleological explanation, (2) is highly elliptical; the canonical form of a teleological explanation is "A ϕd in order to ψ," but in (2) we are given neither ϕ nor ψ—we aren't told what the agent did or what the agent was aiming to accomplish by doing it. Such elliptical explanations are hardly unusual, either in the context of reason explanations or of causal explanations. When they are not isolated philosophical examples, our claims about the world occur in a rich context in which certain facts are assumed and in which explanations "cut to the chase" by giving the new information. In the case of (2), the assumed background information presumably includes something about what child is being discussed, and perhaps information about what action the agent performed. In any event, the explanation suggests that the child in question is in a pitiable condition, and that the agent embarked on some course of action that was intended to alleviate that condition or to alleviate a similar condition in similarly situated children. The information given in (2) can still be construed along teleological lines. Mention of the agent's pity tells us something about the condition of the child, at least in the eyes of the agent, and it tells us something about what was of value about the agent's action. Feeling pity for someone's suffering can be a particularly vivid way of seeing that it would be good if the suffering were alleviated.

Similarly, it is not difficult to give teleological construals of (3) and (4). In (3) we take it that the agent is aiming for a state of affairs in which she has coffee in the way she desires; in (4) we take it that the agent has the goal of gaining fame in the way she desires. The mention of the mental states, again, says something about why these states of affairs were of value from the agent's perspective. While these explanations can and should be construed teleologically, I would not deny that the connectives used carry some connotation of causation. However, I would claim that the connotation is essentially metaphorical. Using a causal metaphor in a noncausal context is not unusual. For example, when speaking of reasons and arguments we say things like the following:

The premises forced that conclusion.

His argument was crushed.

She torpedoed that objection.

If there were no WMDs, that would cause the Administration's official rationale for invasion to collapse.

In each of these cases, we use causal language to provide a suggestive image, but we don't take it literally. Similarly, I suggest that, occasionally, the language used in action explanation metaphorically suggests a causal picture, but that it is not to be taken literally.

In some contexts, construing common-sense language as metaphorical might be seen as a desperate philosophical ploy. But in this case we should keep a couple of things in mind. First, while I acknowledge that some reason explanations employ causal language, many cases of reason explanation contain explicitly teleological language, using connectives such as "in order to," "for the purpose of," and "to." Unless we claim that CSP action explanation is hopelessly schizophrenic, both sides in this debate will have to do some careful interpretation of common-sense language. Second, we reached this point in the debate in a particular philosophical context. Specifically, I argued in chapter 7 that the attempt to reinterpret teleological language in causal terms fails; I argued in chapter 6 that CSP does not have the metaphysical commitments it would need to support causalism; I argued in chapter 5 that CSP does not look like the proto-science it would have to be for causalism to be true; and in the previous chapter and this one I laid out a teleological account of action explanation that, I submit, is plausible, and that answers the common objections against it. With all that in place, it is not much of a concession to admit that causal language occasionally enters, metaphorically, into action explanation.

Appendix: Dancy and Schueler

Two recent noncausal accounts of action explanation deserve close attention, and teleological realism can be clarified by comparison. The first of these is presented in Jonathan Dancy's *Practical Reality* (2000), the second in G. F. Schueler's *Reasons and Purposes* (2003).

Dancy

Dancy's account of action explanation is not causal, but it is not teleological either. Dancy says that explanation in terms of the agent's reasons is "normative explanation" (p. 159). For Dancy, a paradigmatic normative explanation of action would be "The ground on which he acted was that she had lied to him." (p. 132) This explanation cites a feature of the situation—that she lied to him—rather than some state of affairs toward which the agent directs his behavior, as would a teleological explanation. Two things are of immediate note here. First, the cited explanatory factor is a fact rather than a belief or a desire. (I discussed Dancy's claims about desires and the nature of reasons in chapter 9.) Second, the cited fact is something that obtains either at the time of action or before the action. In this sense, Dancy's normative explanation is backward looking, whereas teleological explanation is forward looking.

How do we determine which fact is the reason upon which the agent acted? At least in part, according to Dancy, the reason is the state of affairs that would justify the behavior. By itself, this would leave Dancy open to Davidson's challenge: More than one reason might justify an action, although agent acted on only one of the reasons. How does Dancy determine which one is the explanatory reason? Dancy answers that the reason that explains the agent's action is the one "in the light of which he acted" (p. 163). Dancy acknowledges that he offers "no analysis or philosophical account of the 'in light of' relation" (p. 163). This is analogous to my claim that reason explanation is *irreducibly* teleological and thus not to be analyzed in terms of causal locutions. However, Dancy goes on to note that "it would be good to produce an *account* of the 'in the light of' relation—if one could only think of some way of producing one" (p. 163). I take it that Dancy means that it would be good to have an account of how we make normative explanations, an account that would be analogous to what I called the epistemology of teleological explanation in chapter 9, but that he has no such account to give.

We might try to construct such an account by taking Dancy's metaphorical phrase "in the light of" seriously, but it is not clear that we could get very far. The metaphor is of reasons giving off a certain amount of light; perhaps the reason on which the agent acted was the one that gave off the most light, or simply was the one in whose light the agent chose to act. Either way, the picture of light-giving reasons suggests an agent consciously choosing which of two lamps to follow. Explaining the notion of agency in terms of conscious choice may not seem to have gotten us very far; worse yet, it is highly misleading, since many fully intentional actions are not performed with anything like a conscious viewing of reasons. For example, when I signal before making a turn in my car, I may not be consciously aware of having done it at all, much less am I consciously contemplating some light-giving reason for signaling. Many of our actions are even further from the light of conscious awareness. For example, in the previous sentence I typed the letter 'e' six times. Surely each time I struck the 'e' key on my keyboard it was an intentional bit of behavior; one could even specify reasons for each strike. However, my typing ability is good enough that I was far from conscious of each of these actions.

Whatever account Dancy gives of the "in the light of" relation, his view will run into a further objection. On Dancy's model, a reason explanation cites some fact in the light of which the agent acted, and the explanation is presumably intended, at least in part, to make rational sense of the agent and the behavior. However, citing a previous state of affairs in light of which the agent acted doesn't by itself make rational sense of the action. Consider the example quoted above: "The ground on which he acted was that she had lied to him." That she lied to him may be one part of the story behind what the agent is doing, but it doesn't yet tell us what the agent is trying to accomplish. Or consider another of Dancy's examples: "I am taking my car down to the garage because it is time for it to be serviced." (p. 99) This seems fairly routine, but even in this case there could be more than one end toward which the agent was directing his behavior. The obvious goal would be that of keeping the car in good repair, where the agent believes that this is particularly well promoted by bringing the car in on the manufacturer's recommended schedule. But it might be that the agent thinks that the manufacturer's recommendations are excessive, and that there is no genuine maintenance need involved; instead, he takes the car in on schedule merely to make it easier to resell the car by being able to honestly report that he adhered to the maintenance schedule. Or the fact that it is the recommended time may merely serve as his excuse to bring the car to the garage instead of doing some other task he would rather avoid.

The point is simply this: If we want to make rational sense of an action, we want to know what the agent was trying to accomplish. And that means that we will want a teleological explanation rather than what Dancy calls a normative explanation. Dancy could try to accommodate this point by limiting which facts could be cited in a normative explanation. In particular, he could say that the fact in light of which an agent acts is always a fact about what state of affairs would be promoted by the action. Thus, when we would teleologically explain behavior by saying that the agent ϕd in order to ψ, Dancy would say that the agent ϕd in light of the fact that ϕing would promote ψing. However, even this would still not be quite the same as describing what the agent was aiming at accomplishing. At least on the face of things, saying that one is acting in light of the fact that ϕing would promote ψing is compatible with saying that ψing is a foreseen but unintended consequence. If Dancy then rules out such readings of the "in the light of" relation, it might be arguable that his account becomes a disguised teleo-logical account rather than a backward-looking account. In any event, Dancy's examples indicate that he does have in mind a genuinely backward-looking explanation, and that his account as intended will lead to the objec-tion raised in the previous paragraph.

Another problematic aspect of Dancy's account stems from his insistence that psychological states are not reasons. In chapter 9, I discussed and rejected his claim that desires are never involved in reason explanations. Dancy also claims that even the agent's beliefs are not reasons; rather than citing beliefs, normative explanations will cite *facts* or states of affairs. If a lifeguard jumps into the water because a child is drowning, the lifeguard's reason is the fact that the child is drowning, not her *belief* about the child. This raises another question for Dancy, one of which he is well aware: What about cases where the agent's beliefs are false? Suppose the child was only pretending to be drowning and was actually in no trouble at all, and the lifeguard misread the situation and jumped into the water. How can Dancy explain this behavior? Dancy's answer is somewhat surprising. He says that "explanation of action in terms of the agent's reasons do not require such explanations to be factive" (p. 133). A factive verb is one that presupposes the truth of its object or argument; e.g., "Sue knows that p" presupposes that p is true. Thus, an explanation of the form "The reason why it is the case that p is that q" would be factive if it presupposed that q is true. Causal explanations are presumably factive; causes of an event must actually exist. But Dancy's claim that reason explanation is not factive comes to this: "She did it because p" does *not* presuppose that p holds. So the lifeguard can jump into the water because of the fact that the child was drowning, even if the child was not drowning. Dancy has some subtle and interesting things to say in defense of this view (see pp. 131–137), but I must admit that the view seems virtually paradoxical to me. Given that Santa Claus does not exist, it is very hard for me to see how the fact that Santa Claus exists can explain anything.

The lifeguard case is not similarly problematic for the teleological realist. In a teleological explanation, one explains the behavior by referring to the state of affairs toward which the behavior was directed. These will typically be states of affairs that do not currently obtain, but this does not mean that teleological explanation is nonfactive, for I am not claiming that some future state of affairs explains the present or past behavior. Rather, a teleo-logical explanation answers the question "To what end was the behavior directed?" There is no thing or state that does the explaining here. (See sec-tion 9.4.) So when the lifeguard jumps into the water to save the child from drowning, she is aiming for a state of affairs that does not obtain. But this situation is hardly unusual. Given that the child is not in fact drowning, we also know that she will not accomplish her goal of saving the child. But actions that are doomed to failure are neither paradoxical nor unheard of. We would need a compelling story to convince us that the lifeguard jumped in the water in order to become president, but in the specified circumstances her goal of saving the child was perfectly comprehensible and of intelligible value.

Schueler

Schueler (2003) says that action explanation is irreducibly teleological (p. 56), and in this respect his view is closely related to the one I have been defending. Nonetheless, it will be worth exploring some differences between the two.

Schueler's account of action explanation has a number of strands. He starts with the idea of an object having a purpose: "To say that something has a certain purpose is to say in part that it should do something, or is supposed to do something (i.e., according to the role it has been assigned in some plan or project someone has) ." (p. 6) For example, the system of shelves that surrounds my computer at home has the purpose of organizing incoming mail, and it has that purpose because I assigned it. It could come to have a different purpose, even without any physical change in the structure, if my wife and I were to decide that it would be better used in some other way. Schueler then says that actions are analogous to objects that have been assigned a purpose; he says that "reasons explanations of actions are purposive in the sense of 'purpose' explained in chapter 1 above, the sense in which, in order for something to have a purpose, someone must have a purpose for it" (p. 43).

However, it is not clear what it takes to *assign* a purpose to a bit of bodily behavior. There are some clear cases of explicitly assigning a purpose to behavior—e.g., a baseball coach telling his players that if he touches the bill of his cap that means "Take the next pitch." But assigning purposes in such an explicit and conscious way is surely not *required* for goal-directed behavior. I just now reached for a cup of water and took a drink, but it seems strained to say that I *assigned* my bodily motion the purpose of quenching my thirst. Or, to return to a different example, I performed an intentional action each time I typed the letter 'e' in the previous sentence, but I was certainly not aware of assigning a purpose to each keystroke. Of course, there is a sense in which my typing and drinking motions each played a role in a plan, so long as we don't require conscious awareness of the plan or explicit assignation of roles. But once we make these qualifications, it seems that we have said little more than this: purposive actions are those that are done with a purpose. Although I agree with Schueler that we should not expect a reductive analysis of teleological explanation, we will presumably hope to say more than this.

Later in his book, Schueler presents a more substantive characterization of what we are doing when we make teleological explanations. His discussion centers on an example in which he decides to vote for a tax increase that will pay for subsidized day care. In the example, he reasons as follows:

1. Subsidized day care is a good thing (I say to myself).
2. This proposed tax increase is necessary if there is to be subsidized day care in my community.
3. At the same time, it will cost me some money, which I would like to use elsewhere, if this tax increase is passed.
4. Still it is more important that my community have subsidized day care than that I keep for my own use the few dollars it will cost me each year.
5. So, I should vote for this increase. (p. 69)

As Schueler notes, this differs from the standard practical syllogism in that the reasoning weighs pros and cons. Schueler is quite right that the standard practical syllogism is lacking in this regard, and that the weighing of pros and cons is often a vital element in our practical reasoning. Schueler's claim is that we explain actions in terms of the agent's reasoning, where the agent's reasoning is construed in his way. Of course we do not always reason in the explicit manner Schueler envisages in the example; indeed, I would suggest that such explicit reasoning is comparatively rare. Schueler is under no illusions on this point, but he nonetheless claims that ascribing elements of such reasoning gets to the "heart of the matter":

It is not that an agent must explicitly subscribe to some evaluative premise, aloud or even silently to herself. Nor is it even that she must be willing to agree to some such premise if asked. It is rather that, in trying to understand what she did as an intentional action, we must *ascribe* to her some evaluative thought along the lines of premise 4 . . . if we are to understand her as acting for a reason, that is if we are to understand what she did as an intentional action at all. (p. 135)

In abstract terms, Schueler claims that if we are to see an agent as ϕing in order to ψ, we must be able to ascribe to her the evaluative thought, or *normative judgment* as he puts a bit later (p. 136), that ψing is more important, or better than, the alternatives to ψing. I would agree with Schueler that ψing must be of value from the agent's perspective, and that one part of what we are doing when explaining action is making rational sense of the behavior in this way. However, for a couple of reasons, it seems to me that Schueler takes the point too far.

First, Schueler's picture seems to be modeled on those occasions where we make very explicit and relatively momentous choices, and the picture is less appropriate and rather more strained when contemplating more mundane actions like taking a sip of coffee or getting up to walk to the bathroom. Apparently, for each such action we must ascribe an appropriate evaluative thought or normative judgment. The thoughts need not be conscious internal monologues, but it still seems that, on Schueler's account, there is a whole lot of thinking going on. In particular, Schueler could not attribute purposive action to a creatures unless he is also willing to attribute normative judgments to that creature.

Second, Schueler's account seems to make weakness of the will impossible. He seems fairly explicit about this at one point:

> . . . since practical reasoning necessarily involves a normative conclusion about what the agent should do (in the sense of what she has the *strongest reason* to do, what has *the most* to be said for it), understanding an agent as acting for a reason necessarily involves attributing to her that normative judgment, and hence some evaluations on the basis of which this judgment is made. (p. 136, emphasis added)

So it appears that any time we understand an agent as acting for a reason, we must attribute to her the judgment that she did what she had the strongest reason to do. It would then be literally impossible to understand an agent as acting for a reason but acting contrary to her own best judgment; thus, weakness of the will becomes impossible on Schueler's view. I side with John Searle (2001, p. 10) in saying that weakness of the will, far from being impossible, is actually rather common. If I sit down and watch an inane television show when there is a book to be finished and work to be done around the house, this is not because I judged that watching television is what I have the strongest reason to do. Quite the contrary; I am acting against my own best judgment. The action is still intelligible; there is *something* to be said for watching television. In fact, it might have ultimately been a perfectly rational thing for me to do; perhaps my mind was in need of a break and inane television was just what I needed. (Nomy Arpaly (2003) has shown, through a series of wonderful examples, that acting against one's own best judgment is not always irrational.) Nevertheless, I judged that I ought to do something more productive than watch television, and I then proceeded to watch television anyway. This seems a perfectly ordinary sequence of events, but Schueler's account appears to make it impossible.

Teleological realism has no special problem with weakness of will cases. Suppose that Bob, who is trying to stick to a rigid diet, has a second piece of cake after dinner. Bob may have acted against his better judgment, but his behavior is certainly explicable. He acted in order to satisfy his desire for another piece of cake, and that desire is perfectly intelligible. Given how delicious the first piece of cake was, there was clear value in having a second, even if Bob consciously judged that there would be more value in refraining. Of course, we could ask the further question of why Bob had the cake despite his desire to stick to his diet, and here there may be no perfectly rational story to tell. But, as I noted in chapter 9, the principles underlying teleological explanation do not require that agents be perfectly rational. If the irrationality gets to be too great, then at some point we lose the ability to give any substantive interpretation of the agent or his behavior, but Bob is far from that point.

It may be that I have misunderstood Schueler in some way, and I should emphasize that teleological realism is quite close in spirit to his account. The biggest difference between the two accounts, it seems to me, is this: According to teleological realism, action explanation more directly concerns seeing the effectiveness and value in an agent's behavior, and it leans less heavily on supposedly paradigmatic cases of extremely deliberate and conscious choice.

Hume famously taught that "reason alone can never be a motive to any action of the will" and that reason "can never oppose passion in the direction of the will" (1739/1978, p. 413). According to the Humean theory, the fact that a certain action is morally correct cannot provide a motive for me to perform the action, even if I acknowledge the moral correctness. For me to have a reason to perform the action, I must also have some passion or desire that would be served by the action—perhaps a general desire to do the right thing, or even just a desire to appear to be doing the right thing. (For the classic latter-day expression of the Humean view, see Williams 1981.)

I will argue in section 11.1 that the Humean account of motivation has profound and generally skeptical implications for moral responsibility. In section 11.2, I will claim that the Humean theory is not, on its face, very plausible. In section 11.3, I will point out that the theory would, however, be well motivated by the causal theory of action explanation. In section 11.4, I will argue that the Humean theory looks much less plausible from the vantage point of teleological realism. Hence, the teleological realist will be well placed to fend off the Humean theory's skeptical progeny in moral theory. In a directly contrary vein, Michael Smith has provided an argument for the Humean theory allegedly *founded* on the assumption that reason explanations are teleological. In section 11.5, I will contend that Smith's argument is flawed.

11.1 The Humean Theory and Moral Skepticism

It is customary in this context to distinguish between *motivating* reasons and *normative* reasons. Jonathan Dancy characterizes normative reasons as "features that speak in favor of the action (or against it)" (2000, p. 1). For example, if there is valuable treasure buried in Jack's yard, then Jack has a normative reason to dig a deep hole. Jack has this reason even if he is unaware of the existence of the treasure, and even if there is no way he could reasonably be expected to know about it. Of course, since Jack does not know about the treasure, he is unlikely to start digging deep holes in his yard; that is to say, given his epistemic situation, Jack lacks a *motivating* reason to dig.

Philosophers vary on exactly how to characterize motivating reasons. According to Dancy, a motivating reason is a reason in light of which an agent actually performs a given behavior (ibid.). On this definition, if an agent does not ϕ, the agent therefore had no motivating reason to ϕ. We could define "motivating reason" as Dancy does, but it is somewhat artificial. Intuitively speaking, I now have a motivating reason to go get coffee, for I just glanced longingly at my coffee cup wishing that it were not empty. However, I also want to continue writing, so I decide to stay put. It seems odd to deny that I have any motivating reason to get coffee simply because I decide against refilling my cup. After all, my situation is quite different from that of someone who detests coffee. Thus, I think it will be useful to define "motivating reason" somewhat more loosely than does Dancy. Here I will follow Michael Smith and say that a motivating reason to ϕ is a reason that is "potentially explanatory" of the agent's ϕing (1994, p. 96). The Humean theory, as I have characterized it, concerns motivating reasons. A motivating reason must include an appropriate desire (or other "pro-attitude").

Clearly, one can have normative reasons that are not motivating reasons, as indicated by the case of Jack and the buried treasure. But it is worth making a further point about such cases. By the definition given above, Jack has a normative reason to dig a hole in his yard; however, that reason is not epistemically accessible to him. Not only does Jack fail to believe that there is treasure in his yard, but he also could not reach that conclusion on the basis of any sequence of rational inferences from what he does know. For someone in Jack's epistemic situation, it would not be rational to start digging. Indeed, given what he could reasonably know, we would be worried about Jack's sanity if he started digging up his yard looking for treasure. So the mere fact that someone has a normative reason to ϕ does not imply that he ought to ϕ or even that it would be rational for him to ϕ. (This in turn suggests that the name "normative reason" is not very well chosen, but it has become fairly standard in the philosophical literature by now.)

Indeed, in general, if an agent has no motivating reason to ϕ, then it would not be rational for the agent to ϕ. We can see this as follows. A motivating reason for an agent to ϕ is a reason that is potentially explanatory of the agent's ϕing; in other words, if an agent has a motivating reason to ϕ in a given set of circumstances, then, if the agent were to ϕ in those circumstances, the reason could be cited in an intelligible explanation of the agent's action. So if an agent has no motivating reason to ϕ, then, were the agent to ϕ anyway, there could be no intelligible explanation of this behavior. Thus, were the agent to ϕ without a motivating reason, the explanation of the agent's ϕing would have to be something *not* based on reasons. And when one does something without any reason, it is not a rational action (though this isn't to say that it is necessarily an *irrational* action). So, although we can distinguish between normative and motivating reasons in the standard way, it turns out that if an agent has *only* normative reasons to ϕ, then it would not be rational for the agent to ϕ.

Now suppose that Louis is a teacher of logic and is, at the moment, grading a pile of examinations. We would ordinarily assume that Louis has an obligation to grade fairly, not allowing any biases he might have for or against a particular student to have any effect on his grading. Suppose, however, that Louis reports having no desire whatsoever to grade the exams fairly; indeed, he strongly desires to fail a particular student because he dislikes his habit of wearing dirty baseball caps in class. Moreover, Louis has no other desires that would be served by grading fairly. He has no general desire to do the right thing, nor does he even desire to avoid such punishment as might befall him if his unfair grading is discovered. According to the Humean, motivating reasons for action must consist, in part, in a relevant desire of the agent. Thus, if this is correct, Louis has no motivating reason to grade the exams fairly.

We can, of course, say that Louis has a normative reason to grade fairly, for fair grading is what morality presumably requires. But on the Humean theory of motivation Louis has no motivating reason to grade fairly, and from the point just made above it follows that it would not be rational for Louis to grade fairly. Under these circumstances, how can we hold Louis morally responsible for failing to grade the exam fairly? Surely we cannot hold an agent morally responsible for failing to perform an action that it would not have been rational for him to perform. Holding someone subject to the claims of morality presupposes that we are treating the person as a rational agent (hence our practice of not holding animals and infants morally responsible for their behavior). We are being inconsistent if we hold an agent to the claims of morality (thereby assuming him to be a rational agent) while at the same time holding him morally responsible for failing to perform an action that would not have been rational.

The Humean might reply that, even if we cannot hold Louis morally responsible for failing to grade the exams fairly, we might nonetheless find him morally culpable in some other way. One might say that, although Louis had no reason to grade the exams fairly given his desires, we can nonetheless hold him responsible for having brought it about that he had those desires. Or we might hold him directly responsible for failing to have the right desires. Such moves strike me as dubious. One does not normally arrive at one's desires and beliefs by some sort of intentional action. If one is morally responsible first and foremost for one's *actions*, then it will in general be impossible to hold an agent morally responsible for having the desires he has, for the agent most likely did not come to those desires via intentional actions. Moreover, even if one can change one's desires by intentional action, this presupposes that Louis has reason to do that. And that presupposes that Louis has certain desires that he might not have.

Of course, the point here is not specific to Louis. The lesson is that we cannot hold agents morally responsible unless they have a motivating reason to perform the morally required action, and if they do not have the appropriate desires, then they do not have such a reason. Thus moral responsibility is much more limited in scope than we might have thought; the demands of morality will apply only to those who happen to have the right desires. (For another argument of this sort, see Harman 1975.) Note that this conclusion holds whether or not one is a realist about moral value. That is, even if there are facts about which actions are moral, an agent without the appropriate desires has no reason to perform those actions. Thus, the Humean theory has the apparent consequence that the scope of one's moral responsibility is relative to the desires and beliefs one happens to have.

11.2 Prima Facie Evidence against the Humean Theory

One might well regard the conclusion of the previous section as already something of a reductio of the Humean account, for we are not normally inclined to withdraw all claims of moral responsibility upon the discovery that the agent had no desire to do the right thing. But I will not rest my case against the Humean with this argument. Instead, I will begin by discussing some examples that would seem to indicate the falsity of the theory. (For other apparent counterexamples, see Searle 2001.)

First, suppose that Iris asks John to close the window, and he does so. At first glance, one might surmise that Iris's request is John's reason for closing the window; indeed, it could easily be the case that John himself has no desire to close the window. Of course, the Humean will insist that John had *some* relevant desire—perhaps the desire to satisfy Iris's request. However, we can easily build into the case other factors that make this attribution look strained. For example, suppose that John had consciously decided that he had grown weary of Iris's requests, and that he would not satisfy the next one; moreover, he had also consciously decided that he would like the window to remain open. However, when the request came, John was lost in other thoughts and more or less automatically got up from his chair and closed the window. Under these circumstances, it seems rather odd to attribute to John either the desire to close the window or the desire to satisfy Iris's request. On the other hand, the behavior still looks like an action; he was not coerced, and it was not a reflexive spasm that took him from his chair to the window and led him to close the window. Prima facie, this would seem to be a case of an action performed for a reason where nonetheless there is no ψ such that John desires to ψ and believes that were he to φ he would ψ.

Second, consider how we deal with children, for children are the ones most likely to say "But I don't *want* to!" as if their lack of relevant desire obviates any obligation or responsibility on their part. The following scenario will be familiar to any parent or aunt or uncle: One tells a child to give a toy back to his sister, but the child says "I don't want to!" The details of what comes next will vary with the taste and mood of the adult, but the adult is likely to say something like "It's not nice to take her toy; you must give it back whether you want to or not." The adult might even reply "That's not relevant!" (I once heard my father-in-law give this response to my nephew.) In any event, the adult does not sit back in a quandary, thinking that the child has no reason to give the toy back. Of course, the adult might have searched for relevant desires the child did have—not getting punished, for example. But note that in the example the adult doesn't do this, and it doesn't seem necessary. The Humean might claim that the adult was implicitly searching for relevant desires the child did have, or that the adult was attempting to change the child's desires by deceptively pretending that the child had a reason apart from his current desires. Or the Humean might say that the adult was simply confused for thinking that the child had a reason to give the toy back short of having some relevant desire. My point is not that the example is a knockdown refutation of the Humean theory. It is simply that on the surface the theory does not *seem* to be presupposed in our practice. The adult who doesn't talk like a Humean doesn't look to be confused or mistaken. The Humean view is a *philosophical theory* that needs support; it cannot be simply read off as a commitment of ordinary practice.

11.3 The Humean Theory and the Causal Theory of Action

If the Humean theory of motivation is not an obvious commitment of common-sense practice, from whence does it derive its philosophical motivation? One answer, I suggest, lies in the causal theory of action explanation.
According to the causal theory, explanations citing reasons imply that the
reason *caused* the action. But the cause of an agent's behavior is presumably
some internal state. So we know right away that we cannot cite some state
of affairs external to the agent as the agent's reason for action. Iris's request
that John close the window initiated a causal chain of events that culmi-
nated in John's physical behavior. However, Iris's words didn't push him
across the room in the way that gale-force winds might have done. Rather,
John *heard* Iris's request, and then various internal states of his body, of his
brain in particular, caused his body to move. According to the causalist, reasons must be the cause of the action, but reasons must also justify or ration-
alize the behavior. So the internal state in question, if it is to be a *reason* for
John's behavior, must be the sort of internal state that would justify the
action. But the only sort of internal state that could have both caused and
justified John's behavior would be a mental state of some sort. The causal
theory does not guarantee the truth of the Humean theory in particular, for
a causalist might say that a belief alone could suffice to cause and justify an
action; the causal theory alone does not require that the cause of behavior
be a desire or some other pro-attitude, as claimed by the Humean.
Nonetheless, causalism has limited the scope of reasons to mental states of
the agent, and the Humean might try to find some other argument to show
that a belief alone would not suffice. (For an argument of this sort, see
Smith 1994. I'll discuss Smith's argument in greater detail below.)

So, according to causalism, in cases where an agent does act, her reason
must have consisted in a desire. But the Humean theory was more general
than that, for it purported to tell us what is means for an agent to have a
motivating reason to do something, whether or not the agent acts on that
reason. Moreover, it was this aspect of the theory that had skeptical implications concerning moral responsibility, for the problematic cases involved
an agent who failed to do the right thing, i.e., an agent who did *not* act. So
the more general question is this: Does causalism motivate the Humean
theory's claim that having a motivating reason to do something (whether
one does it or not) necessarily involves having a relevant desire? I think it
is fairly clear that causalism does motivate this position. We have seen that
causalism plausibly supports the claim that any time an agent actually acts

upon a reason, R, that reason must involve a relevant desire. If it were possible for an agent, before acting, to have a motivating reason R that was not a desire, then the causalist would have a very odd situation. Once the agent acts, the causalist cannot cite R as her reason. So what could it mean to say that she had reason R to act before acting, if we could not cite R when explaining her behavior? If R was to properly count as a reason for the agent to act in the first place, R must have involved some relevant desire of the agent. Thus, it appears that the causal theory of action gives firm support to the Humean theory of motivation.

11.4   The Humean Theory and Teleological Realism

The situation looks rather different from the vantage point of teleological realism. Teleological explanations have the form "A φd in order to ψ," as in "Joan went to the kitchen in order to get wine." The explanation cites a *state of affairs,* and Joan's reason for acting was to promote the occurrence of that state of affairs. Thus, on the face of things, when an action is explained teleologically, no internal state of the agent is mentioned. The Humean claim that every reason must include a desire looks to be a nonstarter.

Of course, we do sometimes explain behavior by explicitly citing a desire of the agent. For example, we might have said "Joan went to the kitchen because she wanted a glass of wine." But as we saw in chapter 9, the teleological realist construes such explanations in more explicitly teleological form: "Joan went to the kitchen in order to satisfy her desire for wine," or, better, "Joan went to the kitchen in order to get a glass of wine in the way that she desired." So even in these cases, the desire itself is not cited as the reason for action; rather, on the formal level, the mention of the content of the desire serves to pick out the state of affairs toward which the behavior was directed. Thus, even in cases in which a desire is mentioned in the explanation, nothing about the *form* of a teleological explanation suggests even remotely that all reasons for action must involve a relevant desire of the agent.

However, teleological realism is committed to more than action explanation's having a certain form. In chapter 9, I claimed that, in trying to find a teleological explanation according to which an agent φd in order to ψ, we do the following:

(I$_1$) Find a ψ such that φing is optimally appropriate for ψing, given a viable theory of the agent's intentional states and circumstances.

(I_2) Find a ψ such that ψing is the most valuable state of affairs toward which ϕing could be directed, given a viable theory of the agent's intentional states and circumstances.

I suggested further that, in the degenerate case in which we cannot find a ψ such that ϕing is appropriate to ψing and ψing is of value to the agent, we should then conclude that the behavior was not goal directed. This puts a constraint on when an agent can be said to have a reason to ψ. Given an agent who has not ϕd, we can say that she nonetheless had a *reason*, ψ, to ϕ only if ϕing would be appropriate for achieving ψ, and ψing would have intelligible value, given a viable theory of her abilities, intentional states, and circumstances. If we further assume that the only states of affairs with intelligible value are those states of affairs *desired* by the agent, then we are back at the Humean theory. On this assumption, intelligible teleological explanations will cite only states of affairs desired by the agent, and thus it would be true that the agent, to have a reason to ϕ, must have a desire to ψ, where ϕing is an appropriate means of ψing. Against the backdrop of teleological realism, then, the Humean theory amounts to this claim: Given an agent's abilities, intentional states, and circumstances, a state of affairs can be of intelligible value only if it is desired by the agent.

But there is no obvious reason to assume that the only states of affairs with value are those that are desired by the agent. On the face of things, the notion of *value* is broader than that of *desire*. A state of affairs is valuable, in the broad sense, when it is worthy of action—i.e., when it is worthy of having behavior directed toward it. In *The Last Word*, Thomas Nagel attacks the Humean theory in this way: "Once I see myself as the subject of certain desires, as well as the occupant of an objective situation, I still have to decide what to do, and that will include deciding what justificatory weight to give to those desires." (1997, p. 109) In the present context, Nagel's point comes to this: When deciding what goal is worthy of my action at a given moment, I can take into account all of my relevant desires, then still ask "What ought I to do?" or "What is most valuable?" It is one thing to weigh all my desires against one another and thereby determine what I most want; having done that, I can still ask what is most valuable. Asking this question at least seems to be possible, whereas, if the Humean theory were correct, this further question would have to be literally incoherent.

The Humean might respond by bringing in the notion of a *second-order desire*, a desire that in some way involves other desires. For example, I might desire that I no longer have the desire to eat potato chips, or, more generally, I might desire that my future desires be fulfilled. The Humean can grant that I can question the value of my first-order desires but claim that this is to be cashed out in terms of thinking about my first-order desires in terms of my second-order desires. However, it is not clear that this move helps. Along with Nagel, I have suggested (above) that, having taken into account my desires, I can still ask the further question of what I ought to do, of what is, all things considered, the most valuable. This further question still seems coherent and reasonable, even if taking into account my desires means that I take into account my second-order desires as well. That is, even after weighing my first-order desires as well as my second-order desires (and third-order desires, if I have any and if I can think about them without getting too confused), I might still question what it would be most valuable for me to do. It still seems that the question of what ought to be done and the question of what one desires are conceptually separate.

In fact, when faced with a practical decision, one often does not think explicitly in terms of one's desires. For example, someone who has just turned on a television to watch a baseball game might suddenly think "Maybe I should call my father." She might want to watch the baseball game and not particularly enjoy the prospect of talking to her father, but she also realizes that her father has been feeling lonely lately; with a sigh, she turns off the television and proceeds to the phone. Here there is little explicit weighing of desires. The daughter does not consciously think that it will serve her long-term desires to call her father, nor does she consciously think that she wants to be a moral person and that the moral thing to do is call her father. Instead, she just decides that the most valuable thing would be to call her father. I take it that this sort of scenario is not atypical.

The Humean will have to say one of two things about this sort of case: (i) The daughter was thinking irrationally, in that she decided what was most valuable by thinking about something other than her own desires. (ii) On some implicit or unconscious level, the daughter really was thinking about her own second-order desires, e.g., the desire to have smooth relations with her father in the future or the desire to be a good daughter. The first alternative seems clearly wrong—it would make too many people irrational too much of the time. The second alternative is harder to evaluate, since it is not clear how to confirm or disconfirm claims about a person's unconscious thoughts. But apart from some philosophical *reason* to assume such an account, it seems strained. As I suggested above, the causal theory of action would provide substantial motivation for the Humean view; with the acceptance of that philosophical motivation, we might accept a picture in which much of what practical reason seems to be is actually something else.

But without that motivation, ordinary experience gives no reason to affirm the Humean claim that all reasons for action involve desires.

Given teleological realism, we are free to accept a more liberal view of what has intelligible value, and consequently of what can be a reason for action. For example, doing the right thing can have intelligible value whether or not the agent specifically has a desire to do the right thing under those circumstances. And if that is correct, one can still have a reason to do what morality requires, even if one lacks a desire to perform that action, and even if one lacks a general desire to do the right thing. So one cannot automatically evade moral responsibility by failing to have the right desires.

Of course, in some cases, even on the teleological account, whether one has a reason to do something is relative to one's desires. Since I have a desire to see certain kinds of astronomical objects (distant galaxies, faint nebulae, markings on Mars, etc.), and since I do not possess a functioning telescope, I have a reason to buy a telescope. Someone who lacks the desire to see astronomical objects presumably does not have a motivating reason to buy a telescope. The state of affairs in which one owns a telescope does not have significant value for all people. One might object that we should say the same thing about moral considerations: If one explicitly desires only the improvement of one's own welfare, and one thinks that moral considerations are for the weak and pathetic, then the state of affairs in which one does the right thing likewise has no appreciable value, given that set of intentional states and circumstances. The most straightforward way to reply to this objection is to be a realist about moral value and thus claim that there is always value in doing the right thing. If this is correct, doing the right thing is of intelligible value even to one who thinks that morality is for the weak. The value of doing the right thing is there for the rational person to see, and one therefore cannot escape having a reason to do the right thing. Whether the claims of morality rationally override all other sorts of reasons is a different question; however, on the teleological account, if moral values are real, one cannot completely escape having moral reasons, and one cannot escape moral responsibility.

I have not argued for moral realism; I think it is correct, but that is another matter. Recall that the Humean theory of motivation appeared to make moral responsibility relative to one's set of desires even if one assumed a fully moral realist picture. In other words, the Humean theory suggested a way of grounding a form of moral relativism. My argument here is that this move is unfounded. Given teleological realism, the relativism of moral responsibility follows only if one first assumes some sort of irrealism about moral value.

11.5   Smith's Argument for the Humean Theory

I have argued that the causal theory of action explanation strongly motivates the Humean theory of motivation, but that the teleological account
makes the Humean view look rather implausible. Somewhat surprisingly,
Michael Smith argues that the Humean theory actually follows from a teleological account of action explanation:

> . . . as I see it, the Humean and anti-Humean are precisely engaged in a dispute con-
> cerning what it is about the nature of reasons that makes it possible for reason expla-
> nations to be teleological explanations.
>
> If this is right, then it would seem that there will be only one reason to believe the
> Humean's theory, if indeed we should believe his theory at all, and that is that his
> theory alone is able to make sense of motivation as the pursuit of a goal. In what fol-
> lows I will argue that this is indeed the case. (1994, p. 104)

In the course of arguing that the Humean theory alone allows a teleological conception of action, Smith proposes a conception of the nature of
desire. Since this conception figures crucially in his argument for the
Humean theory, I will begin by explaining this aspect of Smith's view.

Smith conceives of mental states as dispositional states of the agent; i.e.,
states that have a certain functional role (ibid., p. 113). (However, Smith
does not take this conception to commit him to the standard functionalist view, according to which mental states are individuated by their *causal*
role. Smith claims that "it is a substantial philosophical thesis to claim that
desires are causes." (p. 114)) Among mental states, Smith makes a broad
distinction between two types of functional roles, drawn metaphorically in
terms of *direction of fit*. (Smith adopts this conception from Platts (1979),
though Platts himself goes on to reject it. Platts in turn attributes the basic
idea to Elizabeth Anscombe in *Intention*.) Beliefs are said to have a mind-
to-world direction of fit; that is to say, beliefs ideally should be changed to
fit the world. If an agent's belief does not match the way the world is, the
agent should change her belief. Desires, on the other hand, have a world-
to-mind direction of fit. If the world is not in accordance with an agent's
desires, then, roughly speaking, the agent should change the world so that
it matches her desires. Smith spells out the direction-of-fit metaphor as
follows:

> . . . the difference between beliefs and desires in terms of direction of fit can be seen
> to amount to a difference in the functional roles of belief and desire. Very roughly,
> and simplifying somewhat, it amounts, inter alia, to a difference in the counter-
> factual dependence of a belief that p and a desire that p on a perception with the

content that not p: a belief that p tends to go out of existence in the presence of a perception with the content that not p, whereas a desire that p tends to endure, disposing the subject in that state to bring it about that p. (p. 115)

(This formulation of the distinction is still rather vague, as we will see in the course of examining the details of Smith's argument, but for now I will leave it in this form.)

With this background, Smith presents his argument for the Humean theory in three simple steps (p. 116):

(a) Having a motivating reason is, inter alia, having a goal.

(b) Having a goal is being in a state with which the world must fit.

(c) Being in a state with which the world must fit is desiring.

Premise (a) is taken to follow from the teleological account of reason explanation. Premise (b) is said to be true because "becoming apprised of the fact that the world is not as the content of your goal specifies suffices not for giving up that goal, it suffices rather for changing the world" (p. 117). Premise (c) falls out of Smith's dispositional or functional conception of desire. And then, by transitivity of identity, the Humean concludes that having a reason *is* desiring. Thus, when John closed the window upon hearing Iris ask him to, if he had any motivating reason to close the window, his motivating reason must have consisted in his having a goal of some sort; whatever goal this was must have been a state with which the world must fit, and consequently must have been a desire.

The principal flaw in Smith's argument lies hidden in the notion of a mental state's direction of fit.[1] As Smith puts steps (b) and (c), they still contain this metaphor. This by itself is no problem, for, as we have seen, Smith tells us how to cash this metaphor out in more literal terms. Accordingly, the more fully spelled out version of (b) would read as follows:

(b_0) Having a goal is being in a state S with content p such that (i) S disposes the subject to bring it about that p and (ii) S tends to endure even if the subject has a perception with the content not-p.

The more fully spelled out version of (c) would read as follows:

(c_0) Being in a state such that (i) S disposes the subject to bring it about that p and (ii) S tends to endure even if the subject has a perception with the content not-p is desiring.

These formulations, though better, are still somewhat unclear. The unclarity pertains to the word 'state', for there are at least two possible readings of the word.

11.5.1 Weak Reading of 'State'

There is a sense of the word 'state' according to which attributing a state differs only stylistically from simple predication of a property. For example, we might offer something like the following as a characterization of poverty:

Being in poverty is being in a state S such that S makes one unable to afford the basic necessities of life.

However, this language is somewhat stilted, and it might carry some sort of suggestion of reifying the state of poverty, and this suggestion may be unintended by the speaker. In other words, on the weak reading of 'state', the references to a *state* of poverty would be only a stylistic variant on saying that a person is poor. Accordingly, on the weak reading of 'state', the characterization of poverty would be equivalent to the following:

Being poor is being such that the one is unable to afford the basic necessities of life.

Similarly, in (b_0), Smith might intend a weak reading of the word 'state' such that it implies nothing more than the predication of a property. On this reading, we would have

(b_1) Having p as a goal is being such that: (i) the subject is disposed to bring it about that p and (ii) the subject remains so disposed even when she perceives that not-p.

Similarly, if we interpret (c_0) with the weak reading of 'state', we get

(c_1) Being such that (i) the subject is disposed to bring it about that p and (ii) the subject remains so disposed even when she perceives that not-p *is* desiring that p.

On this reading, Smith's argument proceeds from (a) to (b_1) to (c_1), where (a) and (b_1) are said to follow from the teleological account of action and (c_1) is supposed to follow from the nature of desire. A problem for this construal of the argument is that (c_1) is fairly obviously false. The dispositions mentioned in (c_1) can hardly be necessary for having a desire, since, as Schueler points out, "there are plenty of desires that have as objects things utterly outside the agent's control" (2003, p. 34). But it also seems that the two conditions given are not even sufficient for having a desire. I, for example, have a fairly long-standing disposition to forget where I last put my glasses, and I unfortunately continue to be so disposed even on those occasions where it is not in fact the case that I have forgotten where I last put them. According to the analysis in (c_1), it should follow that I *desire* to forget where I last put my glasses. This, I can assure you, is not the case. The problem is simple: One can have enduring dispositions to do or bring about results that one does not desire. The simple dispositional analysis in (c_1) cannot capture all that we mean by attributions of desire. That is, there is more to having a desire than meeting the conditions that (c_1) spells out.

Of course, when I forget where I last left my glasses, I have not thereby performed an *action*. In other words, I did not direct my behavior toward the end of forgetting where my glasses were. Accordingly, perhaps Smith means to be making a stronger claim about desires:

(c_{1b}) Being such that (i) the subject is disposed *to act in order to* bring it about that *p* and (ii) the subject remains so disposed even when she perceives that *not-p is* desiring that *p*.

However, this version of (c) begs the question against the anti-Humean, particularly the anti-Humean who thinks that action explanation is teleological. According to (c_{1b}), one counts as desiring *p* simply by virtue of being disposed to direct one's behavior toward *p*. This is precisely the claim that the anti-Humean denies. For example, in the case of John closing the window, it was granted on all sides that John's behavior was goal directed, in that it was directed at satisfying Iris's request. The question separating the Humean from the anti-Humean was whether John must have had a desire to satisfy Iris's request. But (c_{1b}) would trivially imply that John did have such a desire, since he acted in order to satisfy Iris's request. So the anti-Humean would simply deny this version of the premise.

Thus, on the weak reading of 'state' in (b) and (c), premise (c) is quite problematic. On the most straightforward reading, (c_1), it is clearly false. Interpreted as (c_{1b}), the premise directly begs the question against the anti-Humean.

11.5.2 Strong Reading of 'State'

I think that ordinary (occasional) use of the word 'state' when referring to goals, beliefs, and desires implies only the weak sense. However, it may be that Smith has something stronger in mind. One could read 'state' in contexts like (b) as implying the existence of a particular physical state of the agent, a state individuated by its causal role. This reading of 'state' invites a strong functionalist interpretation of (b):

(b_2) Having *p* as a goal is having a particular physical state *S* with content *p* such that (i) *S* typically causes the subject to bring it about that *p* and (ii) *S* tends to endure even if the subject has a perception with the content *not-p*.

The corresponding reading of (c) would be this:

(c_2) Having a particular physical state S with content p such that (i) S typically causes the subject to bring it about that p, and (ii) S tends to endure even if the subject has a perception with the content not-p is to desire p.

And the argument would proceed from premises (a), (b_2), and (c_2).

Premise (c_2), unlike (c_1), might well appear perfectly acceptable to some, for it basically amounts to a standard functionalist account of the nature of mental states, and (b_2) likewise presupposes an analogous functionalist account of the nature of goals. However, both (b_2) and (c_2) presuppose a causal account of action explanation. Obviously, I think it would be a mistake to accept this account of action explanation and the functionalist account of the nature of mental states; much of the first part of this book was devoted to showing that those are mistaken. Smith himself does not want to commit himself to the claim that desires and beliefs are causes of behavior; hence this reading of the argument presupposes more than Smith intends.[2] In the present context, however, it should merely be noted that on this reading the argument simply presupposes the causal theory of action and thereby assumes that teleological realism is wrong. Since my main purpose in this chapter is to show that teleological realism fails to motivate the Humean theory of motivation, an argument for the Humean theory that simply presupposed the falsity of teleological realism would be irrelevant.

Teleological realism is a nonreductionist account of the mind, an account according to which CSP is logically independent of physical science. The key to teleological realism is the claim that common-sense reason explanations of human behavior are not a species of causal explanation but are instead irreducibly teleological. One might wonder whether one can have nonreductionism for less; in particular, one might question whether an option-3 view must deny the causal theory of action. A number of philosophers have claimed to have nonreductionist accounts of the mind while still claiming that reason explanations are causal. In chapters 6 and 7, I argued directly against the causal construal of reason explanations, and those arguments were independent of one's overall position concerning the relationship between CSP and physical science. If those arguments are sound, then combining a nonreductionist view with the causal theory of action is a nonstarter, since the causal theory of action is false. In this chapter, I will contend that, even if one ignores the direct arguments against the causal theory, it is difficult to combine causalism with a nonreductionist account of the mind. In the final section of the chapter, I also explore instrumentalism, a slightly different attempt to have it both ways.

12.1 Explanatory Exclusion and the Causal Theory of Action

If we maintain that CSP and physical science are independent but also claim that reasons cause actions, we run into a very basic problem. I'll illustrate the problem by first considering an example far from philosophy of mind. In a small apartment, there is a fire and a person is dead. Two very different explanations are offered: The fire department investigator says that the fire was caused by faulty electrical wiring, but a person who investigates allegedly paranormal phenomena tells us that the primary cause was spontaneous human combustion. We can then imagine a debate that might ensue about the relative merits of the two explanations. But what if someone were to claim that both explanations were correct? This would perhaps be even more puzzling than the paranormal explanation taken on its own. The basic problem is that both explanations propose different answers to the same question, and it seems that at most one of the two can be correct.

Now look at the case of human behavior. Joan walks to the kitchen, and we ask why. We are given two different answers, this time one from a common-sense psychologist and one from a neuroscientist:

(1) Joan went to the kitchen because she wanted wine.

(2) Brain state Q caused Joan to go to the kitchen.

On the face of it, these appear to be two different explanations for the same event. Jaegwon Kim puts it as follows: "Two explanations of one event create a certain epistemic tension, a tension that is dissipated only when we have an account of how they, or the two causes they indicate, are related to each other." (1993, p. 253)

The analogy to the apartment fire suggests that we should resolve the tension by determining which of the answers is the correct one, and by rejecting the other. But to do this means accepting option 1, according to which CSP and physical science are inconsistent. The nonreductionist does not want to reject either explanation, so it must resolve the tension in another way.

The teleological realist resolves the epistemic tension by saying that, although (1) and (2) are explanations of the same event, they answer different questions. Explanation (1) answers the question "What was Joan's purpose in going to the kitchen?" Explanation (2) answers the question "What was the efficient cause of Joan's going to the kitchen?" If the questions are genuinely distinct, as I have been claiming, it is no surprise that they have different answers; no epistemic tension or exclusion problem is introduced. (Of course, two distinct questions might possibly have the same answer; the mere fact that one can list two questions here is not enough to rule out causalism by itself.) The option-2 reductionist likewise has no problem here. The reductionist will say that the two explanations are in fact one and the same, and that they just use different ways of referring to the cause of the behavior. Brain state Q just *is* Joan's desire for wine; thus, (1) and (2) ultimately come to the same thing.

The situation is different for the nonreductionist who claims that reasons causally explain actions. If both explanations are causal, then both are answering the same question: "What was the cause of the behavior?" But the nonreductionist cannot say that brain state Q just is Joan's desire for wine, for this would mean that the CSP explanation is identical to, and thus entailed by, the physical science explanation; this would give up the nonreductionism. So it appears that the nonreductionist causalist is forced to countenance two separate causes for one and the same event; this situation indeed gives rise to the tension Kim points out.

I can imagine two sorts of responses to this problem. First, a nonreductionist might claim that human behavior does have multiple causes, one of which is a mental state and one of which is a brain state. Second, a nonreductionist might say that beliefs and brain states cause different things, and that, properly construed, explanations on the model of (1) and (2) should be seen as having different explananda. I consider these responses in the next two subsections respectively.

12.1.1 Multiple Causes

Can we simply accept that Joan's behavior had two different causes, the desire and the brain state? After all, events often do have multiple causes. In general, if an event e has two distinct causes, x and y, there are three possibilities: (1) that x and y are, individually, only partial causes of e, (2) that x and y are independent and individually sufficient causes of e, and (3) that x and y are different links in the same causal chain leading to e. However, when applied to belief states and brain states, none of these possibilities looks very attractive.

An example of the first possibility would be this: In an effort to move a car from an icy parking space, one person presses the accelerator while another pushes the car from behind; each person's action alone would fail to move the car off the ice, but both operating together succeed. But surely desire states and brain states do not work in tandem like this. Rather, physical science will ultimately provide a gapless causal history, a history that appeals only to physical states of the agent. The brain state does not require causal help from some other state of the person.

The second possibility was causal overdetermination. However, it seems clear that brain states and mental states are not independent and individually sufficient causes of actions. Suppose we intercepted the signal sent from the brain to the relevant muscles; were the overdetermination picture correct, we would expect that the desire alone would still have sufficed to produce the action. But that is not what we think would happen; if we interrupt the causal chain between the brain state and the muscles, no bodily motion will ensue.

The third possibility, that the mental and brain states are different links in the same causal chain, likewise seems quite implausible. The brain state causes the agent's behavior by sending the appropriate physical signal to the relevant muscles; the brain state was in turn caused by other physiological states of the organism, and perhaps various irritations of the organism's sensory surfaces. Where would the agent's mental state fit into this causal chain, if it is not to be identified with the brain state? Again, if human physiology ultimately gives a gapless causal history of bodily motions, either mental states are identical to the physiological cause or they are not causes of behavior.

12.1.2 Multiple Explananda

On the second line of response, explanations (1) and (2) ultimately have different explananda and hence are not distinct explanations of a single event. It might help here to take a slightly different example. Suppose that a person pays the bill at a restaurant by signing a credit card receipt. One might suggest a distinction between the agent's paying of the bill and her physical hand motions, on the grounds that the agent could have paid the bill using a variety of different physical motions. The agent might have signed her name in a slightly different way, she might have paid with cash, and so on. In some circumstances, her payment of the bill might have consisted in a simple nod (if, for example, the waiter had said "Shall I bill this to your room?"). If the paying of the bill and the hand motion are distinct events, the causal explanations of these two events could be independent of one another. Accordingly, when Joan goes to the kitchen, one might distinguish between her actual bodily motions and her going to the kitchen. The basic idea behind the distinction is the same as the bill paying case, for a number of distinct sets of bodily motions would have constituted Joan's going to the kitchen. Thus, since the explananda in (1) and (2) are different, the two explanations could be independent of one another.

However, the causalist's distinction between Joan's going to the kitchen and her physical motion might well appear rather implausible. Consider some other ways in which we might describe what Joan did: She left the living room, she walked past the ottoman, she moved fifteen feet closer to Florida, and so on. How many things did Joan do at that moment? According to the current nonreductive causalist position, we already have at least three distinct events, and it is clear that we could indefinitely increase the number of descriptions of the event, and thereby, apparently, increase the number of events. Surely it is more plausible to say that there was just one behavior in question here, albeit a behavior that can be described in a number of ways. (See Davidson 1980; Hornsby 1980.) The mere fact that we can describe an event in a number of different ways doesn't show that the events are distinct. Similarly, I can describe a particular person either as the former president or as the husband of Hillary Clinton, but this doesn't mean that I am talking about two different people.

However, at least for the sake of argument, I'll grant that the bill paying and the hand motion were different events, and that the causal explanations of the events are thus distinct as well. Similarly, I will allow for the sake of argument that Joan's going to the kitchen and her physical bodily motions are distinct. Thus (1) and (2) above have different explananda, and hence, one might presume, there is no essential logical relation between the two explanations—i.e., the CSP explanation in (1) is not implied by the physical science explanation in (2). However, I'll argue that the proposal still fails.

According to the multiple-explananda proposal, brain state Q is the cause of the bodily motion, and the desire is the cause of the going to the kitchen. But what sort of thing is the desire? Is it a brain state? Or is it a dispositional state—a fact defined in terms of the agent's disposition to behave certain ways in specified circumstances? (There might be a third possible alternative, according to which the desire is a combination of a brain state in a given context; in section 12.2, I will consider a proposal based on this conception.) If the desire is a dispositional state, then we are back to the view defended by Lynne Rudder Baker, according to which mental states are dispositional states and kinds of behavior are similarly defined by what the agent would do in various circumstances. In chapter 6, via the artificially constructed example of an agent who shunks and who is shunky, I argued that, on this line, at any given moment an agent will be engaged in an indefinite number of bizarre activities, each of which has its own bizarrely characterized cause, and that none of these causes has any less claim to legitimacy than the agent's mental state. The conclusion of my argument there was that if mental states can causally explain behavior, then mental states must be brain states.

Now suppose instead that the desire is a brain state. Now we have this situation: the desire (a brain state of some sort) causes Joan's behavior of going to the kitchen, and brain state Q causes her bodily motion. However, Joan's action is constituted by the bodily motion, for the fact that a particular kind of bodily motion occurred in a certain set of circumstances makes it the case that she went to the kitchen. Given this, it seems impossible that brain state Q caused the bodily motion and that some other brain state caused the behavior. Thus, Joan's desire must be identical to brain state Q. Accordingly, in (1) and (2), although we have different explananda, we have the same explanans.

But this leads to a dilemma for the nonreductionist. By virtue of what is the desire to be identified with the brain state? What makes it the case that brain state Q is the desire for wine? If there are general facts that suffice for identifying mental states with particular brain states, this begins to look like reductionism again, for physical science could then tell us, in principle, everything we want to know about the causes and effects of those mental states. And if CSP explanations are causal, then the bulk of CSP is entailed by what we can learn from physical science. But such reductive theories are precisely what the nonreductionist denies. So the nonreductionist cannot maintain that there are general facts that independently entail that the desire is to be identified with brain state Q. The nonreductionist seems forced to say that we count brain state Q as the desire for wine because CSP explains the behavior by citing the desire and brain state Q caused the behavior. On this reading, the identification becomes essentially stipulative, for when we explain a behavior by citing a mental state we stipulate that the mental-state term refers to whatever brain state caused the behavior.

However, this line of defense runs into a different objection. According to this line, when we explain Joan's behavior by citing her desire for wine, we are stipulating that "desire for wine" refers to whatever brain state caused the bodily motion that constitutes Joan's going to the kitchen. If we then proceed to explain her drinking of the wine by also citing this same desire, we will likewise be stipulating that "desire for wine," in that context, refers to whatever brain state caused her bodily motion of drinking the wine. For all we know, it might have been two different brain states that caused the distinct bodily motions. By making these stipulations, we would in effect be using the expression "desire for wine" such that it was synonymous with "whatever caused the behavior in question." But this makes the original explanation utterly trivial, for our original explanation now amounts to "Joan's behavior of going to the kitchen was caused by whatever brain state caused her bodily motion." This is scarcely an explanation. Again, things would be different if we had a reductive theory whereby there would be some independent means of identifying the mental state. But when the nonreductionist is forced into stipulating that the mental state is to be identified with whatever brain state caused a given item of behavior, it is mere pretense to claim that the CSP explanation is independent of the brain-state explanation. So this attempt to get out of the explanatory exclusion problem fails.

12.2   Program Explanations

Frank Jackson and Phillip Pettit (1988) have put forward a view of reason explanation that might be thought to evade the objections discussed above. They propose their account as an answer to the problem of how mental states with broad content can causally explain behavior. Based on the Twin-Earth thought experiments, Jackson and Pettit agree that my twin and I have different beliefs when we each look at the cup on the desk and think "There is water in that cup." Since my twin and I then exhibit the same bodily motions when drinking the liquid, the causalist has the problem of finding a distinctive explanatory role for my broad belief that there is water in the cup and my twin's corresponding broad belief that there is XYZ in his cup. Jackson and Pettit's attempted solution involves, first, distinguishing between the narrow content of a belief and its broad content: "For a given broad content B there will be a number of ways of realizing that content by the appropriate combination of narrow content N and environment E, say: N_1 & E_1, N_2 & E_2, ... One of these ways, say N_a & E_a, will be the actual way B is realized." (1988, p. 398) They acknowledge that only the narrowly defined state, N_a, will be causally *efficacious* in producing actual behavior, but they give an account of explanation according to which there is still a distinctive explanatory role for the broad content, B.

Jackson and Pettit argue that "properties may be causally explanatory without being causally productive or efficacious," and that mental properties in particular "programme the result to be explained, rather than actually bringing it about" (1988, p. 400). According to Jackson and Petit, in a program explanation an abstract or higher-order property is cited as causally explaining an event, even though the abstract property itself is not causally efficacious. For example, we might say that an orchestra conductor became annoyed because someone in the audience coughed. In fact, it was the cough of a particular person—call him Fred—that caused the annoyance; i.e., it was a particular cough, rather than the abstract fact that *somebody* coughed. But the abstract fact that someone coughed *programs* the resulting annoyance in the following sense: If someone coughed, no matter who it was, this was enough to ensure that the conductor would become annoyed. So it is reasonable to cite the fact that someone coughed as causally relevant, even though it is not causally efficacious. Jackson and Pettit put the point more abstractly:

Suppose some state A caused state B. Variations on A, say A', A", . . . , would have caused variations on B, say B', B", . . . , respectively. It may be that if the A share a property P, the B' would share a property Q: keep P constant among the actual and possible causes, and Q remains constant among the actual and possible effects. If you like, Q *tracks* P. Our point is that in such a case P causally explains Q by programming it, even though it may be that P does not produce Q. (1988, p. 394)

Reason explanations of action are then said to be program explanations, where the property *P* would be the mental state and *Q* would be the behavior. For example, suppose that I go to the water cooler because I believe that water can be obtained there. My belief has a particular broad content that could be realized by many different combinations of narrow contents plus environments. One of these, say N_a & E_a, will be the actual way in which my belief is realized, and the state N_a will be the causally efficacious state. Nonetheless, Jackson and Pettit contend that the broad content of my belief programs the causal explanation in accord with the abstract pattern given above:

Now each of the N_i & E_i will explain and predict different behavior in the subject, but it may be that there is a common thread T running through these different pieces of behavior. In this case ascribing B explains and predicts T just as well as ascribing N_a & E_a, and does something distinctive besides—it tells us that it did not matter as far as getting T goes that it was N_a & E_a that was actual instead of, say, N_2 & E_2. (1988, pp. 398–399)

According to Jackson and Pettit, if the variations on the broad content share common properties, and there is a common property shared by the behavior to be explained, we can say that the broad content causally explains the behavior, even if it is not causally efficacious.

There are two possible readings of Jackson and Pettit, depending on what it means to say that the variations must share a "common property" or "common thread." First, there is a weak reading on which any property that is shared will count as a genuinely common property. Second, there is a stronger reading according to which the common properties must be *natural* properties. I'll argue that on neither reading will the Jackson-Pettit account allow a nonreductionist to adopt the causal theory of action.

First, consider the weak reading. In chapter 6, I defined the property *shunky* as follows: a person is shunky iff she is disposed to say that Augusta is the capital of Maine, she is disposed to affirm that the pope is Catholic, and she is disposed to deny that Earth is bigger than the sun. Intuitively, these appear to be three very different dispositions, but we can say that they share the following common thread: Each is a disposition shared by anyone who is shunky. Could we, on the weak reading of the Jackson-Pettit account, cite shunkiness as a causally explanatory property that programs certain results? Here is how that would go. First we will define another odd property: A person *pershunks* if she affirms that Augusta is the capital of Maine, affirms that the pope is Catholic, or denies that Earth is bigger than the sun. Now suppose that Margaret pershunks, for when asked whether Augusta is the capital of Maine she says "Yes." It seems that the Jackson-Pettit account allows us to say that Margaret pershunked *because* she is shunky. There were, after all, various states that would have counted as her being shunky, and various events that would have counted as her having pershunked. Given that Margaret had all of the relevant dispositions that constitute being shunky, we can say that her having the abstract property of being shunky ensured that she would have one of the particular states that would in turn cause a behavior that would count as pershunking. So, by the standards of the program explanation account, the fact that Margaret is shunky causally explains her pershunking by programming it. But if the Jackson-Pettit account indeed allows this as a genuine causal explanation, then surely the account has gone awry. "Margaret pershunked because she was shunky" doesn't appear to be much of an explanation, but it especially does not appear to be a *causal* explanation. Moreover, we could repeat these moves with other bizarrely characterized properties, such that we could give indefinitely many program explanations of any given event. So it seems that the weak reading would allow non-explanations to count as causal explanations.

On the strong reading, the common properties in program explanations must be natural properties. This reading would rule out explanations citing shunkiness, for *shunky* is clearly not a natural property; thus the strong reading would evade the objection to the explanatory value of program explanations. However, the strong reading evades this objection at the price of limiting the scope of program explanations to those citing natural properties. This is probably good enough for the example of the conductor's being annoyed at someone's coughing; even if the property *cough* is not itself perfectly natural, most typical coughs presumably share fairly natural acoustic properties, and it seems reasonable to assume that it was the occurrence of an instance of this set of properties that was sufficient to annoy the conductor. Indeed it seems safe to assume that the naturally similar acoustic properties were really doing the work here. A cough that was quite atypical in its sound might not have had the same effect on the conductor (depending on the nature of the sound, perhaps the conductor would have ignored it or would have been too startled to be annoyed).

Thus, I would suggest that the strong reading is enough to cover the typical examples of what appear to be successful program explanations. However, I contend further that the strong reading is too strong to include reason explanations of action. In chapter 5, I argued that mental-state terms do not function as natural-kind terms, and this was part of a broader argument to the effect that CSP does not function as a proto-scientific theory of the mind. The net result is that we have little reason to assume that beliefs and desires form natural kinds. Since on the strong reading of program explanations the cited common properties must be natural, it would follow that mental properties cannot be cited in program explanations. (It might be worth recalling that my argument in chapter 5 was specific to propositional-attitude states rather than affective emotional states or sensory states, so it might be that these could be cited in program explanations.)

Moreover, it is at least arguable that the strong reading is of no help to the nonreductionist. Recall that the question before us in this chapter is whether one can have a nonreductive account of mind that still retains a causal account of action explanation. However, the natural properties are presumably those that can be employed in the physical sciences. Of course, as was highlighted in the opening pages of this book, mental properties do not appear as such in the vocabulary of the physical sciences. So if mental properties are nonetheless natural kinds that can appear in physical laws, this would mean that there must be some way of linking the mental vocabulary of CSP to the vocabulary of the natural properties of the physical sciences. But it is the existence of just this sort of link that the nonreductionist denies. Thus, if program explanations require natural properties, reason explanations of action can be program explanations only if reductionism is true, and thus the Jackson-Pettit account of explanation is of no use to the nonreductionist.

12.3   Baker's Defense of the Autonomy of CSP

Lynne Rudder Baker tries to justify the autonomy of CSP using a very different approach, without invoking multiple explananda:

Garden-variety common-sense and scientific explanations are on a continuum, and what distinguishes one end of the continuum from the other concerns not the nature of the explanatory properties but the justification for taking the explanatory properties to be exemplified. The more that appeal to scientific theories is needed to justify the attribution of a property, the more scientific are explanations that cite the property. (1995, p. 107)

So, according to Baker, CSP is independent of physical science not because it refers to different sorts of properties or asks different questions, but because CSP has a different "justification for taking the explanatory properties to be exemplified." This is a highly problematic line. Recall the example of the apartment fire. According to the fire department investigator, the cause was faulty electrical wiring; according to the paranormal investigator, the cause was spontaneous human combustion. These two investigators use rather different methods and have different sorts of justifications for their theories. Imagine someone defending the paranormal investigator's answer on the grounds that normal scientific explanations and paranormal explanations are on a continuum distinguished at the ends by the justificatory methods employed by practitioners of each field. We can draw a distinction between normal and paranormal explanations if we want to, but the distinction in no way supports actually accepting both answers as adequate. We don't accept both answers, and this is not merely because we distrust the methods of the paranormal investigator; rather, it is because the two investigators propose different answers to the same question, and at most one of the answers can be right. We might explain why the two investigators arrived at different answers by noting the different methods of justification; but, given that only one of the answers can be right, this merely shows that one of the methods of justification must be faulty. Thus, claiming different modes of justification in no way manages to avoid the basic problem of explanatory exclusion.

12.4   Instrumentalism

One might try to preserve some sort of autonomy for CSP in a rather different manner. According to *instrumentalism*, the claims of CSP are not, strictly speaking, true at all; however, CSP is pragmatically quite useful for describing, explaining, and predicting human behavior, and the pragmatic benefits justify its continued use. On this view, CSP would have a certain sort of autonomy, for we are justified in using CSP even if its claims contradict those of physical science. And we could also still say that CSP explanations of human behavior are a species of causal explanation.

Instrumentalist uses of language are relatively common. We speak of the sun's moving across the sky and of its moving through the constellations of the zodiac; we speak of washing machines as temperamental; we think of a chess-playing computer as wanting to win the game and making the moves that it believes will help it win; we predict and explain physical events in terms of Newtonian mechanics; we even tell our children that Santa Claus brings Christmas presents. In each of these cases, we realize that the claims are false, but we continue to employ them because they are useful fictions. The thought behind instrumentalism is that CSP is likewise best construed as a useful fiction; CSP claims are, strictly speaking, false, but it is pragmatically beneficial to use such language, so we are right not to give it up.

To evaluate this proposal, we should begin by looking a bit more closely at the examples I gave of admittedly instrumental language. Some of them are essentially metaphorical. When we say that a washing machine is temperamental, we are presumably saying that its behavior resembles, in certain respects, the behavior of a temperamental person. Similarly, we think that a chess-playing computer's moves resemble those of an opponent who wants to win and makes rational moves with that goal in mind. And the sun's apparent motion indeed resembles that of an object (like a hot-air balloon) moving across the sky. Insofar as we use such descriptions as metaphors, it is certainly not up to philosophers to put limits on when they are appropriate. Saying "Santa Claus was good to me this year" may be poetically lame, but the intent is clear and no philosophical mistakes have been made. However, claims made by CSP certainly go beyond mere descriptive metaphor, for we use the language of CSP to predict and explain human behavior.

There are times when fictions (metaphorical or otherwise) can indeed be useful for explanation and prediction. We can explain and predict events using Newtonian mechanics even though it is false. We can also do quite well in making predictions of various sorts on the basis of the claim that the sun rises in the east and sets in the west; if a washing machine is temperamental, we know not to expect perfectly smooth operation; and few of us would have any luck predicting or explaining the moves of a chess-playing computer apart from treating it as if it were a rational chess player who wants to win. The instrumentalist might say that CSP claims can similarly be used for explanation and prediction.

However, the instrumentalist must tread carefully here. In the above examples, we can *explain* why the fictions are nonetheless useful. Newton's laws are approximately correct, and in most cases they are so close that any error would be essentially undetectable. Talk of the sun's moving across the sky is somewhat different, for, construed literally, such talk is not even approximately correct. Nonetheless, we can cash out the metaphorical description in literally correct terms: Instead of saying that the sun moves from east to west, we could say that Earth rotates counterclockwise (as viewed from above the north pole). We could add that as Earth rotates, an observer on Earth will have to turn toward the west to continue directly facing the sun. These facts *explain* both why the sun appears to move from east to west, and they also explain the basis for any predictions or explanations we might couch in terms of the sun's motion across the sky.

In the case of the temperamental washing machine, we are basically saying that the machine's behavior has in the past resembled in certain ways that of a temperamental human being, where in particular we mean that it sometimes behaves in inappropriate ways. And in making predictions about its future behavior on this basis, we are suggesting that this is a relatively stable property of the machine—that it will continue to be temperamental. In saying this, we presuppose that there is some explanation for its "temperamental" behavior in the past and we assume that this will still hold in the future. The spelled-out version of the explanation and prediction would look like this: The washing machine has typically not worked smoothly, and its variations from intended function are not easily predictable from surface circumstances. On some days it works, and on some days it does not, and there is no obvious explanation in terms of the external circumstances. (In this sense, it resembles the behavior of a temperamental person who, because of quick and not easily predictable changes in mood, will behave a certain way on one day and a different way on another day without obvious differences in external circumstances.) We assume that there is some cause for the washing machine's malfunctioning, and that until this underlying cause is addressed the machine will continue not to function smoothly. And this explains why we can successfully use the useful fiction of speaking of the washing machine as temperamental.

Finally, if I am playing chess against a computer, I will attempt to predict its next move, and I will sometimes contemplate explanations of moves that it has already made. In making such explanations and predictions, I will employ thoroughly intentional terminology. I will, roughly speaking, predict the computer's next move on the assumption that it wants to win the game and that it will make the moves that it believes to be the best. And I will explain its moves with claims like "It moved its bishop so that it would not be taken by my knight." I am not in fact serious about attributing to the computer any desires and beliefs. On the other hand, I have very little idea of how to dispense with such concepts. I know in broad outline a little about how chess-playing computer programs work, but I certainly do not know enough to avoid using intentional terminology. Even for someone who knew the details of the program, predicting the machine's moves by looking at the program would be impractical to say the least—as witnessed by the fact that good chess-playing programs can typically beat their own programmers. However, even though I am unable to dispense with the intentional language, I can still provide an *explanation* for why the intentional language is useful even though it is false. The explanation is simple: I know that the computer has been programmed to imitate the behavior of a rational chess player. Thus I know that, insofar as the programmer was successful, my predictions and explanations will serve my purposes. My predictions will be roughly accurate; my explanations of the computer's moves will be false insofar as they attribute intentional states to the computer, but they will cohere with each other and with the predictions; and, again, the programmer's success in making the computer imitate a human player is what explains this coherence.

So we have seen that, in some paradigmatic cases of false but useful claims, their usefulness has some sort of further explanation. If such explanation was lacking, that would put us into a tough bind. Consider another example. A man and his wife live together in an old house. They hear a number of unexplained sounds, especially at night, and occasionally a picture falls off a wall. The husband believes in ghosts, and he says that these events are the results of a ghost living in the house; he adds that ghosts tend to be more active at night and that some ghosts are known to dislike having pictures on the walls. The wife does not believe in ghosts, but she nonetheless begins to talk as if the husband's theory is correct. Despite her belief that the theory is false, employing the ghost theory in this way might in some ways be useful to the wife. She might, for example, use the theory to gain marital harmony, or perhaps as a subtle way of manipulating the husband's behavior.

Could the wife use the theory to make predictions? Based on the theory, she might, for example, predict that over the course of the next week more pictures will fall at night than during the day. However, insofar as the wife *believes* those predictions, she will need some alternative theory on the basis of which she is making them; if in fact there are no ghosts, she should at least be concerned about *why* the theory can be used successfully for prediction. This concern on her part should be more pressing to the extent that the ghost theory and its predictions become more systematic and detailed. If the ghost theory becomes highly successful and robust in practice, and if she has no clue what alternative explanation there could be for the phenomena, then she has a reason to *believe* the ghost theory. (See chapter 2 above.) At some point, her verbal denial of the theory would become either irrational or mere philosophical pretense. The problems are compounded if the wife purports to use the theory to *explain* events in the house. If a picture does fall from the walls of the house, she cannot, in good theoretical conscience, accept that it fell *because* the ghost knocked it down. She doesn't believe there is any such ghost. She can't accept the ghost explanation (without thereby becoming a true believer in the ghost theory) if she really wants to know why the picture fell.

The basic point is this: If CSP claims are false but nonetheless immensely useful, we need some explanation for this fact. Unlike any ghost theory of which I am aware, CSP is a highly detailed, robust, and successful theory. But we have been given no explanation for why the predictions work and why the explanations cohere. Given our continued full reliance on CSP, any claim to be using it merely instrumentally would be philosophical pretense rather than fact. The instrumentalist picture seems to be this: Every attribution of a mental state comes with a sotto voce disclaimer: "Strictly speaking, there are no mental states." If someone were to hear the disclaimer and ask us to rephrase our assertion in terms that were true, we would have nothing to say. Similarly, if someone were to ask us to explain why CSP works as well as it does despite its falsity, we would have nothing to say. The sotto voce disclaimer would not be indicative of any willingness on our part to withdraw or modify the claim on demand. In fact, the sotto voce disclaimer would seem to have no function whatsoever; it would in effect be a meaningless bit of noise. Given that we know of no way to rephrase our discourse about human beings without presupposing mental states, the claim that we are nonetheless not committed to the truth of such discourse is without any apparent content.

Instrumentalist construals of CSP also run into a further obstacle. In paradigmatic cases of instrumentally useful but false language, there are at least *some* genuine, non-instrumental uses of the language in question. For example, there are things that move across the sky and there are rational chess players; thus, when we regard the sun or the computer as like these things, we at least have some basis for comparison. However, if we construe the intentional language of CSP instrumentally, we are left without any genuine cases of agents with mental states. According to the instrumentalist, are merely saying that it is *as if* people perform purposive actions and have mental states; but if people do not really perform actions or have mental states, then we know of nothing in the universe that does. The only criteria we have for applying intentional terminology are those that we use when attributing such states to one another; if such attributions are actually false, we apparently don't have any criteria for when something would *truly* have mental states. We need not be verificationists to find this rather disturbing. The point is not merely that we cannot define sensory verification conditions for mental terms; we also lack any samples of agents with mental states. We would be in the position of someone who said that it was as if certain people were flurby, but who, when pressed, had nothing to say about when we could truly apply the word 'flurby' and who could not even point to examples of things that were genuinely flurby.

Of course, we cannot point to genuine examples of ghosts either, and this does not hinder us in understanding claims about ghosts, nor does it even hinder us in understanding instrumental uses of ghost language. However, if we were to say that it is as if a ghost were in the house, we would presumably be saying that it is as if there is a person who cannot be seen and who doesn't interact with the physical world in all of the usual ways but has various odd properties. That is to say, without relying on the ghost language itself, we can give a literal description of what a ghost would be. In other words, we can *reduce* ghost talk to person talk plus other perfectly comprehensible properties, like *invisibility*. Similarly, if we could reduce the language of CSP to non-intentional terminology, instrumentalist uses of the language would at least at least be comprehensible, for we would understand what it *would* mean for there to be genuine agents with mental states. Thus, if CSP is quite generally false, and if there are no genuine agents with minds, it seems that we could understand instrumentalist applications of such language only if there were a way to reduce all intentional language to non-intentional language. In other words, an instrumental construal of CSP ultimately presupposes reductionism. However, instrumentalism was supposed to be some sort of halfway house that saved the legitimacy of CSP without going all the way to reductionism. If the coherence of instrumentalism in turn presupposes reductionism, then it seems that instrumentalism cannot be the stable halfway house it was intended to be.

12.5 Conclusion

Nonreductive materialists claim that CSP is independent of physical science—that CSP is autonomous. But the explanatory exclusion considerations highlight a basic objection to this view. On the face of things, common-sense psychology and physical science have, at least in part, the same subject matter, namely the behavior of human beings. How can it be that these realms are not rivals making potentially inconsistent explanatory claims? The teleological realist has at least the beginnings of an *account* of those differences, for we can talk in fairly specific terms about the ways in which common-sense reason explanations differ in form and content from the predominantly causal explanations given in science. But, as we have just seen, things are much more difficult for the nonreductionist who is also a causalist.

In chapter 2, I introduced the simplicity principle:

(S) Given two theories, it is unreasonable to believe one that leaves significantly more unexplained mysteries.

I argued that this principle provides ample reason to reject substance dualism. Substance dualism, at least in some forms, would be one version of an option-3 account of the mind, according to which the truths of physical science are independent of truths about mind and agency. Toward the end of chapter 2, I suggested that the simplicity principle might be taken to provide a strong reason against adopting *any* option-3 account. Any option-3 account will claim that there are truths of common-sense psychology that are logically independent of, and hence not explained by, the truths of physical science. Accordingly, these truths will apparently not be susceptible of further explanation; thus, in addition to whatever mysteries physical science leaves, CSP will introduce further inexplicable mysteries. In contrast, if option 2 is correct, and the truths of CSP are implied by those of physical science, CSP does not introduce any mysteries beyond those of physical science. And if option 1 is correct, the basic propositions of CSP are inconsistent with science and presumably false; so, likewise, no new mysteries would be introduced. Thus, on the face of things, it would appear that any option-3 view will fare less well on simplicity grounds than either option 1 or option 2. The purpose of this chapter is to explore this objection as it relates to teleological realism.

13.1 The Mystery Introduced by Teleological Realism

In a popular book on cognitive science, Steven Pinker makes a vivid case for why CSP seemingly must be ultimately subsumed within physical science:

It's not that common sense should have any more authority in psychology than it does in physics or astronomy. But this part of common sense has so much power and precision in predicting, controlling, and explaining everyday behavior, compared to any alternative ever entertained, that the odds are high that it will be incorporated in some form into our best scientific theories. I call an old friend on the other coast and we agree to meet in Chicago at the entrance of a bar in a certain hotel on a particular day two months hence at 7:45 P.M. I predict, he predicts, and everyone who knows us predicts that on that day at that time we will meet up. And we do meet up. That is amazing! In what other domain could laypeople—or scientists, for that matter—predict, months in advance, the trajectories of two objects thousands of miles apart to an accuracy of inches and minutes? And do it from information that can be conveyed in a few seconds of conversation? The calculus behind this forecasting is intuitive psychology: the knowledge that I *want* to meet my friend and vice versa, and that each of us *believes* the other will be at a certain place at a certain time and *knows* a sequence of rides, hikes, and flights that will take us there. No science of mind or brain is ever likely to do better. That does not mean that the intuitive psychology of beliefs and desires is itself a science, but it suggests that scientific psychology will have to explain how a hunk of matter, such as a human being, can have beliefs and desires and how the beliefs and desires work so well. (1997, pp. 63–64)

Pinker's direct aim, I take it, is to show that it is highly unlikely that CSP will be refuted, rather than incorporated, by science; in other words, he is primarily objecting to option 1. Nonetheless, his example can also be seen as an objection to teleological realism, or to any option-3 view. The objection works this way: On the one hand, CSP can, under certain circumstances, successfully predict the location of two objects two months hence with very good accuracy. On the other hand, predicting the location of two physical objects is exactly the sort of thing that we would expect of physical science. It would be a remarkable coincidence if two genuinely distinct sorts of theories could make the same prediction. If CSP and physical science can both predict the location of the two people in Pinker's example, then, barring some sort of reduction of CSP to physical science, we would seem to have a remarkable pre-established harmony between the two modes of approaching human beings.

To make the objection more precise, we need to step back and look at how CSP makes such predictions. We start with the knowledge that Pinker and his friend are agents. As we saw in chapter 9, CSP makes two fundamental assumptions concerning agents:

(R_1) Agents act in ways that are appropriate for achieving their goals, given the agent's circumstances, epistemic situation, and intentional states.

(R$_2$) Agents have goals that are of value, given a viable theory of the agent's circumstances, epistemic situation, and intentional states.

If we hear the phone conversation between Pinker and his friend, we learn that both agents expressed the intention of meeting at a particular place and time. Fulfilling this intention has value, since friends like to see each other, and there is value in keeping commitments one has made. (R$_2$) tells us that agents have goals that are of value, and (R$_1$) tells us that agents act in ways that are appropriate for achieving their goals; thus we can conclude that each of the friends will perform some appropriate series of actions that will lead them to be in the right place at the right time. Of course, their plans might change between now and then, and any number of things can go wrong, but on the strength of (R$_1$) and (R$_2$), and the knowledge that Pinker and his friend are agents, the observer can have some confidence in her prediction.

A reductionist like Pinker need not deny any of this; in particular, the reductionist can grant that Pinker and his friend are agents and that relevant principles like (R$_1$) and (R$_2$) are true. However, the reductionist will claim that these facts must ultimately be vindicated by—i.e., explained by—physical science. In particular, CSP relies on the truth of (R$_1$) and (R$_2$), and it assumes that being an agent is a stable property of an individual; in other words, in saying that Pinker and his friend are agents, we are not merely saying that (R$_1$) and (R$_2$) have been true of them so far. Insofar as we think of them as agents, we assume that (R$_1$) and (R$_2$) will continue to hold true of them for some time into the future; otherwise, the mere fact that Pinker and his friend are agents now would not aid us in predicting their location in two months. The reductionist will claim that we must be able to give a scientific explanation for the truth of (R$_1$) and (R$_2$). In saying that CSP and teleology are not reducible to physical science, the teleological realist is denying that physical science will explain the truth of (R$_1$) and (R$_2$), or that physical science will explain why being an agent is a stable property of an individual. Without a scientific account of why (R$_1$) and (R$_2$) hold true of certain things in the world, these propositions themselves become irreducible mysteries.

This objection poses, I think, the deepest challenge for teleological realism. To some extent, the objection might stem from a confusion about the nature of the view I am defending; however, even after that confusion is cleared up, a substantial challenge remains. The confusion is this: Talk of a pre-established harmony seems to suggest that (R$_1$) and (R$_2$) tap into some sort of alternative mechanism for producing events—as if physical science dealt with ordinary causation, whereas CSP deals with some sort of non-causal method bringing about events in the world. With this picture, one would indeed have a quite remarkable harmony or overdetermination, whereby two supposedly independent mechanisms both produce the same event. But that is not the right picture of teleological realism. (R_1) and (R_2) do not gesture at some sort of mysterious noncausal means of bringing about behavior. The teleological realist grants that human behavior has physical causes, with brain states presumably playing a central role. Teleological explanations simply do not purport to be identifying the cause of a behavior.

Every event presumably has a cause, so there is a causal story behind the behavior of any object. The behavior of most objects does not conform to (R_1) or (R_2); we cannot, for example, sketch a theory such that the behavior of the planet Jupiter is directed at ends with intelligible value. But the behavior of certain objects in the world does reliably conform to (R_1) and (R_2), and this should rightly seem remarkable. Nonetheless, teleological realism claims that this fact about agents will not be subsumed or implied by physical science. The crucial point is that, although there will be a causal story behind each instance of an agent's behavior conforming to (R_1) and (R_2), these instances will not have a *common* causal story. Each goal-directed behavior will have a causal story, but the stories will not, from the standpoint of physical science, have natural properties in common. So, though physical science could ultimately have predicted each of the individual behaviors, the terms under which they are lumped together by (R_1) and (R_2) are foreign to physical science. If you line up all of the goal-directed behaviors and then line up all of the events that are not goal directed—e.g., planets moving, rocks falling, epileptic seizures, etc.—the goal-directed behaviors will not be a natural group from the standpoint of physical science.

But this still leaves the question of *why* (R_1) and (R_2) hold of certain things in the world (most notably, human beings) but not of other things. If CSP in general and teleology in particular were reducible to physical science, there would be an explanation—in non-intentional and non-teleological terms—for why (R_1) and (R_2) hold. Thus, the objection comes down to this: unless reductionism (option 2) is correct, there is no explanation for why (R_1) and (R_2) hold reliably of certain individuals; that these principles do hold of certain beings in the world is left as an irreducible mystery or coincidence.

13.2   Teleological Realism's Reply

In short, my answer is to admit some of the force of the objection, but nonetheless to reject the conclusion that we should therefore accept strong naturalism. That is to say, I acknowledge that we do and should aim for a simple a theory of the world, where this means that we want our theory to have a minimum of irreducible mysteries. Moreover, teleological realism does accept (R$_1$) and (R$_2$) and contemplates no further explanation for them; the fact that (R$_1$) and (R$_2$) do hold reliably of human beings and other agents is left as a brute, irreducible fact with no further explanation. Thus, in the end the most basic teleological facts and concepts are irreducible and primitive. In and of itself this is not so embarrassing, for all theories, including that of physical science, will leave some basic facts unexplained. However, a theory of the world that managed to subsume (R$_1$) and (R$_2$) by showing that they followed from more basic physical science would, all things being equal, be superior to one that left (R$_1$) and (R$_2$) as brute, irreducible facts. That would indeed be a compelling consideration in favor of causalism *if* one could produce a successful reductive analysis of teleology and the underlying presuppositions. But if (as I argued in part II) this can't be done, we may just have to live with both causation and teleology as irreducible primitives.

The situation here is, to a degree, parallel to the nineteenth-century debate about electromagnetism. David Chalmers describes that episode as follows: "There had been an attempt to explain electromagnetic phenomena in terms of physical laws that were already understood, involving mechanical principles and the like, but this was unsuccessful. It turned out that to explain electromagnetic phenomena, features such as electromagnetic charge and electromagnetic forces had to be taken as fundamental, and Maxwell introduced new fundamental electromagnetic laws." (1996, p. 127) When physicists gave up on the idea that electromagnetic phenomena would be reducible to mechanics, they thereby gave up explaining why electromagnetic phenomena obey the laws that they do.

One must take some care in describing the situation of nineteenth-century physics relative to the simplicity principle. At first glance it seems that physicists decided to accept a less simple theory, for they accepted a theory that assumed without explanation both the laws of mechanics and the laws of electromagnetism, rather than opt for a theory according to which electromagnetic laws were subsumed within mechanics. Thus, the example would seem to show that scientists are sometimes forced to violate the simplicity principle. But that would be a highly misleading characterization of the situation, for it makes it appear that the physicists were comparing two relatively complete theories, one reductionist and one anti-reductionist:

(Rd) principles of mechanics (with all electromagnetic phenomena explained by these principles)

(A-Rd) principles of mechanics plus separate and independent principles of electromagnetism.

(Rd) would leave the truth of the principles of mechanics unexplained, but (A-Rd) would leave unexplained *both* the principles of mechanics and the electromagnetic laws. Thus, faced with these two theories, the simplicity principle clearly would call for us to adopt (Rd). But we were never faced with that choice, for we never had theory (Rd); that is, we never had a theory that explained electromagnetic phenomena in terms of mechanics. The situation was really as follows: *If* we could find a theory like (Rd), it would be far simpler than (A-Rd). This is certainly enough to motivate the search for (Rd), but it doesn't mean we will find it. If physicists had adopted only mechanics, they would have had no explanation for the electromagnetic phenomena. Thus, (A-Rd) was in fact far simpler than any extant alternative theory.

Of course, one can, and sometimes should, plead ignorance: One can admit that electromagnetic phenomena exhibit certain fundamental regularities, and one can admit not knowing how to explain those regularities in terms of mechanics alone, while still being unwilling to state that the regularities constitute laws of nature independent of mechanics. (Pleading ignorance is no violation of the simplicity principle, for, as phrased, the principle merely tells us not to believe a theory that leaves significantly more unexplained mysteries; it doesn't tell us that we must believe the remaining theory.) In this context, pleading ignorance would amount to affirming no theory—one would still use the current version of (A-Rd) for prediction and would work toward something like (Rd), or perhaps some other theory that would unify the phenomena more than (A-Rd) does. And in fact this would have been essentially the right approach to take, for I gather that twentieth-century physics does, in essence, provide one theory for mechanics and electromagnetism, although the direction of reduction is basically the reverse of that sought by the nineteenth-century physicists, for the forces of mechanics are essentially explained in terms of electromagnetic forces.

When should one plead ignorance and believe no theory, rather than believe the extant theory that leaves the fewest mysteries? That is a very tricky question, and there may be no clear, general answer. Presumably, the right approach depends at least in part on the strength of one's commitment to elements of the extant theories and on one's judgment of the likelihood of coming up with a theory that unifies the phenomena. The nineteenth-century physicists rightly had tremendous confidence that both the principles of mechanics and Maxwell's laws were at least approximately correct descriptions of underlying regularities in the phenomena, so they could be quite confident that neither set of principles was going to be rejected outright by some more successful theory. The question of what to believe, then, came down to judgments about the likely success of attempts to unify the two theories in some way.

In the case of the teleological realist (option 3) and the reductionist (option 2), we have a situation similar to that of the nineteenth-century physicists. On the face of things, it looks as if we are comparing two theories, one reductionist and one nonreductionist:

(Rd) principles of physical science (with all truths of CSP explained by these principles)

(TR) principles of physical science, plus separate and independent principles underlying CSP.

Of these two theories, (TR) looks to lose on simplicity grounds, for it posits independent principles (whose truth goes unexplained), whereas according to (Rd) these principles simply fall out of physical science. But, as with the physics example, we have to be careful here. We don't actually have a theory like (Rd). Functionalism and other reductionist philosophical views are at best rough sketches of how such a theory might be produced; no functionalist has ever laid out the actual functional analysis for even a single mental state, let alone the whole network of mental states. We can say that *if* we had a theory like (Rd), that theory it would presumably be simpler than (TR). And, as with the analogous situation in physics, this is enough to motivate a search for a theory like (Rd). If such a theory could be formulated, it would be simpler than (TR); but this is not enough to establish the reductionist's claim.

The objection is not just that no reductionist theory of mind has been completely formulated. If we did have a recipe for constructing such a theory, and if we had reason to believe that the recipe would work, then reductionism would be the right thing to believe. And the objection is also not just that the current recipes seem to have problems (e.g., functional-ism's problem in capturing the content of mental states). In part I of this book, I argued that the objections to reductionism go much deeper, for I argued that CSP explanations of behavior are not a species of causal expla-nation but are instead teleological explanations with a strong normative element. This aspect of CSP makes it look quite unlike theories in physical science and would seem to provide a very principled reason for thinking that no reductionist program will succeed.

As has been mentioned in the case of the physicists, sometimes, espe-cially in the absence of completed theories, one should simply plead igno-rance and keep searching. Thus, while not *affirming* reductionism, one might also be unwilling to affirm an option-3 account like teleological real-ism; instead one might keep working on the reductionist program while remaining officially agnostic. And, in the case of nineteenth-century physics, this would have been the attitude that proved basically correct. However, given the reasons against expecting reductionism to succeed, even that attitude is unjustified here.

13.3 Objection Renewed: The Challenge of Eliminativism

13.3.1 Option-1 Eliminativism

I have argued that we should affirm option 3 over option 2 even when we take the simplicity principle into account. So far in this chapter I have not considered option 1, according to which the claims of CSP will contradict the ultimate claims of physical science, with the presumed further result that we should reject CSP as false. Option 1 would thus be an eliminativist view concerning mind and agency. However, much of part II of this book functions as an argument against both option 1 and option 2. At the outset of the book, I noted that the vocabularies of CSP and physical science dif-fer greatly—that notions like *purpose, goal direction, belief*, and *desire* have no role in physical science. Thus, as I argued in chapter 3, if the truths of phys-ical science are to imply the claims of CSP, there will have to be bridge laws linking the terms of the two theories. But the same point applies for option 1: For the truths of physical science to contradict the claims of CSP, there must be bridge laws linking the terminologies of the two theories.

For example, science cannot show that there are no witches unless we can specify in scientific terms something about what a witch is supposed to be. As I noted in chapter 7, since a witch is thought to be something supernat-ural, we presumably cannot specify a list of naturalistically defined *sufficient* conditions for being a witch; however, we still must be able to specify some *necessary* conditions in the terms of physical science if anything in physical science is to be able to show that there are no witches. In the case of CSP and physical science, much of my argumentative work in part II was aimed at showing that the requisite links between the disparate vocabularies will not be found. For example, by arguing in chapter 7 that there will be no causal analysis of teleological locutions, I argued against the possibility of specifying, in the terms of physical science, necessary or sufficient conditions for behavior's counting as goal directed. If that and the other arguments of part II were correct, this shows both that physical science does not entail CSP and that it does not contradict CSP.

13.3.2 Option-3 Eliminativism

The Objection from the Eliminativist

The challenge of eliminativism is not entirely avoided by showing that the truths of physical science do not contradict those of CSP. Suppose that option 3 is correct, and the claims of CSP are logically independent of those of physical science; so far, it does not follow we should *accept* the claims of CSP. So long as the claims of CSP are not implied by the accepted truths of physical science, the possibility of rejecting CSP altogether remains open. This possibility points to an apparent disanalogy with the case of nineteenth-century physicists. For the nineteenth-century physicists, there was no question of rejecting the electromagnetic laws in light of their failure to reduce neatly to the laws of mechanics, for there were phenomena that could be predicted and explained only by electromagnetic theory. Mechanics alone was clearly insufficient unless the electromagnetic laws reduced to mechanics in some way. Mechanics alone, we might say, did not define a causally closed domain, and this made it obvious that if reduction failed, electromagnetic laws had to be accepted as independent and irreducible, despite the fact that it would be neater and simpler to have mechanics alone. By contrast, in the case of CSP the teleological realist admits that physical science may well define a causally closed domain and that physical science will ultimately be able to predict the motion of a human body in the same way that it can predict planetary motions or weather patterns. If human beings are ultimately constituted by the same physical particles that constitute the rest of the universe, then this result seems guaranteed, unless physical particles suddenly cease to be governed by the normal laws of physics when they are assembled into a human body. Thus, one might suggest that if CSP indeed resists incorporation into a completed physical science there ought to be no call for accepting the principles of CSP as independent from and irreducible to physical science; rather, if reduction fails we should simply reject CSP.

At the current stage of scientific development, it is rather difficult to imagine a wholesale rejection of CSP. But of course the eliminativists are not telling us that we should immediately give up using CSP; they, like the rest of us, would have no idea how we would do that right now. Depending on the brand of eliminativism, the philosopher might suggest that we will never give up CSP in practice, though CSP will be a "second-class" way of describing the world and will, in principle, be eliminable in a way that Maxwell's laws describing electromagnetic phenomena are not. According to the eliminativist, after sufficient advances are made in physical science, the continued use of CSP will, at least in principle, gain us nothing legitimate.

Brain Scanners

I contend that the eliminativist is wrong about the last point. A completed physical science that in no way incorporated or subsumed the concepts of CSP would still miss a great deal about the world. The question for eliminativism and CSP is this: If reductionism fails, would a completed physical science render CSP obsolete? That is, would the claims of CSP be either recognizably superfluous or in some way illegitimate? I contend that we would still have every reason to use and affirm CSP. To see this, I will propose a small thought experiment.

Suppose that one day neuroscience, having made enormous strides, is able to identify the brain state that plays the central causal role in any given bit of behavior; moreover, suppose that neuroscience is able to predict an individual's motor behavior from information about brain states and the person's environment. Of course, insofar as it is impractical to look into a person's brain, the mere theoretical possibility of such accomplishments would leave us little choice but to continue using CSP. But suppose further that it becomes practical and easy to use the new neuroscientific discoveries, a hand-held brain-scanning device having been invented. Using the scanner, one can, with the touch of a button, determine the physical cause of any given behavior; by pointing the device at a person and the immediate environment, one can also use it to generate quick predictions of the person's motor behavior. Even armed with all this information, I suggest, we would have little reason to give up our common-sense psychological practices. Physical science would still not amount to an adequate substitute for CSP's attributions and explanations of behavior, nor would we have reason to think that CSP is massively mistaken. Consider a mundane example: Joan gets up from the couch in the living room and heads to the kitchen.

We want to know why she does so; in particular, we want to know whether her purpose is to get a glass of wine or to avoid the annoying relative who just entered the living room, or something else. The hand-held scanner does not answer this question, for it simply tells us which brain state caused Joan's behavior. The scanner could also give us other information about how Joan would have behaved in other circumstances; such counterfactual information might help us answer our question, but only if the counterfactual conditions are described in intentional terms. For example, it would help to know what Joan would have done if she had *thought* that the annoying relative would stay in the room only a minute; and it would help to know what Joan would have done had she *believed* that there was no wine in the kitchen, and so on. But, given the assumption that reductionism fails, these situations cannot be entered into our hand-held scanner. So the question we had about the purpose of Joan's behavior would simply not be answered by the brain scanner.

The example is symptomatic of a general point: We care about a person's purposes, reasons, beliefs, and desires, but the brain scanner will be able to help us only when our concern is directly related to the person's motor behavior and its physical causes. Much of our reason for caring about CSP categorization is only indirectly connected to prediction of a person's motor behavior. For example, we want to know about a person's purposes, beliefs, and desires when we are evaluating her actions from a moral standpoint; if we want to know whether a person's behavior was morally praiseworthy, blameworthy, or somewhere in between, we typically need to know what she was intending to do and we need to know some of her relevant beliefs and desires. The eliminativist might claim that our reason for engaging in such moral evaluation is so that we can predict what that person will do in the future and act accordingly; such predictions can be handled by the brain scanner without need of CSP categories. But this is surely not the only reason we engage in moral evaluation. We act and think differently toward morally virtuous and morally heinous people, even apart from any direct concern about predicting what they will do next.

Moreover, beyond specifically moral evaluation of actions, we care about understanding people: We hope to understand their character, what drives them, what makes them happy, what interests they have. We want to make *sense* of the behavior of our compatriots. This drive to understand other people becomes most apparent when we see examples of apparently odd or purposeless behavior. If I see people walking about the campus on an autumn day, of course I do not know specifically what each of them is doing, but I know that there are all manner of plausible reasons: to get to a class, to go to lunch, to go back to one's office, simply to enjoy the cool air and the colors of the autumn foliage, and so on. Thus, even though I can't pinpoint any individual's reason for walking about the campus, there is no huge mystery. But suppose that amidst the people on the quad I also see one person running in tight circles around a small oak tree. This will catch my eye. Suppose the person continues in this way for several minutes. I will be filled with curiosity and a desire to know what the person is doing—i.e., what purpose he has in running around the tree. I will be particularly curious (and maybe concerned) if the person is a friend and colleague of mine. Behavior that is apparently purposeless troubles us; we long for an explanation. And our brain scanner's report about which brain state is causing the behavior will not help; we want to know the *reason* for the behavior; we want to understand something about the *person* who is engaged in the behavior. The sort of understanding we want goes beyond what the brain scanner can tell us.

Demons and Disease

The eliminativist might be unimpressed by our concerns, and might respond with an example like the following: Suppose that there is a group of people who believes that diseases are associated with certain sorts of demons or evil spirits. These people have posited an array of demons, and they have various means of determining which demon is present in any given case. However, suppose that the demons are not lined up in a one-to-one way with diseases as classified by medical science; i.e., the array of cases with which a given demon is associated includes diseases of all sorts, and the array seems to have no underlying scientific unity. When members of the group encounter someone with an unusual disease, they want to know what sort of demon is associated with it, and appropriate consultations with the demon theory yield some sort of answer to this question.

We might try to explain to the group the actual physical causes of the disease in question, and the physical causes of other diseases as well. We would be aiming to convince them that demon theory had no work to do, for we could accurately account for all the data with our biological theory of disease; since we need not posit demons as the *cause* of any disease, talk of demons' being associated with various diseases seems to be idle claptrap. Moreover, we would be unable to fathom why demon theorists think that all diseases associated with a particular demon have anything in common. Given a person with a specific disease, the demon theorists are greatly concerned to see which of their categories the disease falls into—i.e., they are greatly concerned to see with which demon it is associated. However, given that their categories seem to us to have no underlying unity, and given that we can determine the causes and cures of a disease without appealing to demon theory, we would not understand why they care about which of their demons is associated with a given person's illness. All of this would seem to provide adequate reason to reject the demon theory.

The eliminativist holding the brain scanner might be similarly impatient with our insistence on asking for the *purpose* of Joan's behavior. The eliminativist will say "Look, I told you the cause of her behavior, and I can tell you what behavior she will exhibit in the future; your concern with her *purpose*—as if this is something on top of or apart from all the physical causes—is idle metaphysical nonsense." Moreover, when the eliminativist looks at the categories posited by CSP, she finds that they have no underlying scientific unity. That is, when she looks at an array of individuals all of whom CSP says have a desire for wine, or an array of behaviors all of which CSP says were directed at obtaining wine, the eliminativist sees nothing that, from a scientific standpoint, unifies the instances within each of these CSP categories. From her perspective as a physical scientist, she is unable to see why we group events the way that we do; given a particular event or person, she would not see any reason for caring about which CSP category applies to that event or person. As with the case of the demon theory, all of this strengthens further the eliminativist's sense that CSP is simply off the mark and is to be rejected. So the eliminativist claims that the sort of understanding we seek through CSP is simply a delusion.

By way of response, let me go to a point emphasized by Quine (1960, p. 4): that theorizing starts in the middle. As an inscription at the front of *Word and Object*, Quine quotes Otto Neurath's metaphor of sailors at sea: "We are like sailors who must rebuild their boat on the open sea, without being able to take it apart in a dock and building it anew from the best components."[1] The point is that we necessarily begin theorizing about the world from the middle of our own overall home theory. There is no "first philosophy" on the basis of which we can construct a theory from the ground up. Of course our overall home theory should and does change over time, but the resources for that change must come from within the theory. In a sense the point is trivial: New beliefs or changes in belief do not get handed to us as from an oracle; rather, changes to our beliefs are mediated at least in part by existing beliefs that we are not changing. This means that any changes to our overall home theory of the world must be made on the basis of other theoretical commitments that go deeper than the beliefs we are changing.

Our commitment to CSP goes extremely deep. CSP informs nearly all of our interactions with other people, and it guides our own deliberations about what to do. To reject CSP would be to obliterate a huge portion of our overall home theory, and the rejection would have to be based on theoretical commitments that run even deeper than our commitment to CSP. According to the eliminativist proposal under consideration, we should reject CSP because it is not subsumed within physical science; that is, we should reject CSP on the basis of the claim that the truths of physical science are the only truths. But if this latter claim is a prima facie commitment of ours at all, it is surely much weaker than our commitment to understanding human beings as persons, as creatures with purposes and reasons. To reject CSP on the thin basis provided by the current brand of eliminativism would be a case of "first philosophy" in the extreme.

Eliminativism and Scientism

The eliminativist's rejection of CSP would indeed follow if we assumed that the only truths are those of physical science; one could then reply by labeling that assumption "scientism" and then denying it. But that would appear to be an unfair caricature of the eliminativist's reasoning. The eliminativist can seemingly argue for her position on the basis of the simplicity principle: Even a completed physical science will presumably leave certain unexplained assumptions or mysteries; but if the basic assumptions of CSP are added to those, we will have a theory that is considerably less simple overall. Or so it would appear at first. But one could reply that in fact physical theory alone would leave far more mysteries, for it simply has no answer to questions like the following: What purpose did Joan have in getting up from the couch? For what reason did the pope declare that women were not fit to be priests? Why is that professor running in circles around that oak tree? CSP can provide answers to these questions; however, if we can't reduce the concept of *reason* or *purpose* to the terms of physical science, physical science will not have answers to these questions. Thus, CSP plus physical science is far simpler than physical science alone. But not so fast! The eliminativist would not admit that there are questions that physical science cannot answer. Rather, the eliminativist *rejects the questions*; according to eliminativism, questions about purposes and reasons are not real questions. According to the eliminativist, these questions contain the false presupposition that purposes and reasons exist.

Thus, the dispute between the eliminativist and the teleological realist comes down (at least in part) to two questions: Are questions about purposes and reasons real questions? If we leave such questions rejected and unanswered, are we leaving inexplicable mysteries? The eliminativist answers "No" to both of these questions. But why? I would say instead that

if it looks like a question and feels like a question, then it is a question—
unless there is some compelling rationale for thinking that the question is
in some sense ill-formed or contains a false presupposition. But apparently
the option-3 eliminativist's *only* reason for saying that the questions contain false presuppositions is the fact that claims about purposes and reasons
cannot be subsumed within physical science. But at this point we are back
to a simple case of scientism after all: the unargued *assumption* that the
truths of physical science are the only truths about the world.

What about the demon theorists? Can they make all of the same argumentative moves that I have made on behalf of CSP and claim equally solid
ground for their demon theory? Before we could reach any firm conclusions
about the demon theory, we would have to ask many more questions. Do
the demon theorists think that the demons cause the diseases? Do the
demons have any sort of power over the events in one's life? If the demon
theorists answer either of these questions affirmatively, their beliefs will
conflict with our well considered scientific beliefs; it will not be simply a
matter of beliefs that are just separate and independent from science. But if
they claim that the demons are not causes of the diseases and they have no
other effects on people's lives, then we would press further to see if we could
connect the concerns of the demon theory with the concerns of our own
CSP. Are the demons associated in some way with the moral character of the
person? If so, further dialogue would be in order to attempt to confirm or
disconfirm these associations. Of course, as a philosophical example, it
would be easy enough to insist that the hypothetical demon theory has no
connections to anything scientific or to anything we care about or value.
Rather, one could postulate that, according to the theory, the demons that
are associated with diseases are in no way connected with anything else in
the world, and have no causal or explanatory role to play even with respect
to the diseases themselves; but the demon theorists simply care about
which demons are associated with which illnesses, even though they can
tell us nothing further about why they care about this. If we were to run
into such people, I think we would be genuinely baffled, and we would
strongly suspect that they were not being honest with us, that they were
playing some kind of joke on us, or that we had failed to translate or understand them properly. To the extent that we thought they were being serious
and that we had properly translated all they had to say about demons, we
would have to reject the demon theory on simplicity grounds as an utterly
superfluous set of claims.

How does our position with respect to the demon theorists differ from
that of the eliminativist toward us? It differs in one crucial respect. The

eliminativist, by arguing with us at all about the status of CSP, has already bought into its concerns. The eliminativist asks for our *reasons* for caring about CSP categories and attributions, and claims not to be able to understand these reasons except insofar as they connect directly with the project of physical science. By engaging in such a debate in the first place, the eliminativist is placing a value on reasons and understanding reasons. When the eliminativist in turn tells us that she can see no reason for adopting the concerns of CSP, she thereby refutes herself, for she is justifying her own argumentative move on the basis of the value of having reasons for one's belief. But *reason, belief,* and *value* are all concepts of CSP that are acknowledged not to be reducible to concepts of physical science. If the eliminativist rejects those notions, she has no reason to say or do anything. If reasons don't exist, one can't have a reason for saying something.

Can the eliminativist say that she is merely adopting the stance of a common-sense psychologist in order to refute the claims of common-sense psychology, in the way that one sometimes establishes the falsity of a claim by reductio ad absurdum? No, because the problem just reasserts itself even in the very description of what has just been done. When we argue by reductio, we assume the truth of something *in order to* show that it leads to a contradiction and thus must be false after all. That is, to argue by reductio is to do something for a purpose. It is not just the eliminativist's argument that in fact presupposes CSP; it is the very fact that she is arguing. That is, we can make *sense* of the eliminativist's words only by assuming that she has reasons for saying them. But if there are no reasons, the eliminativist's words themselves make no sense. And why should we be convinced by something that makes no sense?

13.4 Conclusion

I began with a mystery: It seems that our common-sense talk of mind and agency does not mesh well with our understanding of the world from the physical sciences. I have just argued against the most radical response to the mystery, namely that of rejecting common-sense psychology. But I have also argued that we will not be able to successfully subsume CSP within physical science. That leaves us with the third option, according to which CSP is independent of the physical sciences.

Viewed in a certain way, teleological realism may not seem to do much to resolve the original mystery. If the question is how agents *fit* within the natural order, then my answer is that, in a certain sense, agents do *not* fit within that order. But we must take care in how we describe the situation.

The realm of reasons, values, agency, beliefs, and desires is outside the realm of the natural sciences; that is, there is a realm of facts that employs concepts having no application to most of the rest of the natural world. But this does not mean that we are beyond the physical laws of nature. We are constituted by material particles, and these material particles don't suddenly cease to follow the laws of nature just because they are embedded in the body of an agent. We are every bit as much a part of nature as are the inanimate elements that surround us. But there are facts about what we value, what we think, and what we do, and these facts have no counterparts when the subject is a rock or a tree.

The situation can still seem rather mysterious in some rather distinct ways; that is, the view invites distinct sorts of questions. First, how can it even be possible that there are nonphysical facts about physical objects? Given that we are physical objects, how is it even consistent to maintain that there are facts about us that do not reduce to physical facts? I have tried to answer these questions, largely through the discussion of supervenience without reduction in chapter 8. Thus, although I admit the initial appearance of a mystery here, I think it can be resolved. Second, if CSP is not the same as physical science, then what guides it? If the alternative to science is the realm of faith and intuition, CSP itself begins to look quite mysterious. However, chapter 9's account of teleological explanation is meant to address this question and render CSP less mysterious. To a large extent, the concerns and questions of CSP differ from those of the natural sciences, but this does not mean that anything goes. CSP is constrained by its own internal principles, in addition to the principles of logic and simplicity that also constrain the natural sciences. So again, although there is an initial appearance of mystery, I believe that the question can be answered.

But why are the fundamental principles of CSP true? What explains their truth? That is, by virtue of what are they true of us? I don't have answers to these questions. Part of what it is to have a nonreductionist theory of mind is to have questions like these left unanswered. Of course every theory leaves some questions unanswered, and if questions don't have answers we get nowhere by pretending that they do. Nonetheless, the truth of CSP can seem quite mysterious or magical. Present-day physics has, I gather, no answer to why the mass of the neutron is 1.293 million electron volts heavier than that of the proton, rather than, say, 1.287 MeV heavier. But this may not seem to cry out for explanation in the same way as the truth of the principles of CSP. With the latter, one can even understand a certain inclination toward creation myths, according to which some supernatural agent breathes rationality and value into creatures that are otherwise mere dust, but such myths ultimately provide no explanatory help whatsoever. Perhaps in the end there will be some grand unified physical theory that answers many of the currently unanswered physical questions. And perhaps in the end there will be some even grander unified theory that in some way grounds both CSP and the natural sciences, though I have no idea how a theory of this sort would look. In any event, such a theory would still not constitute a reduction of CSP to the physical sciences. Or, perhaps, in the end, we simply may not be able to provide CSP with the sort of foundation we might want. But that does not mean that the edifice is about to collapse.

Notes

Chapter 3

1. There are some exceptions. The schema "Fx & $\sim Fx$" does imply the schema "Gx"; since there are no interpretations on which the first schema is true, it is thus true that on every interpretation on which "Fx & $\sim Fx$" is true, "Gx" is also true. But this just lets us know that a self-contradictory statement will imply any statement whatsoever, and this is of no use here, since we assume that the statements of science are not self-contradictory. Similarly, "Fx" implies "Gx v $\sim Gx$"; since the latter is true on every interpretation, it is true on every interpretation that makes "Fx" true. But again, this is of no help in the present situation, since we do not expect the claims of CSP to be logical truths or tautologies.

2. The central texts are Hooker 1981, Churchland 1979, Churchland 1989, Churchland 1986, and Bickle 1992.

3. For those interested, I will explain here the recipe I used in making substitutions into schema X such that schema Y results. First, suppose that both X and Y are unquantified, open schemata. The key is that for each term in X, one simply substitutes either the whole of Y, or the negation of Y (or schemata equivalent to Y or its negation, as in the examples in the text). The trick is to figure out whether to substitute Y or the negation of Y for a given term in X. The recipe to follow for that decision is as follows: Find an equivalent of X in conjunctive normal form—i.e., conjunction of disjunctions of terms or negations of terms. E.g., "$(-Ax$ v $Bx)$ & $(-Bx$ v $-Cx$ v $Dx)$." Within the shortest conjunct (the conjunct with the fewest disjuncts), for each unnegated sentence term, substitute Y. For each negated sentence letter, substitute the negation of Y. Proceed to the next shortest conjunct, and do the same, but ignore sentence letters that have already appeared. Etc. Provided that X is satisfiable, this procedure will transform X into a conjunction where each conjunct is either equivalent to Y or to "Y v $-Y$"; the conjunction as a whole will then be equivalent to Y. If X and Y have quantifiers, then things become more complicated, though if (as in Bickle's example) X and Y are conjunctions of universally quantified schemata, then the procedure just outlined works. There is another recipe one can use if X and Y have existential quantifiers, but I will not go into the details of that here.

Chapter 5

1. See Putnam 1975 and Kripke 1980. There is an obvious parallel between the reference-fixing view and the associated-beliefs view on the one hand and the description and causal theories of reference on the other. The parallel is intended, but it has the capacity to mislead. The associated-beliefs view is a thesis about the status of our general beliefs regarding a purported kind; the view is not *committed* to a particular theory of reference. Indeed, I think the associated-beliefs view is consistent with, e.g., a causal-descriptive theory of reference according to which reference is determined by a few descriptions of the causal origins of the beliefs, for these would not be among our general, qualitative beliefs about tigers.

Chapter 6

1. Baker has responded to this argument by providing a criterion that rules out the shunkiness explanation: "In general, if S's believing that p is to explain causally S's doing A, then there must be at least one conjunction of counterfactuals sufficient for S's believing that p that makes no mention of S's doing A." (unpublished, p. 19) Since my definition of 'shunky' does not allow such flexibility, it would not meet this criterion, and thus it could not be cited as the cause of the agent's action. However, I could simply make the example somewhat more complicated and stipulate that any two of the three counterfactuals in the list are sufficient for being shunky.

Chapter 7

1. I am not directly attributing (A2) and its successors to Mele, for Mele never explicitly offers a biconditional analysis of teleological explanations. (A2) and its successors represent a strategy for analyzing teleology that is strongly suggested by Mele's writings (and in the piece co-authored by Mele and Moser) on deviant causal chains and intentional action.

2. At least I take it that Bishop rejects this account. He presents an objection to the account on p. 153; he never responds to the objection, and he seems to take it as decisive. However, when he presents his final account, he seems to allow for either version of the sensitivity strategy.

Chapter 8

1. Thanks to Thomas Gardner for pointing out this problem to me.

2. For further explanation of the relevant concepts, see Boolos and Jeffrey 1980. Briefly, a set is *countable* or *enumerable* if its members can be put into a list such that every member ultimately appears on the list. A set is *denumerable* if it is infinite and enumerable. For example, the set of positive integers is infinite but also enumerable, for they can be put into a list: 1,2,3, ... However, there are some infinite sets that

are not countable or enumerable—whose members cannot be put into a list, even an infinitely long list. Such sets are *nondenumerable*. The set of real numbers is nondenumerable, but the set of linguistic expressions or the set of Turing machines by means of which a number could be computed are each denumerable.

3. I changed the variable in the original quote from P to M for the sake of clarity and consistency with the rest of the chapter.

4. We can see that there are nondenumerably many chessplus positions as follows. First we will find a very low lower bound on the number of possible positions in regular chess. There are eight white pawns, and each can occupy at least six different positions on the board, or they can be off the board, for a total of seven positions. (I will ignore the fact that pawns can, by capturing, go outside their initial file; since I'm just seeking a lower bound, this should be no problem.) Each of these is co-possible—i.e., that one pawn is on a particular square does not prohibit any of the other pawns from occupying any of their possible positions. So there are seven possible positions for the first pawn, seven for the second, and so on, for a total of 7^8, or 5,764,801. Now go to chessplus. Everything remains the same, except that the number of pawns is equal to the number of integers. So the total number of possible positions for the white pawns is $7^{\aleph_0}$, where is the number of integers. This is of course equal to $\aleph_1$, i.e., the number of real numbers. So the lower bound on the number of chessplus positions is nondenumerable.

Chapter 9

1. This account of the form of teleological explanations is adapted from Wilson 1989.

2. Dawkins in turn acknowledges that his discussion was highly influenced by the writings of Daniel Dennett. Dennett's writings, especially those essays collected in *The Intentional Stance* (1987), have also had a direct influence on the views expressed here.

Chapter 10

1. This objection was raised by a member of the audience when I presented this material at the Inland Northwest Philosophy Conference on May 4, 2003.

Chapter 11

1. For related criticisms of Smith's argument, see Schueler 2003 and Mele 2003.

2. Schueler (2003, p. 33) also notes this tension in Smith.

Chapter 13

1. Quine quotes Neurath in German; the translation is mine.

References

Achinstein, P. 1983. *The Nature of Explanation.* Oxford University Press.

Anscombe, G. 1957. *Intention.* Cornell University Press.

Arpaly, N. 2003. *Unprincipled Virtue: An Inquiry into Moral Agency.* Oxford University Press.

Baker, L. 1995. *Explaining Attitudes: A Practical Approach to the Mind.* Cambridge University Press.

Baker, L. Unpublished. "Belief Ascription and the Illusion of Depth."

Bedau, M. 1992. "Goal-Directed Systems and the Good." *Monist* 75: 34–49.

Bickle, J. 1992. "Mental Anomaly and the New Mind-Brain Reductionism." *Philosophy of Science* 59: 217–230.

Bishop, J. 1989. *Natural Agency: An Essay on the Causal Theory of Action.* Cambridge University Press.

Block, N. 1978. "Troubles with Functionalism." In C. W. Savage, ed., *Perception and Cognition.* University of Minnesota Press. Reprinted in Block, ed., *Readings in the Philosophy of Psychology*, volume 1. Harvard University Press, 1980. Page references are to the latter.

Block, N. 1980a. "What Is Functionalism?" In N. Block, ed., *Readings in the Philosophy of Psychology*, volume 1. Harvard University Press.

Block, N. ed. 1980b. *Readings in the Philosophy of Psychology*, volume 1. Harvard University Press.

Boolos, G., and R. Jeffrey. 1980. *Computability and Logic*, second edition. Cambridge University Press.

Bratman, M. 1987. *Intentions, Plans, and Practical Reason.* Harvard University Press.

Brockman, H., A. Grafen, and R. Dawkins. 1979. "Evolutionarily Stable Nesting Strategy in a Digger Wasp." *Journal of Theoretical Biology* 77: 473–496.

Bromberger, S. 1965. "An Approach to Explanation." In R. J. Butler, ed., *Analytical Philosophy*, second series. Oxford University Press.

Chalmers, D. 1997. *The Conscious Mind: In Search of a Fundamental Theory*. Oxford University Press.

Churchland, P. 1986. *Neurophilosophy*. MIT Press.

Churchland, P. M. 1979. *Scientific Realism and the Plasticity of Mind*. Cambridge University Press.

Churchland, P. M. 1981. "Eliminative Materialism and the Propositional Attitudes." *Journal of Philosophy* 78: 67–90.

Churchland, P. M. 1989. *A Neurocomputational Perspective: The Nature of Mind and the Structure of Science*. MIT Press.

Collins, A. 1987. *The Nature of Mental Things*. Notre Dame University Press.

Culver, R., and P. Ianna. 1988. *Astrology: True or False? A Scientific Evaluation*. Prometheus.

Dancy, J. 2000. *Practical Reality*. Oxford University Press.

Davidson, D. 1980. *Essays on Actions and Events*. Clarendon.

Davidson, D. 1984. *Inquiries into Truth and Interpretation*. Clarendon.

Dawkins, R. 1995. "God's Utility Function." *Scientific American* 273, no. 5: 80–85.

Dennett, D. 1987. *The Intentional Stance*. MIT Press.

Dennett, D. 1996. *Kinds of Minds: Toward an Understanding of Consciousness*. Basic Books.

Devitt, M., and K. Sterelny. 1987. *Language and Reality: An Introduction to the Philosophy of Language*. MIT Press.

Dretske, F. 1981. *Knowledge and the Flow of Information*. MIT Press.

Dretske, F. 1988. *Explaining Behavior: Reasons in a World of Causes*. MIT Press.

Fodor, J. 1974. "Special Sciences." *Synthese* 28: 77–115. Reprinted in Fodor, *Representation*. MIT Press, 1981.

Fodor, J. 1981. *Representations: Philosophical Essays on the Foundations of Cognitive Science*. MIT Press.

Fodor, J. 1990. *A Theory of Content and Other Essays*. MIT Press.

Frankfurt, H. 1988. *The Importance of What We Care About*. Cambridge University Press.

Ginet, C. 1990. *On Action*. Cambridge University Press.

Goldfarb, W. 1989. "Wittgenstein, Mind and Scientism." *Journal of Philosophy* 86: 635–642.

Goldfarb, W. *Deductive Logic.* Hackett.

Greene, B. 1999. *The Elegant Universe: Superstrings, Hidden Dimensions, and the Quest for the Ultimate Theory.* Norton.

Guttenplan, S. ed. 1975. *Mind and Language: Wolfson College Lectures 1974.* Clarendon.

Harman, G. 1975. "Moral Relativism Defended." *Philosophical Review* 84: 3–22.

Heil, J., and A. Mele, eds. 1993. *Mental Causation.* Clarendon.

Hofstadter, D. 1979. *Gödel, Escher, Bach: An Eternal Golden Braid.* Vintage.

Hooker, C. 1981. "Towards a General Theory of Reduction." *Dialogue* 20: 38–59, 201–236, 496–529.

Horgan, T. 1993. "From Supervenience to Superdupervenience." *Mind* 102: 555–586.

Horgan, T. 1994. "Naturalism and Intentionality." *Philosophical Studies* 76: 301–326.

Hornsby, J. 1980. *Actions.* Routledge & Kegan Paul.

Hume, D. 1739/1978. *A Treatise of Human Nature,* second edition. Clarendon.

Jackson, F., and P. Pettit. 1988. "Functionalism and Broad Content." *Mind* 97: 381–400.

John Paul II. 1996. "Message to the Pontifical Academy of Sciences: On Evolution." Available at www.ewtn.com.

Johnston, M. 1989. "Dispositional Theories of Value." *Proceedings of the Aristotelian Society,* suppl. 63: 139–174.

Kim, Jaegwon 1993. *Supervenience and Mind.* Cambridge University Press.

Kim, Jaegwon 1998a. "The Mind-Body Problem after Fifty Years." In A. O'Hear, ed., *Current Issues in Philosophy of Mind.* Cambridge University Press

Kim, Jaegwon 1998b. *Mind in a Physical World: An Essay on the Mind-Body Problem and Mental Causation.* MIT Press.

King, M. 1954. "Rediscovering Lost Values." Sermon given at Second Baptist Church, Detroit. Recorded in *A Knock at Midnight: Inspiration from the Great Sermons of Martin Luther King Jr.* Time-Warner Audio Books, 1998.

Korsgaard, C. 1996. *The Sources of Normativity.* Cambridge University Press.

Krauss, L., and G. Starkman. 1999. "The Fate of Life in the Universe." *Scientific American* 281, no. 5: 58–65.

Lewis, D. 1972. "Psychophysical and theoretical identifications." *Australasian Journal of Philosophy* 50: 249–58. Reprinted in Block, ed., *Readings in the Philosophy of Psychology*, volume 1. Harvard University Press, 1980. Page references are to the latter.

Lewis, D. 1983. *Philosophical Papers*, volume 1. Oxford University Press.

Lewis, D. 1989. "Dispositional Theories of Value." *Proceedings of the Aristotelian Society*, suppl. 63: 113–137.

McCann, H. 1998. *The Works of Agency: On Human Action, Will and Freedom*. Cornell University Press.

Mele, A. 1992. *Springs of Action: Understanding Intentional Behavior*. Oxford University Press.

Mele, A. 2000. "Goal-Directed Action: Teleological Explanations, Causal Theories, and Deviance." *Philosophical Perspectives* 14: 279–300

Mele, A. 2003a. *Motivation and Agency*. Oxford University Press.

Mele, A. 2003b. "Commentary on Sehon and Tenenbaum." Paper presented at Inland Northwest Philosophy Conference.

Millikan, R. 1984. *Language, Thought, and Other Biological Categories*. MIT Press.

Nagel, E. 1961. *The Structure of Science: Problems in the Logic of Scientific Explanation*. Harcourt, Brace & World.

Nagel, T. 1997. *The Last Word*. Oxford University Press.

O'Hear, A. ed. 1998. *Current Issues in Philosophy of Mind*. Cambridge University Press.

Okrent, M. 1991. "Teleological Underdetermination." *American Philosophical Quarterly* 28: 147–155.

Peacocke, C. 1979. *Holistic Explanation: Action, Space, Interpretation*. Oxford University Press.

Pinker, S. 1997. *How the Mind Works*. Norton.

Platts, M. 1979. *Ways of Meaning*. Routledge and Kegan Paul.

Putnam, H. 1967. "Psychological Predicates." In Capitan and Merrill, eds., *Art, Mind and Religion*. University of Pittsburgh Press. Reprinted as "The Nature of Mental States" in Putnam, *Mind Language and Reality: Philosophical Papers*, volume 2. Cambridge University Press, 1975.

Putnam, H. 1975. "The Meaning of 'Meaning.'" In K. Gunderson, ed., *Language, Mind and Knowledge*. Minnesota University Press. Reprinted in Putnam, *Mind Language and Reality: Philosophical Papers*, volume 2. Cambridge University Press.

Putnam, H. 1988. *Representation and Reality*. MIT Press.

Quine, W. 1951. "Two Dogmas of Empiricism." *Philosophical Review* 60: 20–43. Reprinted in Quine, *From a Logical Point of View*. Harvard University Press, 1953. Page references are to the latter.

Quine, W. 1953. *From a Logical Point of View*. Harvard University Press.

Quine, W. 1960. *Word and Object*. MIT Press.

Quine, W. 1975. "Mind and Verbal Dispositions." In S. Guttenplan, ed., *Mind and Language: Wolfson College Lectures 1974*. Clarendon

Russell, B. 1921. *The Analysis of Mind*. Allen & Unwin.

Russell, B. 1948. *Human Knowledge: Its Scope and Limits*. Simon and Schuster.

Schueler, G. F. 2003. *Reasons and Purposes: Human Rationality and the Teleological Explanation of Action*. Oxford University Press.

Searle, J. 2001. *Rationality in Action*. MIT Press.

Sehon, S. 1994. "Teleology and the Nature of Mental States." *American Philosophical Quarterly* 31: 63–72.

Sehon, S. 1997a. "Natural-Kind Terms and the Status of Folk Psychology." *American Philosophical Quarterly* 34: 333–344.

Sehon, S. 1997b. "Deviant Causal Chains and the Irreducibility of Teleological Explanation." *Pacific Philosophical Quarterly* 78: 195–213.

Sehon, S. 1998. "Connectionism and the Causal Theory of Action Explanation." *Philosophical Psychology* 11: 511–531.

Sehon, S. 2000. "An Argument against the Causal Theory of Action Explanation." *Philosophy and Phenomenological Research* 60: 67–85.

Smith, M. 1994. *The Moral Problem*. Blackwell.

Sober, E. 1999. "The Multiple Realizability Argument against Reductionism." *Philosophy of Science* 66: 542–564.

Stich, S. 1983. *From Folk Psychology to Cognitive Science: The Case against Belief*. MIT Press.

van Fraassen, B. 1980. *The Scientific Image*. Clarendon.

Vollrath, F. 1992. "Spider Webs and Silks," *Scientific American* 266, no. 3: 70–76.

Williams, B. 1981. *Moral Luck*. Cambridge University Press.

Wilson, G. 1989. *The Intentionality of Human Action*. Stanford University Press.

Winnie, J. 1992. "Computable Chaos." *Philosophy of Science* 59: 263–275.

Wooldridge, D. 1963. *The Machinery of the Brain*. McGraw-Hill.

Index